W9-CRK-670

FRONTIER PEOPLE

To Koen

METTE HALSKOV HANSEN

Frontier People

*Han Settlers in Minority
Areas of China*

UBCPress · Vancouver · Toronto

First published in the United Kingdom by
C. Hurst & Co. (Publishers) Ltd.
© 2005 by Mette Halskov Hansen
All rights reserved.
Printed in India.

Published in Canada and the United States by
UBC Press
The University of British Columbia
2029 West Mall, Vancouver, BC V6T 1Z2
604-822-5959/Fax: 604-822-6083
www.ubcpress.ca

Library and Archives Canada Cataloguing in Publication

Hansen, Mette Halskov
  Frontier people: Han settlers in minority areas of China/Mette
Halskov Hansen.

  Includes bibliographical references and index.
  ISBN 0-7748-1178-1 (bound).—ISBN 0-7748-1179-X (pbk.)

  1. Migration, Internal—China. 2. Migration, Internal—Government
policy—China. 3. Migrant labor—China. 4. Minorities—China.
5. China—Ethnic relations. I. Title.

DS779.215.H35 2005   304.8'0951
C2004-905958-0

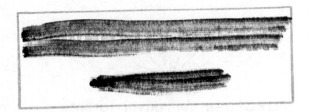

ACKNOWLEDGEMENTS

When I started my study of Han immigrants in ethnic minority areas in 1999 I already had some experience of doing fieldwork in minority areas in Yunnan Province. My new topic of research surprised many of the people I had come to know through these previous fieldwork periods. Studies in minority areas naturally tended to focus on ethnic minorities: their cultures, histories and languages, and sometimes their relation to the state and other ethnic groups, including the Han. Few scholars working in minority areas or with ethnic minorities were interested in the Han settlers themselves. Nevertheless, a number of people and institutions in China did everything they could to help me organise and carry out the field research in which I was interested.

In Yunnan the Yunnan Academy of Social Sciences provided me with the permits necessary to do the fieldwork, and I am especially grateful for the help and assistance provided by He Yaohua, the YACC president at the time, Professor Yang Fuquan and Professor Guo Dalie. During one of my longer field trips to Sipsong Panna, the Jingpo scholar Jin Liyan was an invaluable assistant and colleague. In the province of Gansu I was very lucky to meet Professor Ma Zhengliang and Professor Guo Zhiyi who made my fieldwork possible in the county of Xiahe. Starting up fieldwork in a new location always takes time, and without the help and support of Cui Lei, Xia zhuren and Zha zhuren in the Xiahe Family Planning Committee it would have been very difficult to carry out my numerous interviews with Han settlers in Xiahe. It would also have been less fun! Through the hospitality of all the staff in the Family Planning Committee I was able to live for three months in their office building, taking part in their daily life and special celebrations. They also made it possible for my husband and daughters to join me. This fieldwork period was a very special one in the course of my research. I am grateful also for help from other people in Xiahe, especially Lamojia who introduced me to his village and helped me during research there, and Chen Lijian and Lang Cang from the Tibetan Research Centre.

In Yunnan, as well as in Gansu, I was often amazed by the ways in which Han immigrants received me as a researcher and fellow 'outsider'. Han settlers often reminded me of the fact that we were all 'from the outside' (*waimian lai de*), and this sometimes created a bond between us that made interviewing exceptionally easy and agreeable. Obviously a study of Han immigrants in minority areas relying largely on interviews and informal conversations would not have been possible without these people's willingness to share some of their thoughts and experiences with me.

In the course of my work with the manuscript a number of people have commented on papers, chapters and specific sections related to the project. I especially wish to thank Robbie Barnett, Sara Davies, Steve Harrell and Frank Pieke who have provided me with detailed and extremely helpful comments and timely criticism. I am also grateful to a number of other colleagues and friends who have supported and helped me in different ways in the course of this project: Kristi Anne Stoelen, Oivind Fuglerud, Desmond McNeil, Stig Thoegersen, Halvor Eifring, Rune Svarverud, Christoph Harbsmeier, Liu Baisha, Zhou Yong and Maria Lundberg. In the final stages of the research Michael Dwyer, Christopher Hurst and Maria Petalidou at Hurst & Co. helped me with many improvements to the manuscript.

Scholars cannot live on books alone, and a generous post-doc grant and invaluable financial support for fieldwork and research assistance was kindly provided by the Faculty of Arts at the University of Oslo, the Norwegian Research Council, and the Danish Council for Development Research.

My final thanks are to Koen, my husband, friend and colleague, who helped me during field research, took care of everything at home in periods when I was away, read every chapter, and supported my project in all possible ways. It is a pity that I cannot blame him for errors, mistakes and other deficiencies of this book, which remain my responsibility alone.

Oslo, May 2004   M. H. H.

CONTENTS

Contents

KEY
A. Ganman Tibetan Autonomous Prefecture
B. Sipsong Panna (Xishuangbanna) Dai (Tai) Autonomous Prefecture

1

INTRODUCTION

CHINESE COLONIAL PROJECTS AND THE RESETTLEMENT OF HAN

'Originally, we wanted to develop and change Tibet. In reality, we were the ones who changed.' (Xiao Ji 1996, p. 124)

This is a story about people who have moved—or were sometimes in reality forced to move—to areas that were considered to be on the cultural and political border of their own state. Areas in which their government was carrying out a modernist project attempted at establishing political, economic and cultural control through the counting and classification of people, measuring of land, planning of production, and building of political authority. Some of the settlers were active and conscious participants in what could be termed as an ongoing Chinese colonialist project, some were wives and children of those settlers, and some were individual migrants searching for ways of improving their living conditions. All of the migrants in this book were members of the ethnic majority in China, the Han (*Hanzu*). For various reasons, they left their home towns and villages between the 1930s and the 1990s and settled temporarily or permanently in regions traditionally inhabited by non-Han peoples—regions that were at different times subjected to Chinese rule and incorporated into the Chinese state. Under the People's Republic of China (PRC) they were granted official recognition as 'ethnic minority areas', and within these the Han immigrants experienced geographical, political, cultural and economic conditions that were sometimes profoundly different from the regions they had come from. Through a predominantly colonialist discourse about essential cultural differences between majority and minorities in China, expressed

1

for instance in popular novels about heroic Han settlers in border regions, scholarly books and articles, and primitivist celebrations in the media of 'colourful' and 'natural' minority cultures, Han immigrants were imbued with powerful images of their own role as 'settlers' and 'civilisers'.

Since the 1980s especially, the attention directed by NGOs and international organisations towards the Chinese occupation of Tibet has made some immigrants aware that their own migration history, and the political process of which it was part, have been contested and sometimes strongly criticised. At the same time the migrants were people living their lives, establishing new communities, and engaging in new relations with the indigenous inhabitants and among themselves. In this process they were often finding ways of making sense of their own participation in state projects with profound (though often unforeseen) personal and local consequences. The changing and often contradictory local, national and international discourses on these settlers were relevant to, and inseparable from, the ways in which Han settlers in border minority areas perceived and represented their own situation, engaged in local relationships, continued and established broader networks of communication, and explored and negotiated their own identification as officially recognised members of an officially recognised ethnic majority in China.

In debates among scholars, policy makers, political organisations and NGOs about ethnic relations and minority issues in China, the topic of Han migration to minority areas since 1949 is crucial. It is often brought up and frequently results in heated debates about minorities' rights to self-determination versus Han 'rights' to move freely within the internationally recognised borders of the country. In connection with the household registration system in China there are still a number of restrictions on urban-rural movement in particular, but in practice movements to the border minority areas are subject to few restrictions. Recently, a number of scholars in China have started to argue more explicitly and firmly for the right of all nationalities (*minzu*) in China (defined ideologically as part of the 'Chinese nation', the *Zhonghua minzu*) to freely move to and settle within all areas defined as the territory of the PRC. This obviously raises new questions of how rights of ethnic minorities are perceived, and how problems regarding large-scale movements of culturally and numerically dominant ethnic groups into areas traditionally inhabited by ethnic minorities are going to be addressed in China, as well as in other parts of the world.

The research presented in this book focuses on two specific minority areas—Sipsong Panna in Yunnan Province and Xiahe in Gansu Province. These regions were not chosen because they were seen as being especially representative of the western minority areas of China, but there is no doubt that they may serve as examples of situations which can be found in many other minority areas. I chose to focus on these two specific areas for several reasons. First of all, Han migration to minority areas (especially Tibetan ones) is a politically sensitive issue and it was not easy to gain permission to carry out fieldwork on this topic at all. Rather than carry out short term, unofficial fieldwork in many different locations, I wanted to gain a deeper insight into the consequences of a long term Chinese colonisation process within one or two specific localities. Through long-established personal and research contacts, I was finally given official permission to do research within these two specific areas, and it was therefore partly coincidental that they became the final choice. In one of the areas, Sipsong Panna, I already had long fieldwork experience, and in this book there is therefore a certain bias with regard to the amount of data presented from the two areas and my own feelings of understanding and insight in relation to them. However, through the comparison of these two areas (and drawing on experiences from other minority areas as well) I have become convinced that the Han immigrants' experiences, perspectives and cultural practices, as described and discussed in the context of the two areas of Xiahe and Sipsong Panna, are to a great extent comparable to those of Han immigrants in other minority areas of China which have an equally long history of dealing with a strong Chinese state. Policies resulting in migration to Sipsong Panna and Xiahe have been equally important in many other areas, and research based on these two specific regions will definitely shed light on the consequences of large-scale migration to other western areas within the PRC, including the Tibetan Autonomous Region.

The character of Han migrations to minority areas within China during the period of the People's Republic has largely changed from being predominantly state organised in the 1950s–70s period to being primarily an indirect result of economic changes in the reform period after 1978. However, the political relevance of the issue of Han migrations to ethnic minority areas has not decreased. On the contrary, with the economic restructuring of China, its incorporation into the global economic arena and the consequent increasing need for employment for Chinese peasants and laid-off workers, conflicts regarding Han migration to the rural minority regions on China's frontiers are likely to intensify. These migrations constitute a counter-trend to the much debated rural-urban migration in China and many other developing countries, and with increased pressure on urban immigrants and competition for unskilled work, more rural Han are likely to seek opportunities especially in those border minority regions that are developing cross-border trade relations, tourism and other new forms of industries.[1] As has been seen in some of the new states of the former Soviet Union as well as in Burma and Mongolia, peasants and small-scale businessmen and traders from China are also increasingly seeking working opportunities and establishing themselves in areas bordering the PRC.

In recent years (with the unprecedented opportunities for doing fieldwork in China) minority studies have broadened and deepened our knowledge about the ethnic and cultural heterogeneity of China. They have also contributed to our understanding of the discursive construction and promotion of minorities as a counter-image to the Han majority via the media, education, tourism, etc. At the same time and in the same process, research in ethnic minority areas of China has tended to focus exclusively on minorities, and so, indirectly, largely ignore Han immigrants as agents, or sometimes present them first of all as representatives of official discourse and state policy. In conferences outside China and in political discussions about minority issues in China, 'the Han' have frequently (and often indirectly) been described as a largely homogeneous group of locally intruding power holders who consciously and actively support the central government's goal of achieving cultural and political homo-

---

[1] A large number of publications on rural-urban migration in China have come out in recent years. For just a few of these, see for instance: Croll and Huang Ping 1997, Day and Ma Xia 1994, Ma Xia and Wang Weizhi 1993, Qian Wenbao 1996, Davin 1999, Chen Xiguang 1991, Chen Yimin and Tong Chengzhu 1992, Solinger 1999.

geneity. The result is that while there is now a much more nuanced and complex picture of ethnic minorities living in China than we had before, the Han people in the same areas tend to be construed as a more or less homogeneous group of 'colonisers' or 'civilisers' (depending on the viewpoint) who have seemingly similar lives, cultural practices and ways of identifying with the state and with a 'Han nationality'.

The same trend has been observed in other parts of the world where European colonisers have often been viewed as a largely homogeneous group assumed to express a shared European mentality. According to Ann Stoler ethnographers have been much less interested in describing the cultural complexity and heterogeneity among European colonisers than among those colonised. As Stoler writes, 'colonizers and their communities are frequently treated as diverse but unproblematic, viewed as unified in a fashion that would disturb our ethnographic sensibilities if applied to ruling elites of the colonized' (Stoler quoted in Thomas 1994, p. 13). This criticism applies to a large extent also to ways in which the Han, as people resettled in ethnic minority areas in connection with the state's colonising and civilising projects, have often been represented and described inside as well as outside China.

Many of the Han who live in minority areas of China today have consciously and actively taken part in what could be termed a colonisation project of the Chinese government. Dru Gladney has argued that the concept of 'internal colonialism'[2] can plausibly be used to describe the situation of the Uyghur, Tibetans and possibly other ethnic minorities living today in areas that have been subjected to the Chinese nation-state. As Gladney argues, 'the categorization and taxonomization of all levels of Chinese society, from political economy, to class, to gender, to religion, to ethnicity and nationality represents a wide-ranging and ongoing project of internal colonialism' (Gladney 1998, p. 1 and Gladney 1994). The territories of the vast western non-Han regions, with their various historical relationships to the Chinese empire, have been of paramount interest to the Chinese Communist government as regions containing rich raw materials and as markets for processed industrial products. Their strategic location on the borders with other states, and their potential for

---

[2] A term first evoked in Michael Hechter's study of Wales (Hechter 1975).

absorbing surplus population from other parts of the country, have proved highly significant for the Chinese state. Huge numbers of personnel have been sent into these areas to ensure economic and political control and carry out the 'civilising mission' which, so the state hoped, would ultimately transform these areas and the peoples inhabiting them.[3]

As pointed out by Nicholas Thomas, the word 'colonialism' is still mostly associated with 'intrusions, conquest, economic exploitation and the domination of indigenous peoples by European men', and it is mostly seen as a phenomenon of the past (Thomas 1994, p. 1). Thomas argues against a simple but common assumption that colonialism is primarily a political or economic relationship legitimised through ideologies of racism or progress. Instead, he argues that colonialism should be understood as a cultural process:

> Rather, colonialism has always, equally importantly and deeply, been a cultural process; its discoveries and trespasses are imagined and energized through signs, metaphors and narratives; even what would seem its purest moments of profit and violence have been mediated and enframed by structures of meaning. Colonial cultures are not simply ideologies that mask, mystify or rationalize forms of oppression that are external to them; they are also expressive and constitutive of colonial relationships in themselves. (Thomas 1994, p. 2)

In the context of this book, colonialist projects and culture are understood as an ongoing process carried out by a state that has a history of being colonised itself. My main interest in the Chinese colonial project, and the current colonial culture that is part of it, is directed towards the people who were themselves expected to carry out the civilising project that was hoped to transform the colonised areas and their peoples. I have been more interested in local agency and encounters between indigenes and various settler groups than in official discourse. Still, I include some discussion of specific examples of texts produced by local agents of the Chinese state's colonial project—texts that demonstrate how tension and conflicting attitudes towards the colonial and civilising project are common among 'colonisers'. This is consistent with Thomas' argument that 'Colonialism

---

[3] On the civilising projects in ethnic minority areas of China see Harrell 1995b.

is not a unitary project but a fractured one, riddled with contradictions and exhausted as much by its own internal debates as by the resistance of the colonized.' (ibid. p. 52)

The numerous interviews with Han settlers presented in the following chapters clearly demonstrate that the CCP's civilising mission in minority areas is contested, non-monolithic and viewed differently by different people belonging to the vast group of Han settlers. The Han immigrants in ethnic minority areas may be perceived as participants—conscious or unconscious—in the state's internal colonisation project, but they do not constitute a homogeneous elite. They belong to different social classes in Chinese society and they were often in reality forced to resettle and, afterwards, remain in areas on the borders of China historically inhabited by non-Han groups of peoples. Many were recruited as cheap labour in minority areas, many had no special access to power within the political system, and even those who were granted officially important local positions were often left with no actual choice of remaining in or leaving the area and the occupations they had been entitled to. Many of them told stories reflecting personal feelings of powerlessness and lack of choice, even when they were clearly part of a group possessing a considerable degree of local power and cultural capital. In these senses one might consider many of the migrants in this study as 'subaltern colonisers', or one might at least include this perspective on Han immigrants in minority areas within an analysis of the Chinese—and other—colonisation projects.

By including in my study Han settlers who can hardly be regarded as consciously active participants in the state's civilising project, I have been able to show the degree of similarities as well as differences in the concepts of ethnic minorities, of Han identities, of the state, the government and the civilising project itself among Han who are far from constituting a homogeneous group of people but have in common their resettlement in areas on the periphery of their own state. At the same time, I argue that there is, among the post-revolution Han settlers in ethnic minority areas, a high degree of shared identification as civilisers or, more precisely, as people whose right to resettle in any minority area within the borders of their state and engage in whatever legal economic activity that supports their own income is justified by an assumption that it brings indisputable advantages to

the ethnic minorities. In practically all groups of immigrant Han—
regardless of significant social and economic discrepancies—I encountered a sense of cultural and economic superiority expressed not
merely in negative descriptions of minorities but also in positive evaluations of what were regarded as their 'primitivist', 'natural' inherited
character and tradition. The tendency to express cultural superiority
among many Han was partly due to a long tradition in China of regarding and representing the peoples living on the periphery of the
empire as somewhat uncivilised and uncultured. At the same time,
my research suggests that both the discursive aspects of the Communist civilising mission and the Han settlers' own ways of making
sense of their migration histories and encounters with the minorities
helped to form the current views and attitudes of Han settlers towards
the areas they settled in, the peoples inhabiting them and the state
projects they took part in.

Many of the Han immigrants I interviewed were sent to ethnic
minority areas to fill positions as party cadres, teachers, soldiers, workers, farmers and administrators, and many others followed later in
search of economic opportunities in those developing regions. In
this their experiences are far from unique. During Chinese history,
and all over the world, people have taken part in such government
projects and moved (or been moved) to areas where their own government was expanding its economic and political sphere: Israelis in
Palestine, white settlers in native American regions, Danes in Green-
land, Indonesian settlers in East Timor and so forth. An impressive
quantity of studies have dealt with the impact of colonisation projects on colonised societies, and with so-called post-colonial situations in Africa, Asia and elsewhere. As mentioned above, fewer studies
have from an anthropological perspective been concerned with the
people who themselves took part in the colonisation projects, their
own histories, their own relations with the local people they encountered and with other settlers who followed as a more or less uncontrolled result of colonisation. Historical studies of Han resettlement in
peripheral areas of the Chinese empire are also well known and have
contributed significantly to our understanding of the Chinese state's
colonisation processes during history. However, again very few studies have focused ethnographically on the Han migrants themselves,
whether they were perceived as colonisers or simply as peasants in

search of livelihood.[4] In the historical context Pat Giersch has argued that studies of Qing imperialism have focused on the imperial state as the main actor, generally overlooking the agency of migrants and indigenes (Giersch 2001). He argues instead for an approach that conceives the frontier as 'middle ground', the destructively creative formulation of 'something new' in lands where 'alien cultural and political institutions meet' (Giersch 2001, pp. 88–9). This approach allows for the inclusion of agency on the part of both indigenes and Chinese immigrants, and would provide us with new histories of cultural encounters in the frontiers.

Among the most notable examples of studies focusing ethnographically on recent Han settlers in ethnic minority areas of the PRC are those concerning Han settlers in Inner Mongolia by Burton Pasternak and Janet W. Salaff (Pasternak and Salaff 1993) and Ma Rong (Ma Rong 1987). These studies have shown diversity among Han settlers in Inner Mongolia and described their different ways of adapting to ecological and cultural changes while maintaining, in a changed form, pre-existing rules and understanding of what it implies to be Chinese. Salaff and Pasternak argue that as Han moved into Inner Mongolia many adapted to the grassland ecology, abandoned farming and changed many of the ethnic traditions of what those authors call 'the Chinese Way'. They found that while the Han 'did not cease to be Chinese, and despite the homogenizing role of the state, the new Han cowboys of the Great Wall frontier have forged another kind of society' (Pasternak and Salaff 1993, p. 266).

The striking lack of fieldwork based studies of the recognised large and politically important Han resettlements sparked my initial interest in carrying out a project focusing directly on various Han

[4] Historical studies of Han migration to non-Han areas include, for instance, Qiao Wenbo 1993, Schwarz 1963, Lattimore 1932, Lattimore 1940, Lattimore 1950, Barfield 1989, Wiens 1967, Lee 1978, Lee 1982 and Giersch 2001. Other studies of Han migration to non-Han areas with a sociological, political and, more rarely, anthropological approach to the topic include McMillen 1981, Li Xiaofang 1996, Ma Rong 1993, Chen Yuning 1988, Pasternak and Salaff 1993, Williams 1996, Bernstein 1977, Ma Rong 1991, Ma Rong 1987, Lu Li and Wang Xiuyin 1986 and Li Xiaoxia 1998. Concerning the representation of minorities as a counter-image to the Han, see especially Gladney 1994 and Schein 1997. See Fong and Spickard 1994 and Blum 2001 concerning Han views of ethnic minorities. I return to a number of these studies in more detail in later chapters.

settlers living within ethnic minority areas. A number of questions arose with the collection and processing of fieldwork results, and in writing this book I have asked myself the following questions: how have participants in the Communist Party's various modernist projects in frontier regions responded to their resettlement in terms of engaging in relationships with local minorities and establishing networks among themselves? In other words, what are the cultural dynamics resulting from direct encounters between Han settlers and different local ethnic groups that are minorities in the People's Republic, and between Han settlers from different periods of the PRC, from different regions, and with different social status and access to power? This relates to the broader question of how a specific colonialist culture and civilising project is carried out, perceived, mediated and negotiated by different members of the officially construed and recognised dominant ethnic majority who have, for very different reasons, been resettled within strategically central minority regions.

Fieldwork and fieldwork sites

Anybody travelling, working or doing fieldwork in the so-called ethnic minority areas of China has encountered people in these areas who do not regard themselves as members of an ethnic minority (*shaoshu minzu*) and who are not officially recognised as such. People considering themselves to be Han and carrying an identity card officially testifying that they are Han inhabit, travel to, or work in practically all the areas of China referred to, and officially recognised as, ethnic minority areas (*shaoshu minzu diqu* or simply *minzu diqu*). Western scholars going to minority areas, whether Xinjiang, Tibet, Mongolia or the southwest, have first of all been interested in the indigenous populations of those regions—peoples who in some cases (for instance in the case of Tibet) have their own history as rulers of a previous independent political entity, and in many cases speak different languages from the Han, share different histories, have different cultural practices, and regard the Han as different from themselves. In the 1980s we had very limited anthropological knowledge of many of the societies and cultures of those numerous peoples who had for centuries been described as different categories of 'barbarians' (*yi, man, fan, hu*, etc.) in Chinese chronicles and gazetteers, and later became 'national minorities' or minority *minzu*. The term *minzu* has been translated as 'ethnic group', 'nationality', and sometimes 'race'. Either translation works in different contexts as an explanation of what is meant by the use of the term *minzu* in China. However, in cases where I refer to the special official categories of peoples—resulting from the state's classification work of the 1950s that eventually divided all China's peoples into fifty-six fixed ethnically defined categories—I leave the term untranslated.[5]

Within China, as pointed out by Wang Jianmin, the study of ethnology (*minzuxue*) has to a large extent in practice been the study of minorities (*shaoshu minzuxue*) while, on the other hand, the study of Han Chinese often has been perceived of as sociology (*shehuixue*) (Wang Jianmin 1997, pp. 6–7). In 1983 the discipline of folklore (*minsuxue*) was re-established in China after being banned during the Cultural Revolution and, according to Wang, those Chinese ethnologists who were concerned with the Han were mainly interested in folkloric aspects (Wang Jianmin, Zhang Haiyang and Hu Hongbao 1998: p. 379). Since the late 1980s a number of important new Chinese anthropological fieldwork projects in Han regions have been carried out.[6] Still, Wang argues that often scholars writing about the

---

[5] Until fieldwork became an option, the main entrance for studying the recent history and culture of many of these peoples was the Chinese material produced in the 1950s in connection with the large-scale government sponsored project of classification of the *minzu* and the determination of their stages of development, published in the voluminous series *Five Kinds of Collections on China's Minority Nationalities* (Guojia minwei minzu wenti wu zhong congshu bianwei hui, 1980–1992). Researchers working on ethnic minorities in China are compelled to some extent to take the Chinese official classification of *minzu* in China into account, because all individuals are registered according to it, because it determines significant aspects of people's lives such as education and population control, and because nearly all Chinese publications on minorities use the official designations of *minzu*. For publications on the impact of the official classification of *minzu*, see for instance McKhann 1995, Fei Xiaotong 1981, Gladney 1996, Wellens 1998 and Tapp 2002. With improved possibilities for conducting fieldwork, an increasing number of publications on minorities living in minority areas has been published in the West and in China. See for instance, Mueggler 2001, Jankowiak 1993, Gladney 1996, Lipman 1997, Harrell 1995, Brown 1996, Hansen 1999b, Dillon 1999, Litzinger 2000, Schein 2000. See also Chen Guoqiang 1993, Wang Jianmin 1997, Wang Jianmin, Zhang Haiyang, and Hu Hongbao 1998 for a review of the history of Chinese ethnology.

[6] For a few examples see Chen Guoqiang 1990, Wang Mingming 1996 and Wang Mingming 1997, Zhuang Kongohao 2000.

Han have paid little attention to cultural practices and have rarely employed methods of fieldwork because of the rich historical material about China and the Han (ibid. p. 379). To a large extent the Communist Party of China modelled its ideology and policy related to ethnic groups and minorities on the Soviet Union, and studies of minorities in China were until recently carried out first of all to facilitate policy making. Wang argues that just as Western anthropologists used to focus their interest on peoples whom they regarded as more backward and less modern than themselves, so did Han Chinese ethnologists to a large extent choose the ethnic minorities in China as their preferred objects of studies. Thus in essence Chinese ethnology became the study of minorities and sociology the study of the majority, the Han.

Today there is among Chinese anthropologists and ethnologists a diversity of opinions, theoretical approaches and methodologies that does not justify any sweeping generalisations as to how cultural studies of minorities and Han alike are pursued. However, many local cadres, teachers, administrators and also researchers in minority areas share the view that minorities are the only worthy research object for ethnologists and anthropologists in China, and the positivistic approach to minorities as objectively definable categories still has a strong position among many (though far from all) scholars. Some have argued for a second round of classification that would be more 'correct' than the one from the 1950s, some have embarked on a project of defining the Han as a *minzu* on the basis of the same Stalinist criteria that were originally (in principle more than in practice) used to classify people.

Most Chinese ethnologists working in minority areas are concerned with minorities' cultural practices, and when presenting and explaining my topic of research in minority areas, or to people engaged with local minority policy and research, I often met reactions of surprise as to why I would not rather choose to focus on a minority. Minorities, I was often told, were 'interesting' because they had 'rich and colourful customs' which were unlike those of the Han and unlike my own—in other words, they were not 'modern'. One Han cadre explained me that the Han 'were nothing special' (*mei shenme teshu de*). One American anthropologist, on the other hand, laughingly said that he felt sorry for me having actually to do fieldwork among Han. Among foreign tourists and scholars in minority areas (and even among some Han from larger cities) it is often said jokingly maybe, but as often with jokes not without a hint of seriousness that the Han are less friendly, less communicative and less hospitable than the minorities. At the same time, Han migration to minority areas (especially to Tibet and Xinjiang) has become a debated political issue, sometimes brought up in connection with international human rights disputes, and frequently creating political conflicts between international organisations, governments and international NGOs. Recently, this happened in connection with the much publicised debate (in 1999 and 2000 especially) about the World Bank's possible support for the Chinese Qaidam development and relocation project in Qinghai. This project spurred massive protest from the Tibet lobby and received much interest from the international media.[7] In 2000 China withdrew its request for World Bank support but went on with the project which involved the relocation of about 58,000 poor farmers from eastern parts of Qinghai partly into less populated traditional Tibetan and Mongolian areas of Qinghai.

For reasons such as this, my research into Han migrants and migrations to minority areas was often regarded with scepticism by local cadres and police who feared that my research was intended to support 'Western' criticism of China's human rights record. At one point of my fieldwork I felt that in order to be able to pursue my research in Tibetan Xiahe, I had to agree to an official request never directly to employ the concept of 'human rights' in publications describing the localities of my fieldwork. The issue was brought up not because I was dealing specifically with issues of human rights, nor because local people were particularly concerned with this notion, but because local officials were acutely aware of the potential negative local consequences of publications about their area employing a concept so heavily loaded with political connotations. The human rights disputes between the Chinese and especially the US and Western European governments and international organisations relate to issues of minority rights that inevitably also confront the topic of organised and unorganised Han resettlement in minority areas since the 1950s. Therefore, discussions about migrations to Tibet (and to a certain extent Xinjiang) especially have become so politicised (in

[7] See for instance Dunne 1999 and numerous other media reports.

China as well as in the United States and Europe) that it is sometimes difficult to catch sight of the people behind the discourse—
including Tibetans, Han and other groups which are far from homogeneous groups in terms of status, class, relations to government and
state, and levels of access to power. I do not intend to defend the well
documented increased influx of Han into Tibetan areas or the government's support of this immigration, but simply to add to the research concerning this immigration and its consequences by focusing
on the immigrants themselves, and their relations to the state, government, the colonialist project they are part of and the other ethnic
groups they encounter through their migration.

In the following I do not try to document, prove or disprove previous claims about the scope of Han migration to Tibet, Xinjiang or
any other officially designated 'minority area', though I do refer to
other studies on this.[8] My own research first of all focuses on Han
settlers in two local minority areas—settlers who came after the
1930s and most of them after 1950. A lot of issues discussed in this
book will have specific significance for those two areas, but at the
same time my own and others' experiences in many other minority
areas over the past fifteen years show that there are a number of similarities between minority areas that have been subjected to more or
less the same kind of policy shifts throughout the PRC. In spite of
obvious historical differences in their relations to the Chinese empire between the various regions of Tibet, Xinjiang, Mongolia and
the southwest of China, largely similar policies have been directed
towards all these areas during the past fifty years. Studies of Tibet, for
instance, may therefore benefit from knowledge developed in other
areas inhabited by non-Han, even though many Tibetans may not
regard themselves as a 'minority', or conceive their territory as a 'minority area' in the same terms as different ethnic groups in, for instance,
the southwest. One fundamental characteristic that the areas in which
I have done most of my research share with most other minority areas
is the fact that they have been subjected to Communist modernist
projects that were in effect continuations of a colonising effort involving large-scale immigration of Han. These immigrations have often

[8] Concerning the scale of Han immigration to the Tibet Autonomous Region
especially, see for instance Tibet Support Group UK 1995 and Clarke 1994.

profoundly changed social, economic, political and cultural relations locally. Furthermore, the social outcome of migrations resulting from earlier Communist projects is now being remade under new
conditions shaped by political reform and the shift from the planned
economy to an increasingly open and market oriented economy.

Based on fieldwork studies mainly, as well as on publications and
reports from China and the two fieldwork sites, the research presented in this book attempts to broaden our understanding of what
migration to a minority area implies for the Han settlers themselves,
to what extent and in what ways they are conscious of constituting a
national majority and what, if anything, it means for them to be part
of a national colonisation project. Empirically I focus on how Han
settlers in minority areas perceive and interact with the local ethnic
minorities; what relationships Han migrants form among each
other; how Han identities are eventually narrated differently among
different groups of Han migrants, and how Chinese discourses on
the Han and minorities are reproduced and eventually altered by
Han who themselves live within non-Han areas. This should lead to
a deeper understanding of how Communist modernist projects have
taken shape in frontier regions and what implications changes over
time have had for relations between minorities, majority and the state.
More generally the study hopefully contributes to a more nuanced
picture of what constitutes colonial culture and colonialism outside
the European context and as an ongoing project rather than a phenomenon of the past.

When writing a book about Han settlers in minority areas, one
inevitably encounters the basic question of how it is possible at all to
talk about 'Han Chinese', 'Han people' or simply 'Han'. 'The Han'
is a historically vague category of people that was first of all constructed as a race and dominant majority from the late Qing era and
the Republic, and only recently (in the PRC) officially categorised
as a definite 'nationality' or *minzu*.[9] As pointed out by Susan D. Blum
in one of the few publications specifically discussing Han individuals' views on ethnic minorities in China today, ethnonyms are often

---

[9] See for instance Dikötter 1997b, and Duara 1996. For recent research into various historical self-appellations of Chinese people, see for instance Chen Shu
1986, Chen Liankai 1991 and Xu Jieshun 1992.

'invoked and repeated until they seem to have a hardness or certainty that they scarcely have in some actual cases' (Blum 2000, pp. 148–9).[10] I use the term 'Han' throughout this book knowing that this categorisation is by no means 'hard' or 'certain' and that it is even meaningless in many contexts. My research among the Han living in ethnic minority areas partly aims to show how, when and why the notion of a common identification as Han is important, and why it is at other times irrelevant for people themselves categorised as Han. In any case Han people living among ethnic minorities in areas officially designated as minority autonomous areas are inevitably confronted with a number of situations in which ethnic membership is highlighted: through their own migration experience, in the education system, concerning the policy of population control, in recruitment to government positions, in religious celebrations, and in daily encounters with groups of people with different histories, cultural practices, languages and/or religions. Even those Han immigrants who do not personally experience any significant differences between themselves and, for instance, the local Tibetans or Tai can hardly avoid taking their 'being Han' into account. This is because of their official classification as Han and, more important, the strongly manifested discourse on the differences between 'Han' as a group and 'minorities' as a group, reproduced in the education system, in the media and in other popular sources of communication.

In connection with the dominant nationalist paradigm in China since the late 1980s some scholars in the PRC have started to represent the Han as a *minzu* in very much the same terms and style as the minorities have been described and essentialised as *minzu*. A common Chinese nation, the *Zhonghua minzu*, is actively promoted in the school system as an identity that includes all the minorities as well as the Han, and some scholars have recently constructed essentialist notions of how the Han as a clearly defined ethnic group fit into this overall identity. Some have tried to apply Stalin's well known criteria for an ethnic group (common language, territory, economic life and culture) to describe the Han, largely ignoring the internal differences of history, class, cultural practices, identities, dialects and beliefs of those officially recognised as Han. Xu Jieshun, for instance,

---

[10] See also Blum 2001.

has published widely about the Han as a *minzu* and argues that 'Just as it is impossible to cut off a historical tradition, so it is impossible not to pass on the nature of an ethnic group (*minzu xingge*)' (Xu Jieshun 1992, p. 450). According to Xu, the Han's 'nature', like the 'nature' of all other *minzu*, has its good and bad sides. The Han are characterised by being, for instance, firm and tenacious, energetic and not afraid to sacrifice themselves, honest, introvert, and so forth (Xu Jieshun 1992, pp. 446–56). Xu Jieshun argues in words coloured by Han-nationalist sentiments that since the Han is the largest *minzu* of all, much more attention should be paid to it:

> In the vast world, among all human beings and in the forest of ethnic groups, which is the largest ethnic group? The Han. Which ethnic group has the largest population? The Han. Which ethnic group may be found everywhere? The Han. Which ethnic group has the longest history? Here we can also say, the Han. (Xu Jieshun 1992, p. 50)

> This kind of leading position and main role of the Han nationality in the modern history of China indicate for all the nationalities and people in the country—as well as in the world—that the Han nationality is the mainstay backbone of the Chinese nation. (Xu Jieshun 1992, p. 297)

The essentialised descriptions in scholarly and popular books and magazines of the Han as a *minzu* reach local minority regions through the media, the education system and individuals' interests in these issues. Quite a few Han immigrants in minority areas who were interviewed made references to such objectified descriptions of them as 'Han' with certain inherited characterisations. This supported them in their experiences of being 'different' in the encounter with the indigenous ethnic groups living in the areas to which they themselves had migrated. In spite of other, often more important cleavages and different interests in local minority areas, distinct from those marked by different ethnicity, the impact of the essentialised descriptions of the Han as an ethnic majority group which are part of a long and persistent discourse in China on the benefits of Han resettlement in minority areas tended to enforce ethnic boundaries experienced by Han through their immigration.

Large organised migration from Chinese areas to regions over which the state has tried to establish control is obviously not a new phenomenon. Colonisation projects including large numbers of peasant-soldier resettlers were organised by the Chinese state from the Qin Dynasty (221–206 BCE) onwards. In 221 BCE the first Qin emperor, Qin Shi Huangdi, ordered more than 500,000 military colonists to settle in the south. During the following Han Dynasty (206 BCE–220 CE) the northern border regions of China were thoroughly colonised when more than one and a half million Chinese from the core area of the Han Dynasty were resettled there— the Han government providing them with housing, food, clothing and sometimes even travel allowances (Lee 1978). Often government organised migrants were resettled in state-owned farms and agricultural colonies, for instance in Mongolia and areas covered by today's Xinjiang Province, and the Ming Dynasty (1368–1644), for instance, established military agricultural colonies in Sichuan, Guizhou and Yunnan (Wiens 1967, pp. 196–7). Throughout Chinese history migration has been looked upon as a useful tool for curbing unrest and easing the population pressure in the centre of Chinese territory. The Manchu rulers of the last dynasty, the Qing, tried to prevent Han settlements in the northern Mongolian and Manchu areas with mixed success. They did not succeed in their attempt to keep a kind of 'Manchu homeland' and later this policy was abandoned altogether.[11]

In addition to the government supported or organised historic resettlements in frontier areas of China, large-scale individual migrations have also taken place as a result of overpopulation of certain areas, wars, famines, epidemics, natural catastrophes, etc.[12] According to Lee, private migrations were larger in scale than government organised resettlements after the year 1000 and until the late nineteenth century (Lee 1978, p. 34). For the Communist leadership of the PRC, resettlement of cadres, soldiers and peasants into areas dominated by non-Han peoples was also regarded as a necessity for ensuring political control and efficient administration of those areas, and for developing a country with a unified education system, health services,

---

[11] On relations between Han and Manchu during the Qing Dynasty see Rhoads 2000.

[12] See for instance Wiens 1967 concerning migrations towards the south.

economy and administration. Partly for those reasons, areas traditionally inhabited by mainly non-Han groups have experienced large-
scale government organised immigration since 1949. Since the period of the economic reforms from the 1980s, more spontaneous
and mostly economically motivated resettlements of Han people
have followed. This is part of a modernisation process where local
developments in the field of tourism, trade, agricultural production
and industries have generated new immigrations that are not directly
controlled by the government, but often supported and indirectly
initiated by government activities.

In Inner Mongolia heavy immigration of Han took off especially
after 1911 when the rulers of the Chinese Republic encouraged
Han people to settle there, and it continued well into the time of the
PRC. In 1991, according to official figures, the total population of
Inner Mongolia was 21,647,900 people of whom 18.8 per cent or
4,061,000 people were non-Han, most of them Mongolians, and
80.2 per cent or 17.5 million were Han (Economy Department of
National Minzu Commission *et al.* 1992, p. 60). The Han population had grown from about 5 million in 1949 to over 17 million in
1991, but already before 1949 they constituted the majority. This
increase of Han has mainly been due to the immigration of farmers,
as Uradyn E. Bulag describes:

> The Chinese colonization of Inner Mongolia had many of the
> characteristics of the American opening up of the native Indian
> frontiers though it less frequently involved either ethnic cleansing
> or genocide. The reclaimed 'wasteland' (pasture) was settled by
> Chinese farmers, who were administered by specially established
> county governments. (Bulag 2004, p. 87)

One of the other minority regions with very heavy Han immigration since 1949 is the Uighur Autonomous Region of Xinjiang,
largely inhabited by different Muslim groups. In 1948 the population of Xinjiang was about 4 million with approximately 6 per cent
Han (Barnett 1993, pp. 343–4). As a result of large immigrations of
Han—mainly sparked off by government resettlement projects and
various incentives given to resettlers—this figure has dramatically increased, so that the Han in 1991 officially made up about 30 per cent
of the total population of 15,280,300 people (Economy Department

of National Minzu Commission *et al.*, 1992, p. 60). The number of unregistered settlers in Xinjiang is undoubtedly very high, and an article in the *Far Eastern Economic Review* mentions an unconfirmed figure of approximately 250,000 Han migrants to Xinjiang every year.[13] Today the demographic composition and economy of Xinjiang are characteristic of an internal colony with Han settlers occupying the more prosperous regions and sectors of society. Within the Xinjiang Production and Construction Corps—described by David Bachman as 'an empire almost to itself within Xinjiang with production, military, paramilitary, and "judicial" functions'[14]—about 2.4 million people (most of them Han) reside.[15]

Of all the organised and spontaneous Han migrations to minority areas, the most politically sensitive ones in the relations between China, the United States and Europe have been those to Tibet. These migrations are continuously subject to discussions and criticism. As in Xinjiang and other minority areas it is not possible to find exact figures of the scope of migration to the Tibet Autonomous Region (TAR, established in 1965) and to the areas of Amdo and Kham that today are incorporated into the provinces of Qinghai, Gansu, Yunnan and Sichuan. Tibetan areas within these provinces have mostly been granted status as local autonomous Tibetan counties and prefectures. It is impossible to find exact and reliable figures on immigration to Tibetan areas for several reasons: an ongoing spontaneous, individual and largely unregistered migration; unreliable figures concerning the number of troops; and the fact that many Han who stay for only shorter periods of time, or during certain seasons, are excluded from most statistics.[16] The number of Han settlers and the degree of their increase vary considerably from area to area, and the proportion of Han is much larger in Tibetan areas outside the TAR than inside. According to official Chinese statistics the population of the TAR was 2,217,800 in 1991, of whom only 2.9 per cent were Han (2,152,700 Tibetans and other minorities, and only 65,100 Han). This figure, however, excludes military

[13] Hoh 2000, p. 25.
[14] Bachman 2004, p. 3.
[15] See also Bovingdon 2004 and Becquelin 2000.
[16] See for instance Grunfeld 1996, pp. 218–22 concerning the problems of determining the scope of Han migrations to Tibet.

personel and the large number of unregistered seasonal settlers and business people.

The Chinese researcher Ma Rong has collected a number of figures from China on Han migration to the TAR. His figures suggest that the Han population increased from less than 20,000 before the mid-1950s to more than 120,000 in 1980, when they were supposed to have made up about 6 per cent of the population. After 1980, the number of Han fell again according to Ma, and he believes that there were about 65,000 civilian Han in Tibet by the mid-1990s, or less than 3 per cent (Ma Rong 1996, p. 67). If we look at official figures of Han (again excluding large numbers of unregistered settlers) in all Tibetan autonomous areas together, there were 426,000 in 1953 and 1.5 million in 1990. The increase was mainly due to immigration, and the largest immigration of Han took place in Qinghai province where the proportion of Han in the six Tibetan prefectures seemingly went up from 8 per cent in 1953 to 37 per cent in 1990.[17]

To some extent the situation for Han settlers in minority areas in China between the 1950s and 1970s resembled that of many Russians in the non-Russian republics of the former Soviet Union, especially after the 1930s. According to Pål Kolstø, most Western scholarship on the Soviet Union has claimed that Russians in non-Russian republics made up a common privileged group who enjoyed institutionalised cultural support unavailable to other nationalities living outside their own republics, and had access to desirable jobs without having to study local languages (Kolstø 1995, p. 71). This is disputed by many of the Russians who themselves experienced living in non-Russian republics. The status and position of Russian settlers in the republics were far from uniform or constant over time during the period of the Soviet Union, and important policy changes during the times of Lenin, Stalin, Khrushchev and Brezhnev also affected ethnic relations and the status of Russians living in non-Russian republics (ibid. p. 72).[18] While Russian settlers tended to have only weak notions of a Russian 'homeland' or common Russian ancestors (making them, according to Melvin, an ethnic category with only a dim consciousness of forming a separate, ethnic collectivity) a

---

[17] Based on figures from Ma Rong 1996, pp. 61–3 and Economy Department of National Minzu Commission *et al.* 1992, pp. 833–68.

[18] See also Melvin 1995.

new Russian diaspora (*Rossiiskaia diaspora*) developed after the disintegration of the Soviet Union. Among some Russian settlers this forged a stronger ethno-based identification replacing previous identification with the whole Soviet state (Melvin 1995, pp. 6–10).

Major changes in the status of Russians living in non-Russian areas of the Soviet Union took place after 1933 when Russian migration to the outlying regions increased considerably and the number of Russians in leadership positions rose rapidly—not as a result of direct ethnic favouritism, but as an indirect result of their higher level of education based on the Russian language. Stalin regarded an increase in the number of Russians in the non-Russian republics as a way of strengthening political stability, and 'wherever the Russians moved in, Russian-language schools were opened and Russian-language newspapers and other facilities were established to cater for their cultural needs' (Kolstø 1995, p. 83). One reason for maintaining the Russian language in a special position in all the republics was its unique position as the language of communication within the political centre and administration. Therefore, it also became the language of inter-ethnic communication in the different republics. This is a situation very similar to China, and Mandarin in China, like the Russian language in the Soviet empire, became not merely the *lingua franca* but also the language of success.[19] However, in China, unlike in the Soviet Union, an additional reason for the government's emphasis on the study of the Chinese language (Mandarin or standard Chinese, *putonghua*) at the expense of local languages is the overwhelming majority of Chinese speakers in the PRC. Furthermore, as part of the dominant social-Darwinist discourse on the minorities being less developed than the Han, many scholars and educational cadres in China have insisted that most minority languages are less developed than Chinese and consequently unfit for a modernising society.[20]

There is basis for claiming that many (though far from all) Han Chinese settlers in minority areas after the 1950s enjoyed certain privileges that the local minorities did not. At the same time, it is

[19] The expression 'language of success' is used by Melvin to describe the status of the Russian language (Melvin 1995, p. 8).

[20] Concerning the ways in which this argument has been put forward in China, see for instance Hansen 1999a, chap. 5.

necessary to take a much more varied look at how situations changed over time for those Han, how different people migrated for different reasons and with different backgrounds, how their relationships with their places of origin developed, how they were received by the local communities, and how they themselves perceived their situation and their relation to the state, the government and their new localities. As in the case of some Russians, some Han were 'kept hostage' by government policies and had in practice no choice but to follow suit. Rogers Brubaker has suggested that one of the biggest assets of Russians living in non-Russian republics during the Soviet Union might have been their psychological sense of security, based on their feelings of belonging to the union-wide dominant nationality, rather than the concrete privileges they were enjoying (Kolstø 1995, pp. 103–4, referring to Brubaker). I return in following chapters to this sense of purpose, this sense of being part of a politically important and dominant group with a civilising mission in a minority area, as expressed by some though far from all Han migrants discussed in this book.

The research of this book is mainly based on field research including studies of especially local publications and reports from and about Han settlers in minority areas. Field research was carried out in two different minority areas, namely the county of Xiahe within Gannan Tibetan Autonomous Prefecture in Gansu Province and Sipsong Panna (Xishuangbanna) Tai Autonomous Prefecture in Yunnan Province.[21] In these two areas, the vast majority of Han arrived after the 1950s. I have been interested in settlers' different memories of and various reasons for migration, their relations to their 'old home' (*laojia*), their interaction with and perceptions of the local ethnic minorities among whom they live, their relations among each other and to the state. I have also been focusing on how state institutions,

---

[21] Throughout I use the transcription Sipsong Panna (or simply Panna) which is a common transcription of the name of the area based on the language of the Tai people themselves. The transcription 'Xishuangbanna' is the Chinese name based on the name in the local Tai language. The Tai in Sipsong Panna also call themselves Tai Lue (Le) in comparison with other Tai groups such as, for instance, the Tai Na in Dehong. They are all officially classified as the *Daizu*. Throughout the book I prefer the transcription of Tai in line with scholars who base their research on the language of the Tai rather than on Chinese.

such as the state farms in Sipsong Panna, participated actively in a project to rework into internal publications the experiences, life stories and world views of Han settlers. Rather than focusing exclusively on the dominant Chinese official discourse on minorities I have attempted to understand how a dominant discourse was eventually reproduced, re-formed, re-informed, ignored or rejected by different people, all being conscious of their belonging to the Han majority in China.

Fieldwork in the two areas consisted of a combination of formal interviews, informal talks, all-village surveys and participation in local events. In addition to the structured fieldwork I have also drawn on data collected during several previous years of fieldwork in Chinese ethnic minority areas since 1990. Life histories and settlers' recollections of their own migration made up an important part of the study and highlighted the distinction between '*reality* (what is out there, whatever that may be), *experience* (how that reality presents itself to consciousness), and *expressions* (how individual experience is framed and articulated)' (Bruner 1986, p. 6, my emphasis). The interviewees had their personal histories of migration and their own way of telling them, highlighting certain events, ignoring others, remembering some and forgetting others.

In the stories told by the Han settlers a series of temporal events were recalled so that a meaningful sequence was portrayed, constituting the story or plot of their narrative (A. P. Kerby referred to in Rapport and Dawson 1998a, p. 28). This is what Margaret R. Somers calls 'emplotment' through which the narrative translates events into episodes. The emplotment gives significance to independent instances, not their chronological or categorical order (Somers 1994, p. 616). Most interviewees enjoyed talking about their migration history which clearly played an important role in their lives. Especially for the Han administrators, party officials, teachers and doctors I talked to, moving to their present area of settlement was an event, or an experience, in the sense that it had a beginning and an end, and was articulated or transformed into an expression. It stood out from the ordinary, from the 'temporal flow' of experiences a person constantly has (Bruner 1986, p. 6). It was something to tell stories about—stories where the event was transformed into experience by focus on personal hardships, astonishment at the living style of the local minorities and, for some, memories of being participants in a then important political mission where the collective goals were apparently higher and more honourable than those of any single individual participating in the movement. The 'experiences', as they were recounted and represented to me, were not examples of 'truthful evidence' of what had taken place, but rather stories that highlighted the changing ways in which Han settlers, as conscious or unconscious participants in the Chinese state's civilising and modernisation projects, were able to rework and represent their changing positions as a constructed civilised majority with uncertain and shifting relations to state power.

Many situations during fieldwork made clear the fact that Han settlers in minority areas are highly stratified in terms of class, and have different levels of access to power and profoundly different ways of interacting with the state's various local institutions. This also had consequences for the fieldwork situation itself. By coincidence I was lodging in the Committee for Family Planning's office building during my periods of fieldwork in Xiahe in Gannan. The daily practices at this office were not directly related to my work, but since I was literally living in the midst of the office building I got to know a range of people related in one way or the other to the committee, and had plenty of opportunity to talk to women who came for controls and check-ups related to birth control and the health service. This was not entirely without problems in terms of the fieldwork I wanted to carry out. Especially since my two children stayed with me for some months of fieldwork, everybody in town knew who I was and regarded me as somehow connected with the rather unpopular Committee for Family Planning. While I mostly felt that it was possible to disconnect myself from the committee through longer talks with peasants and traders, my acquaintance with the daily work of the committee made me more aware than ever of how state organisations' intrusion into the private life of people over a long period of time has made many peasants used to receiving 'investigators'. Peasants have become accustomed to people approaching them asking all kinds of questions related to family, education, economic circumstances etc. In the frequent encounters with state organisations carrying out surveys, making propaganda and promoting new policies, peasants have no option of refusing the intrusion into their village or family life. They have to receive the state representatives in their homes, and answer whatever question is asked. Therefore, investigators or researchers are almost inevitably associated with state power by peasants who often routinely receive them and politely supply them with the information they want.

Many of the cadres I knew in Xiahe thought that this was a great advantage for me because, as they said, this made it easy for peasants to handle the fact that I as a foreign woman would also want to carry out my own 'investigation' (*kaocha*). In other words, I was supposedly able to profit from the state's history of intrusion into the lowest levels of people's private spheres. It remains unclear whether most peasants would agree with me that the state's investigations into their life situations could be regarded as intrusion into a private sphere. However, to me the habitual way of managing questions asked by people presumably possessing powers beyond the village created a distance in some of the interviews with peasants, which I had not previously experienced as poignantly as this time, and which could only be diminished through multiple and long-term visits.

The period of reform and modernisation of China of the past twenty-five years has brought a whole range of new social opportunities to peasants and workers all over China—opportunities that may be real, but may also have first of all a strong imaginary appeal to people whose life situations are uncertain. As discussed by Arjun Appadurai, '…the new power of the imagination in the fabrication of social lives is inescapably tied up with images, ideas, and opportunities that come from elsewhere, often moved around by the vehicles of mass media' (Appadurai 1996, p. 54). Imagined life possibilities are often unrealistic, but no less real to the people who imagine: 'Prisoners of conscience, child labourers, women who toil in the fields and factories of the world, and others whose lot is harsh no longer see their lives as mere outcomes of the givenness of things, but often as the ironic compromise between what they could imagine and what social life will permit' (Appadurai 1996, p. 54). For Han settlers (whose lot, to be sure, is generally not as harsh as that of the child labourers Appadurai refers to) the imagination of life possibilities, of imagined opportunities to improve their conditions, played an important role in their own representations of their migration histories and current situation as Han settlers. They experience unprecedented possibilities in China of moving more or less freely in search of jobs, they have access to media praising the opportunities rather than exposing the problems for laid-off workers, and they watch American soap operas in addition to even more popular Chinese soaps that mostly focus on urban middle class people.

But often media descriptions and depictions of social life in China are in strong contradiction to the experiences of laid-off workers and peasant migrants. Likewise many government migrants from the 1950s and 60s felt that they had lost opportunities because of their previous migration that was a direct result of another time's political trend. They tended to represent the past, rather than the present, as a period when one imagined exciting change. It is probably true that 'More persons in more parts of the world consider a wider set of possible lives than they ever did before' (Appadurai 1996, p. 55), but it is of course very difficult actually to *know* what people are imagining. In the study of Han settlers in minority areas I often found that immigrants from the Communist period from the 1950s to the 1970s especially had very strong imaginations about their own life possibilities in the past—imaginations about what had been possible, and what their mission was during the Maoist era. Concerning the present time, on the contrary, some expressed a loss of imagination of alternative life opportunities, and a loss of imagination of the very meaning behind their resettlement. So while imagination was clearly an important part of people's life stories and biographies, to make something meaningful out of this imagination I have sought to study it as an integrated part of people's concrete social life and the historical context in which they accounted for it.

Gannan Tibetan Autonomous Prefecture, Xiahe County. Situated in Gansu Province on the present southwestern borders of Sichuan and Qinghai provinces, the area of Gannan has for long been a frontier area of Tibetan, Chinese and Muslim (Hui) culture. The Tibetan centre of Labrang (in the present county of Xiahe, in the Prefecture of Gannan) borders what used to be the Muslim dominated area of Hezhou (now Linxia) and 'define[s] an ethnic-cultural progression between China and Tibet' (Lipman 1997, p. 13).[22] Migrations

---

[22] See Lipman 1997 for a historical narrative of Muslims in Gansu, especially in Linxia area.

between the area of Linxia and Labrang have been common during history, and the wealth and political power of the Tibetan monasteries in Labrang, Zhuoni and Kumbum (in today's Qinghai) attracted craftsmen, salesmen and settlers up to the 1950s. Today Gannan Tibetan Autonomous Prefecture is made up of the counties of Xiahe (in which the prefecture capital Hezuo is situated), Luqu, Maqu, Zhuoni, Lintan, Diebu and Zhouqu. The prefecture was established in 1953.[23] At this time the government seat was in Xiahe town adjacent to Labrang Monastery. Monks and reincarnated lamas (*tulku* or *sprul sku*) in Labrang enjoyed very high prestige among the Tibetans, and according to interviews with people who were sent to Xiahe at that time in order to establish the new Communist government, it was therefore inconvenient and extremely difficult to build a powerful new political centre in this town. To facilitate the establishment of a new Communist government and remove power from the monastery, the prefecture capital was in 1956 moved to Hezuo which then consisted of a small market town and a temple. Today, Hezuo has developed into the largest city in Gannan with more than 30,000 inhabitants.

In 1953 there were 300,494 inhabitants in Gannan Prefecture of whom 52.7 per cent were Tibetans and 39 per cent Han (Ma Rong 1996, p. 61); in 1982 there were 515,453 people of whom 44.7 per cent were Tibetans, 48 per cent were Han and 6.9 per cent were Hui (Editing Commission of 'A General Survey of Gannan Tibetan Nationality Autonomous Prefecture' 1986, p. 31). Nearly all of my fieldwork was carried out in Xiahe county (in villages around the city of Xiahe and in the county seat itself). I also talked to and interviewed many people who had originally migrated to other places in Gannan Prefecture, and then later moved on to Xiahe.[24] Xiahe county and town are known for the Buddhist monastery of Labrang, syncretistic in architecture and style while wholly orthodox in religious practice and function (Gaubatz 1996, p. 202).[25] Labrang is a

---

[23] From 1953 to 1954 it was called *qu* instead of *zhou*.

[24] I was very interested in doing fieldwork in other parts of Gannan, especially in Zhuoni where there has been Han migration since the time of the Ming and Qing dynasties, but I was not able to obtain permission for this since the area at the time of my fieldwork was not yet open for foreigners.

[25] A recent doctoral thesis (Makley 1999) discusses issues of gender and monastic revitalisation on the basis of long term fieldwork in Labrang. Numerous publica-

national cultural preservation site and a tourist destination, mainly
for Chinese tourists. Tourism is still on a much smaller scale than in
Sipsong Panna, but it has been estimated to bring in over 6 million
yuan annually (Makley 1999, p. 98). Between 1985 and 1992 about
178,000 tourists visited Xiahe, 88 per cent of them Chinese (Commission for Editing Historical Annals in Xiahe County, Gansu Province 1997, p. 958).

Xiahe town is an example of a 'twin city' as described by Piper
Rae Gaubatz. Twin cities develop as a result of occupying forces that
establish a new city or fortified settlement adjacent to an existing indigenous settlement (Gaubatz 1996, p. 175). The original settlement
is not destroyed in the process. As it is a 'frontier of control' rather
than a 'frontier of agricultural settlement' (ibid. p. 20), migrants in
Gannan Prefecture have tended to settle in and develop towns rather
than expanding into the hinterland which was considered hostile
and difficult for them to adapt to. Most of Xiahe and Gannan's hinterland consisted of grassland (making up more than 50 per cent of
the area of Gannan) demanding a kind of production unfamiliar to
the Han. The twin city pattern of a settlement of control is obvious
in Xiahe town today: one part of the town is made up of the monastery of Labrang surrounded by its large residential areas for monks,
while the other part consists of the market, the main shopping area,
and the government seat. A government office was set up under the
Republic in Xiahe in 1926, and already in a Chinese gazetteer from
1934 the twin structure of Xiahe was described:

> Xiahe County is in fact established in connection with Labrang
> Monastery which is really the most splendid place of that county.
> Thus, the county [jurisdiction] may be divided into two parts: one
> is the market street which is the mixed city of Han, Hui and
> Tibetans; the other is the temple which is the religious centre of
> the Tibetans and one of the six large temples of the Yellow Sect.
> (Zhang Qiyun 1978 [1934], p. 87)

When the Chinese government was established in Xiahe town in
1926 it was reported that there were 34,200 people living in the

---

tions in Chinese (often written by Tibetans) about the monastery of Labrang have
appeared for sale in several of the local private bookshops in recent years: for
instance, Dan Qu 1994, Suo Dai 1992, Miao Zishu *et al.* 1987, Dan Qu 1998.

whole county (Zhang Qiyun 1978 [1934], p. 75). In 1928 Xiahe county was established and incorporated into Gansu Province. In 1934 there were reportedly 5,200 people living in the county seat (constituting 15 per cent of the entire county) east of the temple area: about 170 Tibetan families, and 200 Hui and Han families who had all migrated to Xiahe from other places. There were 2,500–2,600 monks and *tulkus* in Labrang monastery (Commission for Editing Historical Annals in Xiahe County Gansu Province 1997, p. 991 and Zhang Qiyun 1978 [1934], p. 77). The population grew to 139,634 people in Xiahe county in 1990, of whom 62 per cent were Tibetans, 26 per cent were Han, and 11 per cent were Hui (based on figures from Commission for Editing Historical Annals in Xiahe County, Gansu Province 1997, p. 526). In comparison, according to estimates from around 1950 there had been more than 90 per cent Tibetans in Xiahe just before the Communist takeover (Ya Hanzhang 1991, p. 40).

Historically Xiahe (and Gannan) formed part of the Tibetan area of Amdo. The monastery of Labrang was established in 1710 by the first incarnation of Jam-dByangs bZhad (known in Chinese as Jiamu-yang). At the same time some Tibetans settled down in the neighbourhood of the new temple, and gradually both the population and the monastery grew. In the early twentieth century there were thirteen villages mainly made up of Tibetan herdsmen who had fully or partly settled in Labrang as farmers (Commission for Editing Historical Annals in Xiahe County, Gansu Province 1997, p. 990). Muslim uprisings in the neighbouring Linxia area resulted in Han (and some Hui) peasants and traders migrating to Xiahe, mainly from the 1930s. At least since the time of the Qing Dynasty there has been agricultural production in Xiahe as well as animal husbandry, but except for a period between 1958 and 1962, animal husbandry on the grasslands has been more important than agriculture. Production in the pastoral areas fell disastrously when after 1958 (during the policy of the Great Leap Forward) more than 22,678 hectares of grassland were changed into agricultural land (ibid. p. 713). As in the rest of the country during this time, grain production was emphasised at any price, and in pastoral areas, mostly unsuitable for agriculture, people suffered immensely because of this.

Until the Communist land reforms were completed in Xiahe in 1953, all agricultural land around Labrang was owned by Labrang monastery and its monks. Peasant families (many of them Hui and Han from the nearby Linxia area) opened up new land themselves and paid part of their production as rent to the various *tulkus* who administered the land of the monastery. Most of the Han and Hui peasant families had come to Xiahe between the 1920s and 1940s and established a living there based on production from land rented from the monastery. According to the local gazetteer from Xiahe, cultivation of land in Labrang before 1949 was divided between 17 families who had independent land; 15.5 families (*sic!*) who were half-independent; and 471 families who rented land from the monastery (ibid. p. 784). The monastery also owned large tracts of forest. This was confiscated as national property in 1958 in connection with the collectivisation of land and the transition into People's Communes (*renmin gongshe*). In the same year Chinese troops crushed armed Tibetan revolts in Amdo, including some parts of Gannan. Although the crushing of religious expressions and revolts during this period was later criticised for being too harsh, publications still insist that this so-called 'battle against feudalism' was necessary in order to promote 'the unity of the *minzu*' (*minzu tuanjie*) (e.g. Editing Commission of 'A General Survey of Gannan Tibetan Nationality Autonomous Prefecture' 1986, p. 149).

Government supported migration to Xiahe increased during the 1960s and 70s, but owing to the unsuccessful attempts to establish larger state farms, the state organised immigration of Han never reached the same proportions as in, for instance, Sipsong Panna. New immigrations of Han took off after the mid-1980s, especially after the rebuilding of Labrang monastery which was partly destroyed during the Cultural Revolution. With the development of tourism, new individual Han immigrants mostly from neighbouring areas have come to work in shops, restaurants, hotels and construction in Xiahe, as well as in other places in the prefecture of Gannan.

Sipsong Panna Tai Autonomous Prefecture.   In 1985, when I first visited Sipsong Panna in the southwestern part of Yunnan Province on the borders of Burma and Laos, I could either catch a three-day bus from Kunming, or take a small and irregular fight from Kunming to Simao and then catch a bus for twelve-hour journey from Simao for the rest of the way to the prefectural capital Jinghong. In 1918 the last part of this trip alone—from Simao to Jinghong—took at least six days with a horse caravan, according to the missionary William Clifton Dodd (Dodd 1992). In 2000 there were six to eight Boeing 737 planes a day flying between Kunming and Jinghong, bringing in crowds of mainly Chinese tourists (and some businessmen) longing to see the legendary sub-tropical Sipsong Panna. On the plane, travellers full of expectations could sing along with the pop-hit 'Beautiful Sipsong Panna' (*Meili de Xishuangbanna*), known all over China from a popular TV series about love and family intrigues resulting from unfortunate love affairs between young Han Chinese intellectuals and local Tai in the 1970s. From being a small Tai kingdom, peripheral to the Chinese state and difficult of access from China, Sipsong Panna has been turned into an extremely popular tourist destination which offers—to the visitor longing for beauty, simplicity, adventure and entertainment—primeval forest (the little that is left of it), restaurants with staged 'traditional' dancing by minority women (or Han women dressed as minority women), 'ethnic villages' (for some of which you need entrance tickets), and plenty of massage parlours and bars. It offers a glimpse into cultures of South East Asia, until recently was inaccessible for the common Chinese citizen.

Li Foyi, a Guomindang official working in Sipsong Panna in the 1920s and 30s, would hardly have believed his eyes. Before the late 1940s the only Han living in Sipsong Panna—apart from some individual migrants who had come before the 1920s and who were hardly recognisable as Han any longer—were the representatives of the Guomindang government. Li Foyi was one of them and he tried to convince more Chinese from South East Asia to go to Sipsong Panna and develop, for instance, tea production.[26] In Burma he told a group of Chinese that a fortune could be made in Sipsong Panna by competent people making proper use of the region's abundant gold, silver, copper, medicinal herbs and fertile land. He argued that since there was plenty of space with only seven people per square kilometre, Panna would easily accommodate 800,000 (Han) immigrants (Hou Zurong 1995). At that time there were probably about 200,000 people living in Sipsong Panna.[27] Most of those were Tai people whose king, princes and government in practice controlled the area together with the other line of administration, that of the Guomindang.

[26] See Hill 1989 concerning the tea trade in Sipsong Panna.
[27] Hsieh Shih-Chung 1989, p. 60.

As today, the Tai mostly occupied the fertile plains engaging in wet-rice cultivation, while other ethnic groups such as the Akha, Blang, Lahu and Jinuo mostly lived higher up in the mountains, depending mainly on hunting, gathering and slash and burn agriculture. By the early 1940s the Han population constituted less than a half per cent according to Chen Han-seng (Chen Han-seng 1949, p. 5).

After 1911 representatives of the new Chinese Republic had established offices in Panna. Following the traditional pattern of settlement in frontier areas, they had built the new government seat at a few kilometres' distance from the traditional centre of the local power holders. The Tai king and government were centred in what was called Xianyigai, down the Mekong River from today's Jinghong town. According to Chen, the Chinese conquest of Sipsong Panna west of the Mekong was still incomplete by 1940 and a two-strata administration by the Tai hereditary chiefs and the Chinese magistrates continued to function (Chen Han-seng 1949, pp. 15–16).[28] However, after 1950 a Chinese city had been established some kilometres upstream on the Mekong River and Xianyigai was eradicated as a power centre. The palace itself was destroyed to make way for a rubber producing state farm during the Great Leap Forward.[29] Like Xiahe town, Jinghong town became a typical 'frontier of control' where the new settlers clustered in the new Chinese town, making little attempt to expand into the hinterland which was regarded as too marginal or hostile to support rural settlement (Gaubatz 1996, p. 21). Only with the establishment since 1956 of rubber producing state farms did new Han settlements gradually expand into the hinterland.

After 1949 the new Communist government wanted to establish firm control in the border provinces, and as a consequence nearly 500,000 persons moved, or were directly transferred, to Yunnan Province between 1950 and 1958 as military personnel, cadres and workers reclaiming wasteland (Li Debin, Shi Fang, and Gao Lin 1994, p. 364). As a border region with natural resources, scarce population,

[28] See also Davis 2003.

[29] In the mid-1990s the local government decided to rebuild the palace and its adherent temple, and protect the little that was left of the primeval forest near the temple in order to promote tourism. When I visited Xianyigai in 1997, this work had not yet started and there were only some ruins of the previous temple to be found. During my last visit in 2000 I found that the plans had apparently been given up.

and potential for developing rubber production, Sipsong Panna was a region of special interest. Whereas the Han population in Sipsong Panna only made up a few per cent before the 1950s, it has been growing steadily ever since. The total population of the area today is 817,000, and according to official population statistics (from the end of 1995) people officially registered as Han make up 26 per cent of the total Sipsong Panna population. In the county of Jinghong[30] they make up 34 per cent, but in the prefectural capital which is also called Jinghong they make up as much as 48 per cent.[31] Since only those who are registered as having moved to Sipsong Panna are counted in these statistics, the actual proportion of Han Chinese is considerably higher. Local government cadres have estimated the size of the unregistered 'floating population' (*liudong renkou*) at more than 32,000 people, in Jinghong county in 1990. The figure today is certainly much higher since the in-migration has increased visibly since 1990. Officially about 24,000 people migrated to Jinghong county between 1982 and 1990; most of them were construction workers, individual entrepreneurs and farmers. Among the migrants are members of the Bai, Hui, Naxi and other nationalities in Yunnan, but the vast majority were, and still are, Han. Today, the Han make up at least one third of the entire population in Sipsong Panna, the Tai make up another third, and the last third is made up of the various other local ethnic minorities such as the Akha, Blang, Lahu and Jinuo.

Already in the 1930s, in order to encourage more Han people to go to Panna, Li Foyi had praised the Tai for being peace loving and hospitable, for liking the Han people, for helping each other and re-garding the fields as common property of the villages.[32] However, for most Han Chinese who heard about Panna at that time the potential attractions of the area were overshadowed by fear of wildness and the uncontrolled. A recent article characterised Panna before the Communist 'Liberation' in this way:

> In the old China, Sipsong Panna was not only characterised by having an extremely backward economy and culture and being difficult to access. It was also a wild and barren place where

---

[30] Since 1996 Jinghong city (*shi*).
[31] Information copied from local, unpublished government statistics.
[32] Hou Zurong 1995, p. 81.

malaria flourished and diseases were like tigers and wolves. It was an awe inspiring and scary place for many people. (Hou Zurong 1995, p. 75).

Today the thrilling mixture of mythical attraction and fear inspired by Sipsong Panna is alive in the minds of many Han from the heartland and the cities. For the local government and inventive entrepreneurs of today, these feelings constitute a resource to be exploited for further developing tourism in an area where the economy has largely been based on agriculture and tax income from rubber production in state-owned enterprises. According to the local government, as many as 1.5 million tourists (mainly Chinese, but also quite a number of Thais, and some Taiwanese, Japanese, Americans and Europeans) visited Panna in 1996.[33] The building of hotels and establishment of all kinds of leisure activities for tourists continued to expand as a response to the encouraging numbers of incoming tourists, but in 1999 the tourist industry started to decline. When I returned to Panna in the winter of 2000 many Han investors and immigrants were complaining about the increased competition in Jinghong and the unexpected drop in the number of Chinese tourists and income from the tourist industry. It had become relatively cheap to buy organised round trips to South East Asia, and Thailand especially had become a popular tourist destination for Chinese who wanted to go abroad and experience a culture different from their own. While many of them would previously have gone to Panna, Thailand was now preferred as cheap, more 'authentic', foreign and therefore also more exciting.

The majority of Han living in Sipsong Panna today are somehow (at least loosely) connected to the rubber producing state farms, either as employees or as relatives of employees. Since the late 1980s an increasing number are individual migrants renting land from local Tai or setting up small stores and restaurants, driving taxis, running the slaughterhouse, and working in jobs related to the development of tourism. The most important part of my fieldwork in Sipsong Panna consisted of interviews and informal talks with a large number of Han who for very different reasons had migrated to Sipsong Panna. Important also was the reading of a number of locally produced books of migrants' stories, histories of the Han in Panna and reports about migration. In particular the state farms were active in

[33] Information from interview with local government representatives.

publishing memoirs of settlers, thereby promoting a certain kind of consciousness among settlers in the state farms of what it meant to be Han in a state farm in a minority area.

Having previously done fieldwork on education in the same area, I was surprised at how easy it was to interview Han immigrants about their resettlement in Panna. I was often told that since they and I were fellow 'outsiders' (*ni ye shi waimian lai de*) I was welcome to ask anything I liked. Many of these Han migrants felt like outsiders, and (quite often correctly) assumed that I shared that feeling. Although our experiences of being from the 'outside' were from very different contexts and of a different nature, it seemed, nevertheless, that a kind of 'invisible community' feeling (Rosaldo 1993) arose from the perception of a shared life experience. This not only facilitated data collection, but also made fieldwork among many of the Han settlers a more pleasant experience than I had expected.

2

HAN IMMIGRANTS AND THEIR WORK IN MINORITY AREAS

The last fifty years of shifting Chinese policies towards ethnic minority areas are partly reflected in the occupational patterns of the Han living there. Before 1950 many of the current ethnic minority areas were only inhabited by a small percentage of Han. Since then, different policies directed at extending the exploitation of natural resources, integrating the areas into the PRC, establishing political control, promoting cultural homogeneity, and later strengthening market oriented economic development have resulted in immigration from the interior and eastern parts of China. Han immigrants from different political periods of the PRC had different reasons for migrating. They found (or were assigned) different kinds of occupation and had highly unequal possibilities for claiming access to resources and political power locally. The occupational patterns of Han settlers in non-Han areas have raised controversy and debate about Han dominance over the most important economic, political and natural resources in those areas. There is still a need for more in-depth research that clarifies the level of economic dominance of Han settlers in various non-Han areas and, not least, specifies the actual level of access to local political and economic power among different social groups of both Han settlers and local non-Han populations. There are very deep social cleavages between different Han settlers that make it problematic to talk about 'Han settlers' as if they constituted a powerful and largely homogeneous group of people. This chapter on occupational patterns first of all attempts to provide a basic overview of the major occupational groups of Han settlers, with their different social positions and status, who were found in

37

the two researched areas, and who will be referred to throughout the book in discussions of concepts of home, minority area, other Han and non-Han.

The data of this chapter demonstrate that the Han settlers constitute a socially heterogeneous group of people who have settled in the ethnic minority areas as a result of very different policies and incentives, and at different periods of time. The chapter also demonstrates how the first government organised large-scale migrations of Han to minority areas between the 1950s and the 1970s have been of paramount importance both for the establishment of powerful Han communities in those areas, and for strengthening new types of Han immigrants since the reform period. Dealing with occupational patterns of Han settlers, the chapter includes some discussions of the private economy of interviewed households. I found, however, that the private economic life of families was one of the most difficult topics to assess, and after years of fieldwork I have come to thoroughly distrust information about the economic status of individuals and families. In some situations it was of course possible to compare information of many informants and reach more or less trustworthy figures. But for a number of good reasons it is often not in the interest of people to account for their actual income and even when some people might tell the truth, it is often impossible to check this. I know of people who lived very poorly and hardly spent any money, but who nevertheless after long acquaintance would reveal tens of thousands of yuan hidden under their mattresses. Official statistics on average income may provide a guideline to levels of income, but often peasants with very low official income had some hidden additional income in the form, for instance, of collected herbs and wild mushrooms or herbal medicine sold on markets. Throughout the book, information on people's income is therefore based on a mixture of official information, interviewees' own accounts, prices observed in shops, and intuition based on general knowledge of income, living standards, and relationship with the people providing information.

Peasants descended from Han immigrants before the PRC

In both research areas a small group of Han were descendants from families who immigrated during the late period of the Qing

Dynasty (1644–1911) or the time of the Republic (1911–49). In Sipsong Panna and Xiahe descendants of such early Han immigrants are nearly all peasants today and live spread around or in smaller enclaves in Akha, Blang or Lahu (but practically never Tai) villages in the mountains of Sipsong Panna, and in Tibetan villages in Xiahe (often also inhabited by Hui who also migrated to Xiahe, mainly during the Republic).

The Han who settled in Sipsong Panna before the Communist period were mainly traders, while some had a criminal background or were for other reasons seeking refuge from neighbours, local communities or state institutions. Sometimes several men settled down together among non-Han populations and married women belonging to the local minorities. According to Giersch, the Qing state often regarded Han frontiersmen in the southwest as threats to stability and it passed laws against intermarriage between, for example, Han and Tai to prevent conflict over sex and property (Giersch 2001, p. 89). In Sipsong Panna, some of these earliest Han immigrants assimilated with the locals, while others remained (with their descendants) distinct for the local population as 'the first immigrant Han'. Today the Han settlers in the mountain villages and their descendants are often called 'mountain Han' (*shantou Hanzu*)—a derogatory term introduced by later Han settlers. In villages where initially Han immigrants settled among local non-Han, a Chinese dialect is often spoken. Descendants of early Han migrants often celebrate both Chinese festivals in their villages and local minority festivals, and the women in the villages often wear minority costumes. The descendants of those immigrants use Chinese family names and tend to follow Chinese traditions of patrilineal descent and heritage. They are not necessarily, as a group, socially or economically better or worse off than the minorities they live among, and they generally have no special privileged access to power. Their situation is largely similar to the 'remote Han' in Liangshan described by Stevan Harrell: 'In both economic and educational terms, then, life for the remote Han is not much better or worse than it is for their minority neighbors.' (Harrell 2001, p. 301)

However, some informants who were themselves descended from a Han father and a non-Han mother in a mountain village pointed out to me that they had had certain advantages related to language when starting school. Some had become low-level cadres in local administration, and they partly attributed their success in escaping the much-despised peasant life to their Han descent. This, they argued, had given them privileged access to the language of success, Chinese. Han educators who had helped set up schools in Panna in the early 1950s also recalled that they would deliberately, and often with success, specifically cooperate with local Han in the mountains when promoting schooling in villages. They also felt that the descendants of early Han immigrants had certain advantages in terms of language, and some claimed that they had maintained a tradition of valuing learning of the Chinese language, something which made them more inclined to send their children to newly established schools. Apart from this, I found no special contacts or feelings of community expressed between the peasants who had Han ancestors and had lived for generations in the mountains and the Han workers and cadres of very different social status who immigrated to Panna after 1950. Being a descendant of a Han did not in itself create a feeling of unity with recent Han immigrants. On the contrary, several descendants of the earliest Han migrants pointed out that in spite of certain educational advantages in being brought up in an environment where a Chinese dialect was spoken, by the mid-1980s it had become even more important to be able to register children as minorities rather than as Han. The few cadres I talked to who had Han ancestors and were brought up in a Han/minority village in the mountains were all careful to register their own children as minority *minzu* members because of the minorities' special treatment, especially in education.

Whereas I managed to do only sporadic interviewing among the descendants of the earliest Han immigrants in Panna, I carried out a number of interviews with descendants of pre-1949 immigrants in a pure Han village in the Tibetan Xiahe in Gansu Province, and conducted an all-village survey supplied with in-depth interviews with selected families in a mixed Tibetan and Han village, as well as in a mixed Tibetan, Han and Hui village. Almost all of the Han families living in those villages were relatives and descendants of Han who had fled Muslim uprisings in the late 1920s and '30s.[1] Most came

---

[1] Concerning the Muslim uprisings and a history of the Hui, see especially Lipman 1997.

from neighbouring Linxia (then Hezhou), and many of the Han (as well as Hui) started small hotels and restaurants, or worked with handicrafts, at a time when Xiahe with its significant Buddhist Labrang monastery was still an important trading centre for goods such as tea, horses, tobacco and alcohol traded between Tibet and China.

Trade in the Xiahe area was known from the time of the Tang Dynasty but flourished especially during the nineteenth century when Labrang became an important political, religious, economic and cultural centre in Amdo. Since the eighteenth century Labrang had already established a market, and traders delivered certain amounts of money or goods as taxes to the *tulkus* controlling the land. Apparently no differences were made between Han, Tibetans and Hui as to the amount of taxes they had to pay to the *tulkus* of the monastery for using their land. In the 1930s, when hundreds of Han escaped to Labrang from Linxia, private trading in Xiahe was lively and the number of Han and Hui trading families continued to grow. According to statistics from 1937, there were more than 180 small and large businesses in Labrang, most of them run by Han and Hui (no author 1993, p. 3). There were about 34,000 people in the whole of Xiahe county, of whom about 2,600 were living in the commercial area of the county seat and a similar number were connected to the monastery. The town seat, excluding the monastery, was made up of 45 per cent Tibetans, 36 per cent Hui and 19 per cent Han (Zhang Qiyun 1978 [1934], p. 38). By the time of the Communist takeover at least 800 Han and Hui trading families had become locally known as the 'eight hundred families of traders' (*ba bai jia maimai ren*) (Commission for Editing Historical Annals in Xiahe County, Gansu Province 1997, p. 1048).

According to interviews with old Han and Hui peasants, Han immigrants in the 1930s from Linxia either engaged in local trade and business or became peasants renting and opening up new land from the monastery, and most of them settled in newly established villages rather than in already existing Tibetan villages. Older settlers remembered that before the first real road from Lanzhou to Xiahe was built in 1952, business was particularly good because travelling took a long time and traders needed to rest and eat on their way to Xiahe. However, after 1952 the number of Han cultivating land increased, and more Han started to settle in villages together with Tibetans who were already engaged in agriculture. Several families recalled that there was enough land available in Xiahe to make a living, and that it was only after the Communists' collectivisation and the complete end of the system of land renting from Labrang that food became a scarcity. As in other Tibetan areas virtually no Han migrated to the nearby grasslands where the production methods and living style of herdsmen were profoundly different from what Han peasants were used to.[2]

In spite of the fact that a number of new Han villages were originally founded separately from Tibetan villages by immigrant peasants in the 1930s there is today, to my knowledge, only one larger pure Han village in the county of Xiahe. This village was founded in 1938 by three different Han families after they had been kicked out of a Tibetan village (literally, according to one of the women of the village who was sixteen years old when she came to Xiahe with her husband). Today this village has 150 Han families from a number of different lineages. One of the main reasons why so many other villages today are inhabited by Han, Tibetans and often Hui is the administrative changes that were introduced under the PRC. The following example from one Han-Tibetan village exemplifies how such political changes of administration resulted in new ethnically mixed villages: in River Village[3] there were in 1997 twenty-six households of which twenty belonged to families with only Han members; two were families of only Tibetans; two were Tibetan families where one Han had married into the family; and one family was Han with one Tibetan who had married into the family. However, like several other villages, River Village had only recently become ethnically mixed. During the Great Leap Forward in 1958 one Han and one Tibetan village were united into one production team, but geographically and socially they remained separate entities. However, in 1976 a few Tibetan families from the Tibetan village of the production team moved down to the Han village that was nearer to the river and road, though further away from the grasslands. This

---

[2] See Pasternak and Salaff 1993 about Han settlers on the grasslands of Inner Mongolia.
[3] Pseudonym.

move was accepted by the Han villagers because the two villages were anyway part of one common production team and therefore economically dependent on each other. However, in 1979 the production team was divided into two teams based on the original geographical structure of the two villages. Therefore by that time, owing to the earlier movement of the Tibetan families, the River Village that had originally been purely Han was now a mixed one.

Today, the twenty Han houses in River Village are owned by nine different family names which according to the Chinese tradition have split up the families (*fenjia*) and built new houses for sons and daughters in law in the village. While the Han families tend to expand in the village, the Tibetan families remain more or less stable because often one son in the Tibetan families becomes a monk and the other sons and daughters do not necessarily stay in the family or even in the village after marriage (map 1 of households in River Village). Many other villages had become ethnically mixed owing to administrative changes under the PRC, and within villages peasants belonging to different ethnic groups continued to have somewhat different strategies for generating additional income.

After they had worked in collective fields for more than twenty-five years, land was distributed to peasants in Xiahe (like in the rest of China) in 1981–2, and by the late 1990s the households in River Village had approximately 1.8 *mu*[4] of land per person who was in the household at the time of distribution. However, most land was in mountainous areas and one *mu* of land produced only about 200 kg of grain per year.[5] While most families had increased in size since 1982 the amount of contractable land had not, and all peasant households pointed out that they now needed additional income to support their families. One way to increase income that was employed mainly by Han families had been to open up new land on the nearby mountain slopes. Although this land was not officially contracted (*chengbao*) by peasants, nobody normally objected strongly to this practice until the changes in reaforestation policies in 1998. Whereas the Han had sought to expand their agricultural land, some Tibetans

---

[4] One Chinese *mu* is equivalent to 0.0667 hectare—15 *mu* is one hectare.

[5] Most important crops are wheat, highland barley and to a lesser degree red beans, mainly for the animals, and soya beans. Some farmers also grow carrots and potatoes.

had instead managed to profit from the original distribution of grassland and animals in 1981–2. Although by that time the Han families
had lived for generations in the Tibetan area, they had never become seriously engaged in raising animals on the grasslands like their
Tibetan neighbours. Therefore, most of the grassland and sheep that
belonged to the collective were distributed to Tibetan families in
1981–2. After the early 1980s the price of sheep and goats rose
considerably and some Tibetan families were thereby able to make a
fair income.

In River Village the development of the market oriented economy benefited especially those families that already had certain occupational skills to provide them with an additional income—skills
that were sometimes learned through apprenticeship (*xuetu*), but
mostly informally transmitted from father to son. These were especially the blacksmith in the village and other Han families who
made shoes for the lamas in the temples and the painted wooden
dar-lcog[6] used by the Tibetans in connection with festivals for mountain spirits. Normally, families would make approximately 15 yuan
per day on this, something considered very good in the village. Since
a competent person with these skills could normally earn quite well,
an apprentice only received very low wages during his learning period. The few women who were able to provide extra income to
their families mostly sewed for other people. Therefore, almost all
families considered it very important to have able men in the family
who would go out to do manual work (*dagong*). Very few young
women seek work outside the county, and the poorest families were
always those without younger men capable of providing an income
in addition to agriculture and herding. After having planted the
wheat before summer most young men, Tibetan and Han, went out
for five to six months (before the harvest season) to do all kinds of
work in construction, transport, road repairs after landslides etc.,
usually within the county or prefecture. They would only rarely
seek work in areas at a longer distance from their home, for example
in large cities such as Lanzhou or in other provinces. Workers would
normally get between 8 and 15 yuan a day for performing unskilled
manual labour, but by the late 1990s everybody was complaining
that it was getting increasingly difficult to find this kind of work.

[6] Locally called *jianban* in Chinese.

Xiahe had no local industries employing large numbers of people, and the county government had few strategies for developing industries apart from tourism. Its economy was therefore strained and by the late 1990s the government was rarely rebuilding roads or engaging local people in larger public works as it had used to do. As in many other remote rural areas of China larger public projects (in transport, electricity, communication, etc.) had been cut down since the responsibility for, and the financing of, many such projects had been decentralised. Furthermore, the increasing number of unemployed and laid-off (*xiagang*) workers in China had resulted in larger numbers of migrants coming into Xiahe competing for work. Often they were better skilled than locals at work in construction for instance, and if not employers and entrepreneurs still tended to prefer Han and Hui workers from outside Xiahe and Gannan, for instance from neighbouring Linxia. Han peasants from Xiahe generally looked for work in small towns within their own prefecture, and were rarely found among the so-called 'floating population' (*liudong renkou*) in the large, developed cities.[7] They had no connections in the cities, and were rarely wanted for larger construction works. I interviewed a large number of migrant workers in Gannan, as well as people hiring workers, and they all confirmed this view. One construction worker from neighbouring Linxia, himself working temporarily in Xiahe, formulated his deep scepticism about the ability of the local Gannan peasant labourers in this way:

> 'Practically all men in the countryside of Linxia go out to find manual work most of the year. It has become more and more difficult. With the policy to lay off workers, more and more people are looking for this kind of work. Therefore, we just go wherever there is work, whether it is Lanzhou, Xinjiang or Lhasa. Here in Gannan the locals do not understand how to do this kind of work. They do not have the brains for it [*naozi bu tai hao*]. Therefore they [the employers] prefer to recruit people from Linxia. People in Linxia can do all kinds of work. They can do anything, and therefore they are popular workers in Gansu, even in Qinghai and Xinjiang. Linxia people know how to endure hardship [*chi ku*].'

[7] See especially Solinger 1999 for one of the most comprehensive recent monographs on the topic of rural-urban migration.

Often workers in the minority areas, who had come from other rural areas, were willing to work longer hours than the locals since they had anyway no possibilities of being with their families in the evenings. Han entrepreneurs in particular often consciously recruited Han workers (and only rarely minority workers) from outside, and those local peasant Han and minority people who were interested in finding work in their own areas often had disadvantages because they were regarded as being less skilled, having less experience, and being illiterate. They generally had a bad local reputation as workers.

The descendants of the earliest Han immigrants who had settled in rural areas before the time of the PRC still constituted a smaller part of the local population in both research areas. During decades of interaction with the other ethnic groups within the area and their villages many of them had developed close social and economic relationships with their non-Han neighbours, and they largely shared the same working conditions and social positions. It was only after 1949 that they were outnumbered locally by new groups of Han taking part in the new large-scale state organised migrations to ethnic minority areas.

Modernist projects and mass immigration

From the mid-1950s millions of Chinese became actors in state projects involving mass resettlements that reflected the Communist leadership's grand vision for the frontier regions and their incorporation into the PRC. The leadership envisioned a Communist modernity that would transform the areas considered to be on a lower evolutionary stage of development through the input of more advanced technology, improved means of production, Chinese education, the dissemination of ideas of mass participation in politics guided by the CCP, and new notions of citizenship in the Communist state. The Communists' imagination of change was modernist in the sense that it pointed strongly to the passage of time and expected a constructed archaic and stable past to be replaced by what Bruno Latour has referred to as 'a new regime, an acceleration, a rupture, a revolution in time' (Latour 1993, p. 10). The leaders of Communist China shared a 'high-modernist' ideology that implied faith in the legitimacy of science and technology:

[High-modernist ideology] is best conceived as a strong, one might even say muscle-bound, version of the self-confidence about scientific and technical progress, the expansion of production, the growing satisfaction of human needs, the mastery of nature (including human nature), and, above all, the rational design of social order commensurate with the scientific understanding of natural laws. (Scott 1998, p. 4)

James C. Scott has convincingly showed how four elements combined may account for some of the world's most tragic results of state-initiated large-scale social projects, including the disastrous Great Leap Forward in China in 1958–9. High-modernist ideology is one of these elements that when combined with the administrative ordering of nature and society (mapping, counting, standardising...), an authoritarian state and a prostrate civil society make it possible to put into practice ambitious centrally directed and controlled plans of radical social change:

In sum, the legibility of a society provides the capacity for large-scale social engineering, high-modernist ideology provides the desire, the authoritarian state provides the determination to act on that desire, and an incapacitated civil society provides the levelled social terrain on which to build. (Scott 1998, p. 5)

Numerous top-down state projects of the Communist era in China fit well into this description, without necessarily resulting in the kind of human disaster that followed the Great Leap. As actors in the large-scale modernist projects in frontier regions huge numbers of Chinese were imbued with the *imaginaire* of a state, government and Party that provided them with means to transform their own role as ordinary citizens, peasants, soldiers and cadres into that of civilisers, developers and self-sacrificing people who were 'supporting the borderlands' (*zhichi bianyuan*[8]).

The first Han Communist cadres in government and Party. Before the Communist takeover in 1949 the Guomindang administration in Xiahe cooperated closely with the leadership in Labrang monastery which remained the local *de facto* political power up 1949. Apa AbLo

---

[8] Popularly shortened to *zhibian*.

(Huang Zhengqing), the brother of Labrang's fifth reincarnation of Jam-dByangs bZhad, was put in command of the local Guomindang army and Tibetan guerrilla troop in 1928, and later received the position as the local Security Command (*bao'an siling*) as well as a number of other high level positions in the local Guomindang government. The Communist Party operated in Xiahe from the early 1940s, and by 1942 approximately 150 people participated in the CCP's secret revolutionary organisation in Labrang (Commission for Editing Historical Annals in Xiahe County, Gansu Province 1997, p. 1248). A Party branch was established in Xiahe in September 1949 and courses were set up to educate so-called minority cadres (*minzu ganbu*) who would work for the new Communist government. New Communist work teams and military groups arrived as soon as the Guomindang and local opposition was suppressed. Those of the early revolutionaries who ended up staying in Xiahe eventually received high positions within the administration and Party. Most of them married other Han while a few married local Tibetan women. Their children were always brought up primarily learning Chinese, going to Chinese schools, and most of them later became local cadres themselves.

Han people working in local government and Party administration only constituted a small minority of the whole population, but owing to their political elite status they have obviously had a considerable influence on the economic, political and cultural changes in those areas since the 1950s. Cadres (of all ethnic groups) working in government institutions and Party organisations in 1990 made up 1.6 per cent of the whole population in Xiahe county.[9] As generally in China, the vast majority of cadres in Xiahe have been men, with only 15 per cent women in 1962 and 29 per cent in 1990. Among the 18,800 members of the CCP in Xiahe in 1984, 35 per cent were minority people (ibid. p. 100). Reforms since the 1980s have helped to ensure a more clear division between the work of the government and the Party than in earlier periods of the PRC. Still, all cadres interviewed agreed that in the case of discrepancy between local government and Party, the Party leadership in practice had the final word. According to the national autonomy law the heads of autonomous

[9] Based on figures from Commission for Editing Historical Annals in Xiahe County, Gansu Province, 1997, pp. 1 and 1394.

prefectures belong to the minority that has been granted the 'autonomy', but this rule does not apply to the local Party branch and most
often Party leaders in minority autonomous areas have been Han.

As in many other minority areas the percentage of so-called minority cadres in Xiahe has grown markedly since the 1960s due to
conscious efforts to include minorities in the administration. In
Xiahe there were 18.4 per cent minority cadres in government institutions in the mid-1950s and 33.8 per cent in 1986. The policy of
placing trained minority cadres in official positions in minority areas
has obviously been very important to the government, partly because it helps to legitimise claims that minorities have autonomy and
control their own autonomous areas, but also to ensure that local
cadres are able to work as middlemen between the Party, higher levels of government, and the local minority population. In both research areas Han cadres continue to play an important role in policy
making and implementation, and it was often suggested by minority
cadres interviewed that while minorities possess the leadership positions in the government, it is often the Han cadres in officially lower
positions who have the strongest say in policy and decision making
processes. Many of these younger Han cadres were themselves children or descendants of the earliest government and Party organised
Han immigrants. I was not able to obtain figures on how many of
the current cadres in the two areas were in fact children of earlier
government organised Han migrants from the 1950s and 60s, but
on the basis of interview data a considerable proportion certainly
were. According to several high level cadres working in Xiahe they
even constitute 'the majority' of cadres today. In that connection
many of the earlier Han immigrants, who were themselves cadres or
retired cadres, argued that one of the few real benefits they had had
within the minority area was the improved opportunity to have
their children educated in the best local schools, and to use their own
cadre status to improve their children's chances for employment in
the state sector.

While the proportion and number of minority cadres have generally increased, the situation in earlier periods of political radicalism
was different. According to information from local gazetteers, during such periods the number of cadres in general increased while the
proportion of minorities in cadre positions fell. In Xiahe this happened most notably after the Tibetan uprising in several parts of

Gannan (and Amdo in general) against the Chinese government in 1958—a revolt that was violently crushed by the Chinese military and resulted in a mass exodus of Tibetans. Although the reaction of the military was criticised later in the early 1960s and again in 1979 for being too harsh, a local gazetteer written in 1990 (by local government cadres, some of them ethnic Tibetans) maintained that the crushing of the revolt was in reality justifiable because it was 'a battle against feudalism' (*fan fengjian douzheng*). The revolt was, according to the text, 'reactionary' and directed against 'the Party', against 'Socialism' and against 'the people' (Commission for Editing Historical Annals in Xiahe County, Gansu Province 1997, p. 112). Therefore, the temporary drop in the number of Tibetan cadres could also be justified, and 'minority cadres' were clearly only wanted as long as they lived up to the expectations of Party loyalty and fulfilled their role as middlemen between Party politics and the local population.

In Sipsong Panna the Guomindang administration in the 1940s encouraged Chinese peasants and soldiers to resettle in Panna, and it granted special economic privileges to Chinese peasants from Thailand who would grow tobacco. It also set up new Chinese schools, recruited Chinese teachers and supported Chinese traders and workers who wanted to develop tea production, trade and open up wasteland.[10] But none of this resulted in concentrated large-scale immigrations of Han. In Panna up to 1949, the CCP was active in the mountains among the minorities who had the least contact with the Guomindang and its administration. These early Communist revolutionaries in Panna operated in groups of men and a few women who were trained as guerrilla soldiers. After the establishment of Communist power the situation for those of the early revolutionaries who stayed in Panna was rather similar to those who were sent to and remained in Xiahe. They received important positions within the government and Party, and were responsible for building up the new political system while recruiting and training members of local minorities both from the local elites and from the common people

---

[10] See Chen Han-seng 1949 concerning Panna during the Republic, and Davis 2003 for an interesting discussion of the continuance (in new forms) of traditional institutions and folk practices among Tai in post-modern China. See also Hill 1998 concerning the history of Yunnanese caravan trading into Southeast Asia, also going through Sipsong Panna.

to function as employees and cadres connected to the new government and the Party. The early revolutionaries who remained within Panna established families in the area, most married other Han, and most of them hoped to bring up their children to become educated cadres themselves. The basis for the political impact that many of their children actually later gained as cadres was thereby laid by their parents, the earliest political recruits of the Communist Party who were sent to the areas in the early period of the PRC or even before its establishment.

State farms and large-scale immigration. While the Han immigrants employed in state and Party administration still only constituted between one and two per cent of the entire population in the two researched areas by the mid-1950s, their work laid the ground for further large-scale immigration initiated and organised by the new Communist government. New policies to establish state and military production units in various minority areas were partly a result of the Communists' ambition to transform nature to suit the purpose of progress.[11] They were also aimed at further ensuring military and political control over the minority regions while at the same time promoting production that would satisfy some of the needs of the state. These policies involved resettlement of an unprecedented number of mainly Han people into areas designated as ethnic minority areas, from the early and especially from the middle 1950s.

Military state farms (*budui nongchang*) were started in the Tibetan county of Xiahe in 1958 in connection with the sweeping social, economic and political changes introduced with the Great Leap Forward. Already between 1955 and 1957, following central decisions to transfer so-called 'capitalist enterprises' into state-owned or collectively owned enterprises, most private shops had been collectivised and a few larger ones had become state-owned. By 1958 all shops were state-owned and the private market in Xiahe stopped. The crushing of the Tibetan uprising in Xiahe in 1958, and the radical leftist policies after 1958 especially, had devastating consequences for the political and economic development in Xiahe and the whole of Gannan. While nomadism and animal husbandry had often in China been regarded as a barbarian means of production

---

[11] See also Shapiro 2001.

incompatible with Chinese ways of life, policies in the late 1950s especially were directly aimed at transforming nomads into settlers and grassland into agricultural land. In Xiahe, as in the rest of China, People's Communes were established in 1958, 'grain became the key' (*yi liang wei gang*), and 'agriculture was the most important' (*yi nong wei zhu*). Up to 1960, 34,000 *mu* of grasslands in Xiahe were transformed into agricultural land and animal husbandry as a means of production fell drastically with devastating consequences for the Tibetan herders especially. In Xiahe county alone, one of the disastrous results was the death of more than 18,400 livestock and a meagre harvest of grain in a region unfit for Chinese traditional grain agriculture. The situation was somewhat repeated with massive death of livestock in 1970 during the Cultural Revolution and a new period of emphasising grain production (Qie De'er 1991).[12]

In the radical periods of the 1950s, 60s and 70s large numbers of settlers were sent by the government from the interior of China to many of the frontier regions to open up wasteland and develop agriculture, for instance in new military state farms. In Xiahe state-owned forestry centres (*linchang*) were also established, mainly with Han workers from outside Xiahe, and timber was transported to central China on a large-scale from 1958. These forestry centres were transferred to the county level of administration in 1986, and owing to the relative scarcity of forest in Xiahe they did not attract or recruit workers on a large-scale from the beginning of the 1960s. Grain producing state farms established in Xiahe in 1958 were not at all adapted to local geographical conditions and they did not succeed in raising production. According to local people's memories, the vast majority of Han who arrived to work in these state farms quickly left because production was quite a disaster. A number of those Han immigrants who stayed on were provided instead with jobs in road construction, which was also a high priority to the government at this time.

While agricultural state farms in Xiahe only lasted for a short period of time, and the remaining forestry centres were on a very limited scale and therefore also recruited only a limited number of Han workers, state farms in Sipsong Panna have had an immense impact on social structures, the natural environment, and the ethnic

[12] See also Ma Jiang 1993.

composition in the area.[13] This is due to their size, scale, importance to the central government in earlier periods of their establishment, and ability to later survive in and partly adapt to the market oriented economy. Keen on breaking China's dependence on rubber imports through expanding its own domestic production, the Communist government started after 1949 to experiment with rubber production in Guangdong and Hainan Island. Experiments suggested that the sub-tropical Sipsong Panna (and Dehong in Yunnan) would also be suited for rubber plantations, and after initial investigations the first larger group of 1,697 soldiers from the People's Liberation Army (PLA) was sent to Panna in 1955 to start the first rubber producing military state farm (later just a state farm) in the area. By 1959 more than 3,000 workers and cadres had been sent as part of military troops to establish and work in state farms, all of them recruited outside Panna. Groups of women were especially recruited as potential spouses from the interior of Yunnan to improve the situation for the soldiers who were mostly unmarried young men.

The state farms and their population had an immense impact on the environment of the area where jungle was cut down on a large-scale to make way for new rubber plantations. In 1990 the whole Wasteland Department administered 135,000 *mu* of rubber divided among ten state farms.[14] The surplus of the state farms in Panna belongs to the state rather than the local community, but taxes from the state farms make up a major part of the local government revenue. The state farm population has changed the ethnic composition of Panna considerably, and today it makes up more than 17 per cent of the official population of 817,772.[15] The state farms of Panna have always been on a smaller scale than the Production and Construction Corps in Xinjiang (PCC), but basically they have carried out the same functions as these, and like the PCC they have always formed an 'overwhelmingly Han organization' (Bachman 2004, p. 175).

From the early establishment of the state farms in Panna the policy of sending large numbers of Han to the border area was welcomed

[13] This was also the case in Xinjiang, see for instance Bachman 2004 and McMillen 1981.

[14] Though most of the state farms in Panna today mainly produce rubber, there is also important production of tea, fruit and grain in state farms.

[15] According to official statistics from 1995 copied by hand from the local Prefecture Statistical Department.

by the revolutionary cadres already stationed in Panna. They saw in this a great potential for further developing the economy, people's political consciousness, the local educational level and what was regarded as the relatively 'backward' culture and customs of the minorities. But first of all, they saw this as a policy to support the new Communist state through the exploitation of essential natural resources. Contacts between local Han Party leaders and administrators and the newcomers in the state farms were initially warm and supportive. They were united in a feeling of participating in the same mission. As interviewees recalled, there were now more people around to share the experience of having left home. They were all among natives with different social customs, and shared the experience of being regarded with a certain scepticism. This made it easier for them to bear the 'primitive' and unfamiliar conditions. And many more workers were to join in, making the state farms the most concentrated Han communities in Panna.

From the beginning many settlers in Yunnan and other southwestern areas were recruited in Hunan Province, and in Sipsong Panna the majority of state farm workers and cadres came from two counties in Hunan. However, life in the jungle seems to have been harder than many of the recruited Hunanese workers had anticipated. Between 1960 and 1962, at least 18 per cent of them returned home. According to those who stayed behind, the returnees were 'longing for home' and found it difficult to adapt to the very different geographical and living conditions in Panna. Peasants who had been used to growing grain were now planting rubber and it was difficult for everybody to adapt. Therefore the Land Reclamation Department (*Nongken Ju*), responsible for the state farms, introduced new methods to make it more attractive for the new workers to stay on the farms. They let the workers have what they called 'a little bit of freedom' (*xiao ziyou*) to grow a few vegetables of their own and raise pigs for themselves, and they tried to satisfy the special local needs of the people from Hunan who liked, for instance, to 'eat hot peppers' and 'wash themselves in warm water' (Land Reclamation Department 1997, p. 22). The state farms' problems of making their Hunanese workers stay in Panna were by and large solved by 1963. Since then state farm workers from Hunan have tended to settle permanently in Panna and their sons and daughters were until 1993 guaranteed employment in the state farms as well.

During interviews it became clear that most of the over 145,000 people living in state farms by the late 1990s either came from two specific counties, Liling and Qidong in the province of Hunan, or were children of workers or cadres from those two counties. Between 1959 and 1960 nearly 37,000 people were sent from Liling, Qidong and Qiyang counties in Hunan to work on state farms in the southern parts of Yunnan. The majority of these (nearly 22,000 people) were sent from the counties of Qidong and Liling to work in Sipsong Panna.[16] Equally, 60,000 other Hunanese, mainly peasants, were recruited to go to the province of Xinjiang to work in state farms (see for instance Li Debin, Shi Fang, and Gao Lin 1994). Later on a number of family members of the Hunanese state farm employees migrated to Panna as well, though not necessarily to find work on state farms. Often state farm employees found ways to help family members from their places of origin to rent land or set up shops in Panna, in order to unite the family and support their relatives.

From their beginning the state farms functioned as political and social units independent of the local government and administration. They had their own schools which had nothing to do with the new Chinese schools established among the local Tai, Akha and other ethnic groups, and all employees lived on the farms which were organised as Chinese units (*danwei*). As state farms developed the employees had access not merely to their own schools but to kindergartens, medical services and leisure time activities. Especially after the gradual introduction of a market oriented economy after 1979, several state farms in Panna developed into enterprises that, in addition to their agricultural production, produced rubber, electricity or mineral water, processed latex, timber etc., and moved into the tourist industry. During the 1980s the income of the state farms increased, not without causing resentment among many local people who complained about the ways in which state farms were profiting from local resources because of their technical skills, resources and investment opportunities which the locals lacked. In discussions about the current development of state farms, the luxurious housing standards of the leadership compared with ordinary workers and

[16] Workers from Qidong, Liling and Qiyang were also sent to the districts of Simao, Honghe, Dehong and Lincang, all in the province of Yunnan.

especially villagers were often brought up, as were state farm leaders' activities within luxury hotels in Jinghong.[17]

While state farms were always dominated by Han people, some minority workers were also recruited, especially after 1979. State farms promoted this new trend as a strategic attempt to improve ethnic relations between Han in state farms and minorities. The more concrete reason behind the decision to recruit minority workers was the new labour situation that developed within the state farms when, in 1979, most intellectual youth (*zhishi qingnian*) sent to work in the countryside left the state farms for good. This created an unprecedented acute demand for large numbers of new workers, who were then found mainly among the local Akha. Later, in the 1990s there were also cases where state farms in need of new land 'invited' whole villages in the mountains (Akha villages for example) to move downhill to work within the state farms in separate new units. In return the villagers had to hand over their fields to the state farms which needed them because their workers were entitled to get a small piece of farming land for private use. Since the Tai people were reluctant to join the farms and give up their fields, state farms were more likely to seek agreements with the people living in the mountains under much poorer conditions than the Tai in the plains. There is certainly also a possibility that the relocation of Akha villagers in this period was not as voluntary as presented by state farms, but I was not able to find reliable data confirming this.

Large-scale immigration from regions outside Panna to the state farms is now a phenomenon of the past, because it has become increasingly difficult for state farms even to secure work for their own current employees. The second generation in state farms is no longer guaranteed work there, and some farms have even started to lay people off (*xiagang*). International competition in the rubber business is hard and the Chinese government is reluctant to support rubber production in China when cheaper rubber is available on the international market. State farms now have to sell their products to companies which compare prices and quality of products from elsewhere, for instance Malaysia. As state institutions, rubber farms in

---

[17] As in many areas of China, locals vigorously complained about widespread corruption among Party and government leaders regardless of nationality, but also among cadres within state farms.

Panna have to provide their employees with schools, hospitals, leisure activities, cheap housing and pensions for an increasing number
of retired employees, and this makes it more difficult for the state
farms to compete on the free market.

The central government has made clear to the local state farms
that they should not expand rubber production further, and the increasingly insecure economic situation has started to influence the
second generation Han's behaviour on the labour market. Many are
no longer interested in trying to find work within state farms, but
prefer to find jobs either in the local administration (called *difang* as
opposed to *nongchang*, the state farms) or in the private market.
While schools in the state farms have always been considered the
best in the area, several well educated teachers belonging to the second generation of state farm employees have now started to seek
employment in the local keypoint schools where wages and conditions are largely dependent on state support rather than on the uncertain future economic development of state farms. Some state farm
parents are now even willing to pay extra to have their children enrolled in one of the better secondary schools outside the administration of the state farms—a radical change from the situation in the
mid-1990s[18]. Some locals have started to lease rubber forests to engage in private small-scale rubber production, but so far the state is
maintaining its large-scale farms, its control of rubber production,
and the responsibility for the farms' employees. Nevertheless, some
state farm employees have started to express doubts as to the possibility of maintaining a future for these farms that have had such immense impact on the environmental, political, economic, cultural and
demographic changes in Sipsong Panna's recent history.

Although immigration of Han directly connected to the state
farms has stopped, the reform policy of the 1980s and 1990s has promoted new kinds of migration which are directly related to the earlier establishment of the state farms: employees in state farms often
actively help their family members, friends and neighbours from
Hunan to rent land and settle in Panna or start small businesses, and
many young men seeking work in Panna have married local Han
women from state farms and settled permanently in the area. Especially since the late 1980s it has also become quite common for

---

[18] See Hansen 1996b.

elderly and retired employees in state farms to help relatives from Hunan to resettle in Panna, renting land for small-scale agriculture or doing business. In Panna, they say, the climate is pleasant, crops are good, the family can be united, and for Han people with established families with good connections in Panna it is still relatively easy to find work. This is a different situation from that in the Tibetan Xiahe where Han settlers were much less likely to work actively for the immigration of relatives, because the climate was considered unhealthy, the area poor and unlikely to develop, and because it was much more difficult for Han settlers to find work there than in Panna.

Intellectual youth. About 1.2 million urban youths were resettled in the countryside of China between 1956 and 1966, most of them between 1962 and 1966. Then, between 1968 and 1975, as many as 12 million youths were sent to the villages during the 'up to the mountains and down to the villages' campaign (*shang shan xia xiang*) (Bernstein 1977). These campaigns, which aimed at solving problems of surplus labour in the cities, increasing disciplinary control over youth after the high tide of the Cultural Revolution in 1969, and teaching urban youths about peasant life, had an immense influence on a whole generation of school graduates. This has been reflected in the countless novels, reports, scholarly works, films, documentaries and collections of memories related to these people and their experiences.[19] Ideologically the intellectual youths were to receive education from the peasants and at the same time contribute to rural development by influencing what were seen as outdated customs and habits and introduce more modern forms of education and technology. Many of the young graduates were settled in suburbs around the cities, and most of those who went to minority areas, including Sipsong Panna in Yunnan and Gannan in Gansu, did so either because they were not able to get accepted for places closer to the cities, or because they deliberately applied to be sent to the areas considered to be the most backward, remote and rough. Going to such areas was sure to bring status as a truly devoted Communist and child of Mao.

---

[19] For just a few of the more recent Chinese collections of memories of the time of the *zhiqing* see for instance Cao Chunliang *et al.* 1998, Hao Haiyan *et al.* 1998 and Cheng Jiang 1998.

Gannan prefecture in Gansu had its share of intellectual youth, but owing to the failure of several state farms the number was smaller than in Sipsong Panna, and only very few intellectual youths settled down permanently in the county of Xiahe. In 1958, after the central government had issued decrees about how youth from the cities should help establish socialism in the border and minority areas, more than 3,000 'intellectual youth in support of the borderlands' (*zhibian qingnian*) were sent from Henan to different counties within Gannan to work in state-run mining and in agricultural and live-stock husbandry state farms (*nongmuchang*). By late 1959 the number of intellectual youths from Henan had reached more than 40,000. They all worked in the newly established collectives and opened up new land for agriculture. In the aftermath of the Great Leap Forward they, like other peasants and herders in the region, started to suffer from the lack of food, and they returned in large numbers. Already by 1961 more than 60 per cent of these earliest intellectual youths had returned to Henan, while some of those staying were given jobs in the transport sector and others in forestry. During the Cultural Revolution new groups of youth arrived in Xiahe but, as in Panna, nearly all of them left during the late 1970s.

Within Yunnan Province Sipsong Panna was one of the areas that received the largest number of 'intellectual youths', who for a short period came to make up as much as 56 per cent of all employees in state farms. Sipsong Panna was well known among intellectual youths in Yunnan, and to intellectuals and school graduates Panna seem-ingly offered the challenges of true remoteness and backwardness. At the same time it was one of the only minority border regions in Yunnan to have well-established state farms that would provide both a steady income and a concentrated community of other Han im-migrants. The first group of 550 intellectual youths (the youngest of them aged only fifteen) came to Panna from cities in Yunnan in 1956, and like all those to follow they settled in one of the state farms. In 1965 the first large group of 1,500 youths came from Chongqing. They started as ordinary workers in the state farms, but even with their often relatively short education they were better trained than most local Han in the state farms and were quickly channelled into positions such as teachers, doctors or drivers. Many had only nine years of schooling and hardly any specific training beforehand for the new jobs they carried out, but in a border minority area with a limited level of Chinese education their skills were appreciated by the developing state farms:

> 'We intellectual youths had a very big influence on the civilisation [*wenming*] and culture [*wenhua*] of the border areas. It was also very useful for ourselves to be sent to these areas. We learned a lot, and we spread a lot of knowledge. Therefore we also got all kinds of work. Of course some were not good, but most did a good job spreading culture from central China [*neidi*]. Most cadres and ordinary people had not been to school at all, or maybe only for a few years. If you had graduated from primary school at that time it was considered to be really good. Only the second generation in the state farms got a good education.' (Interview with a female former intellectual youth who had married another intellectual youth and stayed in Panna because they were not allowed to return to the same city in 1979, and because special treatment was provided to those who agreed to stay)

The biggest influx of intellectual youths in Panna came in early 1969 when ten large groups with as many as 52,941 youths arrived— more than 30,000 from Shanghai and more than 15,000 from Chongqing. All worked on state farms which therefore experienced a sudden crisis when in 1979 all intellectual youths were suddenly allowed to return home. Within a few months the number of employees in the Land Reclamation Department responsible for all state farms dropped by 47.2 per cent, and by 1993 only 1,170 of the original intellectual youths were still employed in the state farms.[20] Almost from one day to the next, the state farms lost teachers, doctors, administrators and other people in positions that ideally demanded some kind of specialised training. They solved this by upgrading workers within the state farms to those positions previously held by the intellectual youths, while at the same time recruiting large numbers of new workers, mostly from Hunan Province. However, as mentioned above, a new method of recruiting workers was also introduced: the provincial government accepted that more than 6,000 ethnic minority people should be recruited from villages in or near Sipsong Panna to fill the gap in the workforce. This policy was used ideologically for

[20] All figures are from Land Reclamation Department, 1997, pp. 20–21.

what it was worth to promote the 'unity of the nationalities' (*minzu tuanjie*). The state farms emphasised that they were now recruiting 'brother nationalities' (*minzu xiongdi*) to repair the damage inflicted by the Cultural Revolution on the relationship between the state farms and the locals. This was the last time that the Land Reclamation Department recruited such large groups of people from outside Panna and from villages within Panna, because after that new workers and cadres were mainly found among the so-called 'second generation' (*di er dai*), the children of the Han immigrants in state farms.

The second generation. Between 1982 and 1993, 33,716 people belonging to the second generation were employed in state farms (Land Reclamation Department, 1997, p. 23). Growing up in the state farms in Panna, the children of the Han settlers from after the mid-1950s became the first large group of Han in the area who were not themselves immigrants. As discussed in the following chapters, their ideas of 'native place', 'home' and 'local *minzu*' were profoundly different from their parents'. As a group they became locally known as 'the second generation'. In Xiahe this second generation of the Han settlers from the Communist period was far smaller than in Panna and was not locally categorised as a group called 'the second generation'. However, having grown up with migrant parents in the Tibetan area, and not having many opportunities for leaving it, they shared some of the same ideas of constituting a new 'local *minzu*' (*bendi minzu*). In Xiahe most of those belonging to the second generation of Han settlers from the Communist period worked as lower and mid-level civil servants in schools, banks, the Party and different kinds of administration. Thus most of the local Han cadres were either themselves migrants from the 1960s or 70s or children of such migrants. Similarly in Panna the second generation of the Han settlers belonging to the group of 'local cadres' (*difang ganbu*)—as opposed to cadres in the state farms—had received an education that had enabled many of them to get positions in local administration, schools, banks, hospitals, etc. However, until recently it was less common for members of the second generation of state farm settlers to get employment in local administration, because they used to be practically guaranteed work within the state farms. Between 1982 and 1993 state farms, by and large, only recruited new workers and staff from the second generation. After 1985 they were normally employed on a contract basis since state farms did not have the capacity to guarantee life-long employment to all people from the steadily growing second generation. After 1993 they were not guaranteed work at all in the state farms, and some state farm cadres started to complain that it was too difficult for the second generation to accept the fact that the 'iron rice bowl' (a synonym for life-long job security) was no longer available for them:

> 'The biggest problem here is the attitude of people. People's minds are too narrow. I do not know much about the situation in *difang* [the local area outside the confines of the state farms], but here in the state farm people's minds are definitely too traditional. They are afraid of making investments and giving up the idea that because we are a state run enterprise we can take care of everything. They still prefer the iron rice bowl.' (42-year-old cadre in state farm, himself belonging to the second generation)

Since the 1990s, more and more people belonging to the second generation in the state farms have had no choice but to try their luck on the free market. Many worked in service jobs connected to the tourist industry and could often earn better income or find work less physically demanding than in the state farms. Having grown up in the close-knit state farm society, they often had networks and contacts that helped them in the search for jobs and on the competitive market. They were capable of renting proper shops and houses, getting loans etc., and in interviews they often expressed strong opinions on their own rights as 'locals' compared to the huge number of new incoming Han also engaged in businesses and often competing with them for jobs. Thus, as I explain further below, the various people locally categorised as a group called 'the second generation' seem to have developed a kind of common identification based on their common situation as the first Han to be born in the area. While the differentiation between *locality* (*difang*) and *state farm* (*nongchang*) used to define Han settlers' and their descendants' work, living conditions and social affiliations, most people aged between twenty and forty-five, from within and outside the state farms, are now competing for work on the same market. And they are competing with an increasing number of individual Han immigrants, who are not able to claim status as a local 'second generation' or as 'local Han'.

Individual immigrants since the 1980s

Minority areas that had potential for developing tourism, industry or trade or had available land that could be opened up or rented for agriculture experienced new kinds of immigration from the mid-1980s. As noticed by some scholars, the tendency to move only from the west of China to the east in the early 1980s has been reversed, with an increasing number of migrants now seeking instead working opportunities in the vast minority areas in the west.[21] Many expect that this trend will be further reinforced owing to the campaign launched in 1999 to open up, or develop, the western regions (*Xibu da kaifa*), a campaign that also emphasises the need to import 'qualified personnel' into the western areas. While government organised immigration on a large-scale was stopped in Xiahe and Sipsong Panna after the end of the Cultural Revolution—and generally decreased in all minority areas of China from that time—new individual, mainly economically motivated migrations to the border regions have taken over, often with tremendous impact.

The scale of this migration is not captured in official population statistics because many migrants come only temporarily or during certain seasons. And while many obtain temporary residence permits, most do not register at all. The government tries to keep track of the migrations through ordinary registration, but since immigration is normally regarded as favourable for promoting local economic development, the attitude towards unregistered migrants in minority areas as compared to those in urban centres is by and large relaxed. Many people have reported that favourable provincial loans have been granted to support settlers in various minority areas, but to my knowledge settlers in Sipsong Panna and Xiahe had come on their own initiative with their own collected or borrowed capital to rent land, start shops or work in construction or service industries. The dynamics of modernisation of trade and industry in these areas have generated economic activities, or potential for such activities, that attract settlers without the government having to actually give them direct incentives to resettle. The impact of the state farms, the tourist industry and individual earlier settlers, as well as many Han entrepreneurs' undisguised preference for Han rather than minority

[21] See for instance Tian Fang and Zhang Dongliang 1989, p. 77–8.

labour, are all elements that combine to promote further immigration of individual Han migrants seeking work often far away from their places of origin.

At all levels of administration cadres and governments tend to regard these new migrations towards the western border regions in a predominantly positive way. Similarly, in the Chinese media discourse on 'the floating population' and other internal migrations, movements from the eastern and central parts of the country to minority areas in the west are mostly evaluated positively. In Jinghong County in Panna in 1990 the population had grown about 24 per cent since 1982, to 338,465 people (Office in Charge of the Fourth Census of Jinghong County 1990, p. 5). In addition the local statistical bureau estimated that there were 32,446 people belonging to the so-called floating population that had not settled permanently and had not registered in the area. More than 85 per cent of these had probably already been in Jinghong for more than a year, while the vast majority had their household registration outside Panna. More than 63 per cent were estimated to have been in Panna for more than five years (ibid. pp. 126–7). Two-thirds of the floating population came from rural areas, but since many came from rural areas in Zhejiang and Jiangsu—areas more economically developed than Panna and most other minority areas—they were described as having a positive influence on the further development of Panna.

At the same time an unpublished report from the local statistical bureau emphasised some of the problems found to result from the immigration of peasants. Some immigrants had gone bankrupt, sold drugs or become prostitutes, and some had evaded birth control, becoming part of the much criticised 'moving guerrilla of people having too many children' (*chao sheng youjidui*). Other more general social arguments connected to the acceptance of large-scale immigration of peasants from other areas of China were also brought forward: first, immigrants took work away from the locals; secondly, with the immigration of women who came to marry, the population would increase further when couples had children; and thirdly, immigrants with low education should be restricted while immigrants with higher education and more qualifications should be encouraged (ibid. p. 10). But problems, such as the above mentioned ones, were much less frequently highlighted by cadres than the advantages of supporting further Han immigration. Although unskilled peasant workers are needed and often accepted in the metropoles for carrying out low-status and low-income jobs that the local urban population often does not want to perform, there have been many reports about widespread negative images of these immigrants as 'rural', unskilled, uncontrollable and poorly educated people.[22] However, in the context of Han peasant migrations to minority areas negative descriptions of the results of migration were much rarer, and the immigrants' impact on the development of the minority areas' economy and culture was normally always evaluated positively by local cadres especially.

Some Chinese scholars have gone so far as to argue that the advantage of large-scale Han migration to minority areas is so great that the time is ripe for starting up new government organised and controlled migration, especially to Xinjiang which is known as one of the most conflict ridden minority regions and which has already experienced extremely large immigration of Han. In the official discourse on migrations to minority areas the earlier large-scale migrations are normally praised without reservation for having promoted development and progress. Referring to America's history of settlement, Tian Fang and Zhang Dongliang have compared the European settlements in North America to the Chinese settlements in Xinjiang. Referring to the statement that 'without migrants there would be no America', they comment:

> Consequently people [in America] often associate migrants with vigorous development. This view is definitely correct, and regarding Xinjiang we may also say: 'Without migrants the Xinjiang of today would not exist'. (Tian Fang and Zhang Dongliang 1989, p. 208)

Tian Fang and Zhang Dongliang argue that while Xinjiang in the 1950s helped solve the population pressure in eastern parts of China by providing land to a growing number of Han people, this way of supporting immigration is not valid under the current conditions. Instead, new immigration should be encouraged when it is 'to the benefit' of the people already living in Xinjiang and for the general

---

[22] See for instance Davin 1999 on concepts and images of peasant immigrants in large Chinese cities.

development of the area (ibid. p. 208). This implies, they argue, that more people with higher technological knowledge and better education (*suzhi gao*[23]) should be organised to settle in Xinjiang, while labour movement should mainly be organised internally in the province. This view largely corresponds with the government's reasoning with regard to Han migration, connected with the more recent policies of developing the western regions. According to Tian and Zhang, with a proper supply of water Xinjiang could still accommodate organised migration of several million people who would at the same time support the ongoing Chinese civilising project as they see it: only when Han people arrive in larger numbers, they argue, are they able to speed up the modernisation of the minorities' lifestyle (ibid. p. 206).

In spite of various government sponsored projects in recent years, involving resettlement of poor peasants and some support for resettled trained personnel, the suggestions for new large-scale government organised migration to minority areas have not yet (by early 2002) been followed up by concrete government policies. However, in recent years the government has again started to favour government controlled modernisation schemes that imply more conscious and systematic efforts to centrally direct and guide cultural as well as economic change in minority areas. The recent campaign to develop the western regions is known to many people in the minority areas as a grand ideological project that is initiated and directed from above, and has very few channels open for suggestions or demands from below. The project is widely publicised in western regions where most cadres and intellectuals seem to be patiently waiting to see what will come out of it.[24]

Within the cultural field, and closely connected with the renewed emphasis on larger hegemonic campaigns, are the centrally guided efforts to speed up the promotion of standard Chinese (*putonghua*) as the first language of all people in the PRC. This campaign is not exclusively directed towards minorities and minority areas and it is not

---

[23] This often used term refers here mainly to educational level, though often it is also used to refer to more unspecific characteristics related to moral and social behaviour.

[24] Concerning the project to open up the west (*Xibu da kaifa*) see for instance Jhaveri 2001.

directly connected to policies regarding migration of Han to minority areas. However, it is frequently argued that an increased proportion of Han in minority areas also works in favour of the spread of Chinese language among ethnic minorities. Many officials in minority areas are running out of patience, having previously believed that minority languages would gradually and naturally (with assistance from the education system and the media) be superseded by the presumably more modern and developed Chinese language. As pointed out by, for instance, James C. Scott, a distinct language is a powerful basis for claims to autonomy and it represents a 'formidable obstacle to state knowledge, let alone colonization, control, manipulation, instruction, or propaganda' (Scott 1998, p. 72). With renewed threats of internal conflict and potential claims for autonomy, the government is speeding up its demands to promote a unified language that would also, many interviewed local cadres believed, facilitate cultural and economic 'progress'. In many places the renewed emphasis on standard language and education has to some extent already resulted in decreased local investment and interest in supporting the learning of minority languages in schools, in publications of books in minority languages, and in developing media in minority languages and promoting research in bilingual education.

The policies towards the minorities and minority areas in the 1980s and early 1990s emphasised the need to decentralise and left more of the responsibility for directing cultural and economic development to the local administrations than in previous periods. In addition to being part of the general reform policy since 1978 to open up and modernise China, this was a response to the oppressive campaigns of the 1950s, 60s and 70s that had intensified ethnic conflicts (especially between Han and minorities). In the 1990s, with the government's ever increasing need to legitimise its power and compensate for the politically dangerous and deepening gap between levels of economic development in the eastern and western regions, new kinds of top-down projects directed towards minorities and minority areas were initiated. Ongoing policies of language, education and culture directed towards minority areas are closely related to projects focusing first of all on economic development, such as the campaign to develop the west. The expected increase in immigration of

Han to western border regions in connection with this project is regarded, by some Chinese researchers and cadres, as favourable also
for promoting Chinese language and culture, which they hope will
serve to prevent increased demands for autonomy and self-determination from some minorities in some of the border areas.

However, so far the vast majority of Han who migrate every year
to the western minority areas are still mainly individuals and families
from towns and villages in rural regions of China who migrate on
their own initiative. As for the total number of individual migrants
(permanent as well as temporary) in the two areas, it was impossible
to find exact and reliable figures. According to the local Department
for Industry and Commerce, Xiahe county gave in 1998 temporary
residence permits, as well as permission to open private enterprises
(*getihu*), to more than 1,500 people.[25] But the Department was also
aware of the much larger actual number of short- and long-term
residents doing business and working mainly in construction. Most
had come from other places in Gansu or from the provinces of
Zhejiang, Jiangsu, Henan, Shaanxi and Sichuan.

Sipsong Panna as a prefecture is a much larger area than the county
of Xiahe, and it has a much more developed tourist industry. According to the local administration of individual enterprises, in 1997
there were 12,000 officially recognised individual enterprises and an
estimated 100,000 people from outside Panna doing all kinds of
business and work in the region (excluding people working on a
contract basis for the state farms). Most were from Hunan, Sichuan,
Zhejiang or places within Yunnan. The typical immigrant in Sipsong Panna by the late 1990s was a young Han Chinese man, unmarried or with a young wife and one or more small children who
would stay with their parents until they reached school age and then
return to their grandparents in the family's village of origin. He was
from a rural town or village, had some years of primary or lower middle school education, and was capable of working in construction,
doing different kinds of manual work or engaging in small-scale business. He had come on his own initiative, but with some help from
family members already living in the minority area, and he was likely

[25] In comparison there were only about 30 *getihu* in the whole county in 1980
(interview with Department for Industry and Commerce, Xiahe, 15 May 1998).

to have experience as a migrant in one of the larger cities, maybe even in the eastern coastal areas of China, prior to his migration to the western border area. He had brought with him a small capital which could be used for setting up a small shop or renting some land, or else he worked in construction. He was likely to reside in a crowded room with people from his own province or even his county of origin. He was also likely not to have registered as a settler in the minority area.

The 'typical' Han immigrant in Panna was welcomed by the local government. It hoped and planned for the further establishment of about 30,000 private enterprises (most of them on a small-scale with only a few employees). To support this development they granted permanent residence permits to those who invested more than 200,000 yuan in Panna in 1997, or who simply possessed that amount of money. As one of the administrators said, 'We want to develop Panna, so we are very unrestrictive when allowing people to come here, settle and do business. We make it very easy for them to bring their family as well.' (Han cadre) Special policies were indeed needed if the government was to expand investments according to its plans. According to the Department for Industry and Commerce a number of private enterprises had gone bankrupt before 1997 and many people crossed the borders, especially into Burma, to set up businesses there. Since the late 1990s the tourist industry in Panna had started to decline, partly owing to the increased opportunities for Chinese tourists to visit Thailand and other countries in South East Asia, and an increasing number of Han immigrants were seeking their luck across the border in Burma.

Why did individual Han migrants choose a minority area as their destination? In Sipsong Panna interviews with large numbers of recent migrants showed that most of them had come from Hunan Province, especially the areas of Qidong and Liling (but also neighbouring Shaoyang, Mao Zedong's home county) where the vast majority of government organised migrants in the state farms had also come from decades earlier. Very many migrants interviewed referred to often distant family members when explaining why Panna had become their choice of current settlement. In this aspect patterns of Han migration to minority areas resemble those established in other areas with large-scale Chinese migration, both in urban centres in China, in Southeast Asia and in other areas outside the PRC.[26]

In terms of occupational patterns of peasant immigrant labour in the minority areas there were obvious differences from those described by other scholars in larger cities. In her study of peasant migrants in large cities, Dorothy Solinger identifies six major occupations in which so-called floaters were frequently found: construction, manufacturing, working as nursemaids, marketing and services, cottage-style garment processing, and begging and scrap collecting (Solinger 1999, p. 206). In the minority areas where I did my research most peasants found jobs in the county and prefecture capitals in sectors that were directly or indirectly connected to the development of tourism. Manufacturing was obviously not very important in these areas with few industries apart from tourism, state farms and a few local factories, and there was not a large market for nursemaiding either. Construction, on the contrary, was one important sector for peasant immigrants, especially in Panna where large numbers of hotels, restaurants and roads were built in the late 1980s and 90s especially, but also in Xiahe in connection with the tourist industry and the expansion of Labrang monastery. Many recent immigrants were engaged in small-scale trading and services (bicycle repairing, electricians, workshops, small shops and restaurants) which were expanding in both areas, owing partly to tourism and higher living standards. Also the transport sector (cycle-rickshaws, ordinary taxis, buses, etc.) was largely dominated by Han immigrants. Another popular business for peasant immigrants was in agriculture in Panna, where land was rented from local peasants and crops sold locally or in nearby provinces and cities. More well-educated immigrants in Panna, often from other cities in Yunnan, would act as entrepreneurs and engage in the tourist industry. Some worked in the numerous private tourist offices and centres, guiding Han tourists and organising tourist activities. Others started or managed larger restaurants and hotels.

[26] Recent publications on Chinese international migration, transnationalism and diaspora include for instance Ong and Nonini 1997, Benton and Pieke 1998, Wang and Wang 1998 and Pan 1994. See also Zhang 2001 on the ways in which rural immigrants in the cities of China form associations and support people from the same places of origin.

Peasants renting land. In villages around the prefecture capital of Jing-hong in Sipsong Panna it was quite common for Tai peasants to rent their land to Han settlers from other areas, mostly from Hunan and Sichuan. They still maintained their contracted land in their places of origin, but most did not have enough there for the entire family to survive on. Many said that they only had about four *fen*[27] per person in Hunan, and they had therefore decided to rent their own land to other people in their village and migrate. In Panna they had nearly all been introduced to Tai families renting out land through relatives engaged in work in a neighbouring state farm because, as one farmer said, 'The Tai will not rent their land to somebody whom they do not know.' The price of land depended largely on the availability of water. One family had rented 12 *mu* of land in a very attractive place—close to the river, but far enough not to be affected by floods—and this cost them 2,400 yuan per year in 1997. This was not considered to be a very large sum by immigrant farmers, but income was always insecure since the area was often affected by drought. Nevertheless, owing to the sub-tropical climate of Panna more kinds of vegetables could be cultivated and they could be harvested faster than peasants from Hunan were used to from home. In Hunan they sold one kilogram of Chinese cabbage for one jiao,[28] in Panna they sold it for seven jiao in 1997. According to peasants this difference in price was first of all a result of competition. In Hunan transport was a lot easier, and therefore local peasants were competing with peasants from outside who brought in more vegetables for sale from other areas of China.

Peasants renting land normally renewed their contracts every year and most interviewees planned to stay only as long as they were convinced that they could make a steady income from growing and selling vegetables. The Tai families who rented out their land had alternative means of income. They raised domestic animals, sold fruit, worked in the service sector, or in some cases contracted rubber plantations. A number of Tai, as well as Han, peasants pointed out that the Tai farmers were disadvantaged on the free market because it now demanded vegetables favoured in traditional Chinese diet

[27] Chinese units of area: one *fen* is 66,666 square metres. 10 *fen* is one *mu* which is equivalent to 0.0667 hectares.
[28] 10 jiao is one Chinese yuan.

rather than the kinds of plants, vegetables and rice traditionally cultivated by the Tai. With the large number of Han peasants ready to
cultivate the land of the Tai and compete in an increasingly fierce
market, many Tai families (at least around the Jinghong prefecture
capital) seemed to prefer to rent their land to them and withdraw
from agriculture. In some other villages development of enterprises,
mostly related to the tourist industry, also resulted in government or
enterprises buying up the right to use land.

Private shops, stalls and restaurants. In 1997 I carried out a street survey
in Jinghong in Sipsong Panna to find out who ran the various shops
in one of the major shopping streets, and where they came from.
The particular street was chosen because it had a whole range of different kinds of shops and was not, as some others were, mainly lined
with one type of enterprise. Some restaurant areas with small restaurants were mainly run by, for instance, Sichuanese; several Shanghai'ese
ran larger restaurants, hotels and bars; streets with fashion garments
were dominated by entrepreneurs from Zhejiang; the market area
had many people from Hunan selling vegetables, meat and fish, etc.
In comparison, the street chosen for the survey clearly had people
from different areas of China running different kinds of shops, and in
addition there were many small-scale traders with stalls or simply
selling or repairing goods from a seat on the pavement. In each shop
or stall along the street at least one person was asked to participate in
the survey which only inquired about the shop or stall owner's place
of origin, gender, age and ethnic affiliation and, when people had
time and interest in talking more, about their history of migration to
Panna and reasons for starting business there.

As seen from the table below, there was a total of ninety-five shops
and small stalls along the street, ninety-two of them privately owned
or contracted (*chengbao*). Two (maybe three) were brothels disguised
as beauty parlours; the others were mainly restaurants, food stalls, repair shops, pharmacies, jewellers, shops selling electronic articles and
clothes shops. Of the ninety-two privately run shops eighty-four
were run by Han Chinese, thirty-seven of them from Panna, which
normally meant that they belonged to 'the second generation'. Three
shops were run by members of the Hani nationality (two Akha and
one who called himself a Biyao), four by Tai (one of whom was not

SURVEY OF A SHOPPING STREET IN JINGHONG, 1997

	count	%
Total private shops/businesses[29] in survey (not including 3 state-owned enterprises)	92	100
Shops owned by Han	84	91.3
Shops owned by Tai	4	4.3
Shops run by Hani	3	3.2
Shops run by Yi	1	1
Owners' place of origin		
Sipsong Panna	42	45.6
Yunnan (outside Sipsong Panna)	11	11.9
Sichuan	24	26.0
Guangdong	5	5.4
Hunan	4	4.3
Zhejiang	2	2.1
Shanghai	1	1.0
Burma	1	1.0
Guizhou	1	1.0
Fujian	1	1.0

from Panna), and one by a Yi. The survey showed that many shops changed owners within relatively short periods of time, something which was mostly explained as a result of rather fierce competition. Many interviewees explained that it was becoming increasingly difficult to do business in Jinghong and many were considering moving to the counties of Mengla and Menghai in Panna or even to smaller towns in these counties. In other shopping streets of Jinghong also, shops and restaurants run by Tai or other local minorities constituted a small minority, while there was still a considerable number of Tai and other minorities selling especially vegetables and food products in the market area. According to interviews with people working in the government office responsible for the administration of private entrepreneurs, an estimated 80 per cent of people selling goods (including clothes and vegetables) at this market were nevertheless people from outside Panna, who mainly bought their goods through contacts in larger cities and brought them into Panna for sale.

Han interviewees selling goods at the market generally found that they were treated well by the local administration and that it was relatively easy to set up shops or sell goods at the market even if you

[29] Including the small private stalls run only by a person sitting in the street.

were not officially registered. As for the level of economic success among entrepreneurs there were big discrepancies depending on the kind of trade people were engaged in, but also depending on management and capability to adapt to local market demands. Some Han restaurant owners were profoundly frustrated about their failing efforts to make money, whereas others were able to make up to 15,000 yuan a month in rather small restaurants. An entrepreneur's level of contacts in state farms and the local administration played an important role, and those who had relatives in cadre positions in state farms or in local administration were clearly more likely to attract large parties wining and dining at the expense of the state. In terms of investment there were obviously also huge differences between establishing a shop selling valuable jade or starting a small bicycle repair shop.

From the late 1990s new economic pressure on state employees and the increasingly large number of laid-off workers resulted in new types of entrepreneurs and small-scale traders coming into the two areas. In Xiahe it was not uncommon to encounter people employed in the state sector selling plastic goods on the street during weekends, or laid-off workers coming all the way from coastal cities to sell, on the street, cheap electronic gadgets otherwise unavailable in Xiahe. However, approximately 70 per cent of those who got permission to open shops in Xiahe were Hui coming mostly from other places in Gannan or neighbouring Linxia, according to information from the Department for Industry and Commerce.[30] Through its training programmes and in the media, the government encourages laid-off workers and cadres to be creative in their ways of dealing with the loss of work and income. With the pressure on jobs in the cities in the east one way to deal with discontent is to support people going west to participate in what is launched as a grand scale modernisation project. In that connection I have heard both journalists and scholars mention that central and provincial authorities sometimes provide support in the form of special loans or grants to individuals who want to move to a minority area. Nevertheless, during my research I never actually met Han immigrants who had themselves received any kind of financial support from the state for moving individually to a minority area. Neither did I manage to find written reports or rules concerning such decisions.

---

[30] This trend is also noted by Makley in Makley 1999.

Service and transport. The development of tourism and trade in the two areas researched has resulted in a greater demand for transport facilities. In both areas there were plenty of taxis and they were practically all driven by Han. The importance of personal connections, accumulated capital and also preference for (and indifference to) certain types of jobs helped to explain why this sector was almost entirely dominated by immigrants. One of the characteristics of the street scene in Jinghong in the 1980s and 90s was the numerous tricycles that functioned as cheap and convenient taxis used frequently by locals as well as an increasing number of tourists. The tricycle drivers in the late 1990s were nearly all from Jiangxi (estimated at around 80 per cent) or Sichuan, and no locals were engaged in this kind of business. Biking up to ten hours a day with a load of up to three people in the heat was not surprisingly considered to be extremely hard work. Many local Tai looked down upon the people who would accept to do this low-status service job. But for many Han peasants, biking was after all an attractive business, and until rumours spread in late 1997 that tricycles would soon be prohibited in Jinghong (which they eventually were by 1999) they were popular items because an official permit to bike for commercial purposes was included when one bought a tricycle.

The practices related to the buying and selling of tricycles illustrate how connections related to common place of origin were decisive for gaining access to certain sectors of economic life. People planning to sell their tricycle, normally had several interested buyers from their own township or county of origin, usually in Jiangxi or Sichuan. Buying a tricycle from a fellow villager included getting help to settle down in the Tai village of Manjinglan where most drivers from Jiangxi or Sichuan lived together in rooms rented from Tai families. Thus one would get help from fellow villagers to establish both a social and a professional life in the new home place, and within the community of tricycle drivers most people preferred newcomers from their own areas of origin.

In 1997 a tricycle cost between 10,000 and 20,000 yuan and renting small living quarters (basically one room next to between ten and twelve other small rooms under a traditional Tai house, together with other tricycle drivers) amounted to around 90 yuan per month per room. A couple where the man biked at night and the woman during the day could make between 500 and 1,500 yuan per month.

The government restricted the number of tricycles which would otherwise most certainly have been much larger than the 600 allowed, and this helped increase the price of tricycles. In 1997 approximately one thousand people were connected to this business, most of them men. When the tricycles were prohibited in Jinghong from 1999 in favour of ordinary car taxis, those who had accumulated enough capital sold their bikes and bought cars instead. Many others moved on with their bikes to other places within Panna (Mengla and Menghai) that were in the process of developing trade and transport (at a level like Jinghong approximately ten years before). Most people losing business in Jinghong preferred to move south to other areas of Panna with less competition, rather than returning to their places of origin. Again, the government generally supported this trend as it was seen as a means to modernise the region, now also in the areas further away from the capital of Jinghong.

Recruited labour. While a large number of recent individual migrants had come to the minority areas on their own initiative, some were also directly recruited as labour in newly established enterprises. Especially in Panna, the tourist industry had generated a demand for people working in construction, in various service jobs connected with tourist activities, hotels, bars and leisure parks, and in privately contracted rubber plantations. In 1997 the Office for Rural Enterprises was responsible for approximately 40,000 workers, mainly Han immigrants employed in various rural enterprises.[31] Several entrepreneurs pointed out that poor Han peasants were among the most reliable workers, because they were recruited from outside Panna. They were willing to work long hours, had no family to return to in the evenings, and were anyway so poor that they were satisfied with relatively low wages. In particular the county of Mojiang just north of Panna was known as a very poor region. Both Hani and Han people had come to Panna from this area to work, and in particular Han from poor Mojiang villages had been recruited as labour for enterprises in Panna. These were often peasants with no capital and no opportunities for establishing their own shops or restaurants. They often had only a few years of schooling, and the jobs they found in Panna were of low status and badly paid. Moving to Panna as recruited labour—as a Han immigrant worker—was not a guarantee of

---

[31] Information provided in oral communication by one of the leaders of the office.

high income and living standards. It did, on the contrary, sometimes have devastating social consequences. The following case of a pure Han village in Sipsong Panna, called Mojiang Village after the county of origin of the villagers and established in 1988, illustrates this.

Mojiang Village obtained its name because all of its inhabitants had come from Mojiang. It was a village with only Han inhabitants and I became aware of it through an interview with a retired female worker in a state farm. She had introduced her cousin and his relatives from Mojiang to a local township-owned rubber plantation in Panna which was looking for workers in 1988. Although these peasants came from an extremely poor area, the woman was appalled by the situation that these recruited Han peasants ended up in as a result of their migration. In 1988, her cousin and his family, together with twenty-five other families from Mojiang, gave up their land in their home township and settled down together near the rubber plantation in Panna where they were going to work. The reason behind their decision to move was explained by one of the men in Mojiang Village: 'In Mojiang the mountains are high, communication is bad, there is a lack of water, and we had no electricity.' In their new home place they hoped for a steady income, and they settled down building simple straw huts in what became a new village in the area, and one of the few pure Han villages in Sipsong Panna today.

In the late 1990s when I visited this village all the women were illiterate while most of the men had attended primary school. In the beginning, the people from Mojiang worked for the township's rubber plantation, making 150–200 yuan a month, which was clearly better than their original income from agriculture. They were paid according to how much they worked and how much rubber they produced. Then in 1992 the township government gave up this business because it was not profitable and wages were consequently frozen. The villagers still took care of the rubber trees because they hoped that they might be able themselves to take over the entire plantation. This did not happen, and after a while the plantation was contracted first to a private investor from Sichuan and then, shortly afterwards, to a local Han. The plantation was still not able to compete on the rubber market and wages were still not paid. At the time of interviewing in 1997 the village was clearly extremely poor. The villagers had their household registration changed after they settled in Panna and had therefore no land to return to in their place of origin. Since they were employed to work for a rubber producing enterprise they also had no land for agriculture in Panna, and they had no accumulated capital. They had no possibility of renting fields from the local minority people but had instead found temporary work in the fields labouring for other Han who had rented fields from local minority people. Some found temporary work on a daily basis in the neighbouring Hani villages where people wanted to start rubber production themselves.

The villagers of Mojiang clearly defined themselves as peasants (*nongmin*). They argued that they were the worst-off peasants in the entire Panna because their families had rural household registration but no access to land. From being a village of recruited rubber plantation labourers, Mojiang Village had become a village of landless peasants. The case of Mojiang Village was a rather exceptional one because most other recruited labourers kept their fields in their original homes and rented them out or let relatives use them temporarily. But many recruited workers in Panna (mostly Han and Hani) were living under poor conditions and were exploited by entrepreneurs who preferred their labour precisely because they were easier to control than local minority people with relatives and friends within the area. Many interviewed labourers from the poorest Han areas were themselves very disappointed about their economic, social and working conditions in their new home place. Generally, those who had been actively recruited from the poorest Han villages to work for entrepreneurs had harder living and working conditions than those who had come on their own initiative with some capital to start business or rent fields, and they expressed less optimism about their potential for improving their and their families living conditions.

Most areas inhabited by ethnic minorities and officially designated 'minority autonomous areas' have experienced large-scale immigration of people from other areas of China, especially since the establishment of the PRC. Policies of different periods of the Communist era have brought different groups of migrants. The vast majority of immigrants in the past fifty years have in common that they are classified as Han and refer to themselves as Han—as members of the officially recognised ethnic majority as opposed to the ethnic minorities they settle among. However, as shown in this chapter, in terms of occupation, social status, income and level of access to political and administrative power, they cannot be regarded as a homogeneous group of people, or as equal participants in the state's projects to establish control over and direct further developments in the minority areas. The era of grand state controlled modernisation projects from the mid-1950s to the late 1970s involved organised resettlement of large numbers of people, some of whom were granted prominent positions in local political leadership and administration or in organisations set up to control the exploitation of natural resources. Workers recruited from the interior of China in the same period settled down with their families and helped establish new communities of Han, but at the same time the relationship between Han workers and cadres, when analysed within the state farms for instance, commonly showed the same discrepancies in levels of power and social status as that, for instance, between cadres and commoners in other parts of the country.

Later groups of individual immigrants, following in the wake of economic reforms, were often peasants with low incomes and insufficient amounts of land from inland provinces where they had found few possibilities of generating alternative sources of income. Relaxed policies on movement, and new trading and working opportunities in some border regions, attracted groups of people who were not conscious participants in the state's modernising and civilising efforts in minority areas. These people often lived poorly within the minority areas and had no special advantages with regard to obtaining political or economic power. Thus, as shown in this chapter, seen from the perspective of Han immigrants' local economic, social and political positions, diversity and inequality, rather than homogeneity, characterised them as a group.

In terms of numbers, the individual migrants and their families constitute the most important group of Han immigrants in minority areas today. While few immigrants are now organised by the state, an increasing number of laid-off workers and peasants seek new work and life opportunities in the developing western regions of China. However, those of the earlier migrants organised and sent by the government and Party who have remained within the minority areas have secured important political and economic positions. They continue to be very influential within the government, the Party, the education system and the local economy. Their children—the second generation Han—have benefited from this and generally they manage well in the new market economy and the local bureaucracy.

3

DYNAMIC ENCOUNTERS

BEING HAN IN A MINORITY AREA

'The concentration of population in planned settlements may not create what state planners had in mind, but it has almost always disrupted or destroyed prior communities whose cohesion derived mostly from non-state sources. The communities thus superseded—however objection-able they may have been on normative grounds—were likely to have had their own unique histories, social ties, mythology, and capacity for joint action. Virtually by definition, the state-designated settlement must start from the beginning to build its own sources of cohesion and joint action. A new community is thus, also by definition, a community de-mobilized, and hence a community more amenable to control from above and outside.' (Scott 1998, p. 191)

When Han interviewees who settled in Panna or Xiahe between the 1950s and late 1970s were asked to recall their first encounters with local non-Han people, they tended to stress their surprise at pro-found differences in style of living, languages, customs, food, clothes and religion. They had seen and heard little beforehand of the areas they moved to, and they represented their experience as a movement in distance as well as time, to a remote world and a time of the past. At the same time they emphasised that they had taken part in a larger scheme instigated by their government, and that their movement was therefore endowed with a specific and important purpose. The world they came from had provided them with answers as to how the new world they moved into should be thoroughly changed for the better. Their defined goal was to bring about a movement in time from the dark ages to the bright era of Socialism, and their per-ceptions of and relations with the minorities were marked by the ideological weight of their mission. Their ways of living, working, marrying and speaking were closely related to their very participation in the state controlled and state organised modernisation project. In comparison earlier and later migrants (from before the 1940s and after 1980) were far less directed in their ways of interacting with the local people they encountered, because they had moved on their own initiative and had often had to find their own means of establishing their lives and sometimes families in the new place of living. For those moving after the 1980s, transport was eased considerably and moderns means of communication from the start made more direct contacts with family members in other parts of China possible. Thus the early state organised migrants and later individual migrants had different ways of engaging in the local social life of the ethnic minorities living in the area, and in interviews they also represented their relations with local people in different ways.

Zygmunt Bauman, in his discussion of how the time of communication has shrinked so much during the globalisation era that space and spatial markers have lost their importance for the elite (but not necessarily everybody else), also describes how troublesome it can be to find oneself being in a place truly far away with all the uncertainty this might bring:

> Near, close to hand, is primarily what is usual, familiar and known to the point of obviousness; someone or something seen, met, dealt or interacted with daily, intertwined with habitual routine and day-to-day activities. 'Near' is a space inside which one can feel *chez soi*, at home; a space in which one seldom, if at all, finds oneself at a loss, feels lost for words or uncertain how to act. 'Far away', on the other hand, is a space which one enters only occasionally or not at all, in which things happen which one cannot anticipate or comprehend, and would not know how to react to once they occurred: a space containing things one knows little about, from which one does not expect much and regarding which one does not feel obliged to care. To find oneself in a 'far-away' space is an unnerving experience; venturing 'far away' means being beyond one's ken, out of place and out of one's element, inviting trouble and fearing harm.
>
> Due to all such features, the 'near-far' opposition has one more, crucial dimension: that between certainty and uncertainty, self-assurance and hesitation. (Bauman 1998, p. 13)

For the migrants participating in the state projects, in what appeared to many of them to be remote, isolated and unfamiliar border regions, as well as for those moving mainly in search of increased income, the minority areas on the borders of the PRC represented neither something entirely 'near', 'usual' and 'familiar', nor something fully incomprehensible or 'far away'. And displacement was clearly not experienced in the same way across time and space and did not unfold in uniform fashion.[1] For many individual economically motivated migrants of the 1990s, the minority areas were not first of all sites of cultural difference or fixed points of arrival. They were areas en route to fulfilment—in an undefined future—of hopes for economic advancement. The areas they had chosen just happened to be inhabited by peoples with different histories, languages and to some extent cultural practices from those of the migrants themselves. This, however, often did not play a major role for Han immigrants in the 1980s and 90s because they would, within the minority area, find the same television stations as in other parts of China, the same content of school education for their children, the same language (standard Chinese) used in media and in official communication and, with few variations, the same political system of administration as they came from. With the technological development of media and new means of communication, Han immigrants in areas commonly presented in China as isolated corners or borders of Chinese civilisation were able to some extent to stay in touch with friends and relatives in their areas of origin.[2] At the same time, they were often forced for economic reasons to live for years far away from their families and children, many of them only being able to afford a visit to their homes of origin once a year or even less often.

Experiences from minority areas have led many foreign students, journalists and scholars to conclude that 'the Han' living in minority areas hardly ever learn the local languages, have racially discriminating views of minorities, rarely intermarry with them and either ignore their festivals or exploit them as resources for ethno-tourism. Studies of minority areas have provided important insights into the effects of the Chinese civilising projects in minority areas, the dominant discourses on minorities, and especially minority elites' ways of engaging in the construction of minority identities.[3] But few studies

[1] With reference to Lavie and Swedenburg 1996a, p. 14.
[2] See for instance Rouse 1991 and Olwig 1997 for different perspectives on how modern technology has changed migrants' ways of identifying with place of origin.
[3] See for instance Harrell 1994, Schein 1997, Gladney 1994, Litzinger 2000, Hansen 1999b.

have focused on the Han settlers in minority areas and their own ways of representing ethnic minorities and engaging in relations with them. Many of the data I collected during fieldwork among Han migrants to a certain extent supported the image of the Han migrant who patronises local minorities, regarding them as groups of people less civilised and less developed than mainstream Han. But at the same time the data pointed to strong individual differences as well as significant dissimilarities between groups of migrants in unequal social positions in society. Cultural and social contacts and relations between Han immigrants and minorities, as well as Han attitudes towards the non-Han peoples, were largely defined by education, social status, occupation and reason for migration. While Han immigrants' views of the local non-Han people will be specifically discussed in Chapter 6, this chapter focuses on how different groups of Han adapted to life in the minority areas—how they settled, celebrated festivals, used the education system, and perceived the differential policies for minorities and Han that they directly encountered in their new place of living.

Patterns of settlement

The physical organisation of different immigrants' housing facilities and living quarters was closely connected to the very reason behind their resettlement. State employees in state farms and other work units were automatically provided with housing within secluded work units, while peasant migrants had to find rooms or apartments to rent individually. Workers recruited for new private enterprises were often provided with collective living quarters in the vicinity of their workplaces. To a certain extent the physical structure of housing determined ways of direct social interaction between immigrant Han and the people already living in the area.

When the first state farms in Panna were established the pioneers had to clear the jungle to plant rubber trees and to build their own housing facilities. The state farms were normally organised according to a hierarchy where the central administration of the state farm (where also the highest level of schools, medical facilities, etc. was found) was situated in one of the larger towns. Sub-branches of the state farms (*fenchang*) were situated in rural areas closer to the main rubber plantations of the farm. Thus workers in state farm branches lived in rural areas in the vicinity of minority villages and had to interact more directly with the local people than did state farm employees in the county capitals. However, since all farms were organised as special units that would eventually provide their employees and their families with housing, schooling and medical facilities, there was very little need for people within the farms to actively try to socialise with the local villagers. Children from state farms went to their own schools, and some people from state farms recalled that as children in the 1960s and 70s they used to fight rather than play with the neighbouring Tai children. In Panna sub-branches of state farms were mostly established near Tai villages in the plains where it was convenient to build roads and secure water supplies. Nevertheless, social contacts between state farms and villages were mostly sporadic, especially with regard to villages higher up in the mountains where state farms would normally just go on representative tours once in a while, for instance to prevent conflicts over access to forest areas, or to mediate in situations of disagreement. The neighbouring Tai were sometimes invited to participate in state farm festivals and vice versa, but generally the state farms functioned as separate small societies.

The style of housing in the rural state farms—low, long rows of similar brick blocks and sometimes taller buildings for the administration—was always easily distinguished visually from local Tai villages with houses built in traditional style on poles, mostly in wood but now sometimes also in stone. Within the state farms there was also a clear hierarchical distinction reflected in housing standards. The highest cadres had secured larger, modern apartments built after the 1980s in modern Western style. Lower cadres lived in houses of mid-level standard, while houses of workers in the rural sub-branches in particular were much more simple. Most of these houses were originally built during the Mao era and were kept in the Communist style with no local flavour.

From early on the state farms had to engage in so-called 'nationality work' (*minzu gongzuo*) which was first of all aimed at ensuring cooperation from the local minorities and minimising the risk of open conflicts. Several interviewees recalled that within their farms just one person, normally belonging to an ethnic minority himself, had this task. Other people within the state farms normally felt no need to engage in local relationships outside the state farm, but a few recalled how they occasionally met with Tai peasants working close to their rubber plantations and how they would sometimes have a smoke and play cards with them. However the separation of state farms from the rest of society, differences in language and, in the view of state farm interviewees, villagers' sceptical attitude towards state farms normally prevented close relationships from developing. The employees in state farms had come to work and live in state organisations as part of a government programme. They had no reason to try to adapt to life outside their farms which anyway provided the basic needs for all the families working there. Conflicts between state farms and local populations were numerous in periods of establishment and to some extent during the Cultural Revolution.[4] Therefore, in the early phase of the reform period after 1980 it was decided that all state farms should organise a 'nationality unit' working specifically for improving Han-minority relations. They started activities such as a yearly party to 'unite the nationalities' and an official 'month of unity among the nationalities' (*minzu tuanjie yue*) (Dongfang State Farm 1988, p. 18). Furthermore, state farms were encouraged by the government to help local Tai people set up their own rubber plantations and teach them rubber producing techniques. Schools in state farms were also partly opened up to minority people willing to pay tuition fees for their children. Descriptions in state farms' internal publications of these various activities indicate that relations between Tai and Han were actually rather strained, and support fieldwork data showing that very few individuals from the rural state farms had closer social contacts with minority people who were not in some way connected to the state farms themselves.

While interviews suggested that a large number of conflicts took place especially before 1980 between state farms and local minority villages, only a few concrete incidents were ever made public. Only when stories of conflict could be used in the propaganda for successful 'nationality work' have they been publicised. One of them was described in the journal *Nationality Work* in 1993 (Fan Wenwu and Deng Zhiren 1993) and it illustrates how the physical, economic and social division of state farms and villages resulted in numerous clashes over access to local resources. In the late 1970s relations between a local Akha village and the nearby rural state farm were bad

[4] There were struggles between fractions within state farms during the Cultural Revolution, and Red Guards (locally and from outside Panna) took action to demolish local temples and other 'remnants of feudal culture'.

because of conflicts over resources. As a consequence, local Akha people tore down some houses belonging to the state farm and started to collect guns to prepare for battle against the state farm employees. However, when the intellectual youth working in state farms left in 1979 and there was a sudden urgent need for new workers, the state farm decided to try to make peace with and cooperate with the local Akha people. The Akha village was incorporated into the state farm and, according to the article, within a short time the average income of Akha peasants increased to more than the double that of other peasants in the nearby mountain areas. The policy of incorporation of the dissident Akha had, according to the article, been successful. In recent years there have been other cases where state farms have sought to incorporate local Akha villagers within them, mostly in order to gain access to more land and fields. But even in these cases the physical structure of housing continued to reflect the strong division between state farm employed Han and local minority villagers. Within the farms special housing and working units were established for the Akha villagers because, as one interviewee said, 'The Akha have a very different way of living and working, so it is better to let them have their own units.'

The Han living in state farms probably constitute the group of immigrants who live most secluded from the local minorities inhabiting Panna. Even Han working in government and administration seemed to have more social contacts with members of local minorities because they worked together, and shared social positions and living quarters with minority people employed within their units. The members of the local political elite, whether Han, Tai, Tibetans or other minorities, have areas of common interests and obvious opportunities to engage in personal relationships across ethnicity. Because of their positions as cadres they mostly live together in the cities within their working units.

In Panna the tens of thousands of individual traders and workers mostly have to find rooms themselves to rent, and this has changed not only the economy of local families but the organisation of living space in some Tai villages close to the cities. During the 1980s and 1990s especially, many Tai families in the Tai village within Jinghong town rebuilt their traditional houses in order to house immigrant Han. Houses were traditionally built in wood on poles, providing space for domestic animals under the living quarters. By the late 1990s, a number of Tai houses had been rebuilt to contain instead up to ten or fifteen small brick rooms under the traditional living quarters. These rooms were then rented to immigrant Han. Mostly groups of immigrants from similar places of origin and with similar kinds of jobs would live together under one or several Tai houses, and they would themselves organise the shifting of rooms when some people left and others arrived. Under the Tai houses, rooms were organised to the side, and in the middle was a common space shared by all the immigrant inhabitants. These were meeting places for immigrant Han, and most of my interviews were conducted in such common, semiprivate zones where many immigrants would gather after working hours. This common space was normally not shared by the Tai hosts who would stay in the living quarters above, but many interviewees among Han immigrants renting cheap and simple rooms under Tai houses pointed out that they had developed good relationships with the Tai landlord family above. While it was first of all a business relationship, Han and Tai individuals and families lived so close to each other that mutual respect and exchange of food and favours were seen as positive, even necessary, for ensuring peaceful and friendly coexistence. One typical Tai house of this sort would host a family of five to six Tai people above and between ten and twenty immigrant Han living below. All Han interviewees living in these quarters saw this as a temporary stage in their lives and had no intentions of staying permanently. Many were couples with only small children, because children of school age would normally be sent back home to the grandparents in the villages of origin where they had their household registration and could attend school without paying fees.

The village mentioned above is an example of how living quarters were adapted by Tai villagers themselves to respond to the growing demand for housing among an increasing number of individual and not very wealthy Han immigrants. In other sections of the cities of Panna individual immigrants found cheap rooms in small hostels mainly owned by other Han immigrants or people from the second generation of Han, or in different kinds of buildings restructured to house large groups of immigrants with little money and modest demands as to their living standards. Individual immigrants were by and large struggling to save money and were rarely willing to pay more than the absolute minimum for their housing facilities. Some families interviewed lived with up to ten young employees together in one room while making several thousand yuan every night in their popular restaurants. Han peasants in Panna renting fields from the Tai did normally not live within the Tai village. They built their own small huts directly on the fields and lived there because it was cheap and convenient for access to the fields, and because there were few opportunities for finding equally cheap housing within the rural Tai villages.

In the Tibetan Xiahe state employees, whether Tibetan, Hui or Han, also tended to live in the same housing quarters within work units, while individual immigrants rented rooms from locals within the county capital. As in Panna those Han who lived together with minorities in rural villages were normally people descended from immigrants who had come before the Communist period. In the agricultural villages of Xiahe a number of early Han immigrants and their descendants had settled and built houses which were often similar to other houses in the village, Tibetan or Hui, built in various local styles, and it was first of all in these villages, among peasants living for generations together, that closer social contacts between Han and Tibetans across lines of ethnicity were found.

Celebrations and religious practices

Han cadre: 'After 1958 [and up to 1970] we [government-organised Han migrants in Xiahe] did not celebrate any festivals, not New Year, not Tomb-sweeping Day [*qingming jie*], no, no, no, that was not possible [laughs]. That was superstition. Of course every year everybody participated in ceremonies for the dead heroes of the revolution. That was not superstition. That was a way of remembering and honouring them. The Hui and the Tibetans could also not celebrate festivals, but maybe you did anyway, at home?'

Hui friend: 'Yes, we did it at home. And in our hearts. In 1958 all the ahong, lamas [sic] and Christians fled. Many were killed and those who stayed resumed secular life. So we could not pray in public, but we did it at home.' (Interview in medical shop with early Han immigrant and his Hui friend, both men about fifty-five years old)

Two Tibetan peasants in their mid-thirties looking around in a local Chinese temple:

A: 'All our old temples were destroyed. Mao Zedong did that.

Our history, religious monuments... He took care that everything was destroyed. Is that not right?'

B: 'Yes'.

A: 'Now it is all coming back. But not nearly to the same extent
as before. When I was a child we were not allowed to participate
in Buddhist activities. But our parents whispered in our ears and
taught us behind closed doors. Now it is coming back. But on a
much smaller scale than before.'

B: 'They have quotas for the number of monks these days.[5] It is
like in the state sector. People have to leave their jobs (*xiagang*),
and in the temples it is just the same. They want fewer monks and
they don't want the temples to grow large.'

These are familiar stories about radical periods of the PRC. In
Xiahe as well as in most other areas of China during the Cultural
Revolution, temples were destroyed, monks fled or were forced to
resume secular life, and cadres themselves belonging to ethnic minorities had to take part in struggle sessions and meetings criticising
old habits and reactionary cadres. The Tibetan monastery of Labrang was destroyed during the Cultural Revolution and a road was
constructed through the temple area. According to one of the cadres
from that period every working unit had to choose a few people
who would participate in the destruction, and many middle school
students actively took part as well. According to local accounts, the
Party secretary of Xiahe at the time—a Han man—was worried that
leaders would later get into trouble because of the destruction of an
important historic relic such as Labrang monastery. He managed to
convince the local military leaders, whom the Red Guards did not
dare to go against, to save one building.

As in other parts of China and Tibet, the end of the Cultural
Revolution and the beginning of the reform period brought new
and more relaxed policies on religion. In 1979 religious activities in
the monastery of Labrang were restarted and from 1982 the monastery was partly reconstructed with government money and support
from the local population. Several thousand monks were connected
to the monastery in the late 1990s, and it was frequently visited by
monks and Buddhists from other parts of China and the rest of the

---

[5] In Labrang the quota was 800 while in practice there were many more monks
attached to the monastery.

world. Today the monastery of Labrang is a national preservation site and without comparison the main tourist attraction in Xiahe and Gannan.[6] But what happened to the religious activities of the Han immigrants after the revival of Tibetan Buddhism in Xiahe?

In addition to the Tibetan monasteries there were mosques and Chinese temples in Xiahe before the Cultural Revolution. The Han immigrants from the 1920s and 1930s, together with their descendants, normally practiced Tibetan Buddhism and participated in the same festivals as their Tibetan neighbours. At the same time they had their own temples for worshipping, and during the Republic Apa Abho, the head of government and brother of Labrang's fifth incarnation of Jam-dByangs bZhad, supported the establishment of a Chinese temple that also hosted a local Tibetan mountain deity. During the Cultural Revolution this temple in Xiahe town (similarly to some other temples) was used as a primary school connected to a production team. Years after the rebuilding of Labrang and other Tibetan monasteries, the Han community of mainly early immigrants and their descendants (with support from some Han cadres) started in 1988 to collect money for rebuilding the Chinese temple. In 1989 the temple was repaired, and in the early 1990s a Daoist priest from neighbouring Linxia, known for its large numbers of Daoist priests and monasteries, was invited to serve in the temple.

In the late 1990s the temple was actively used by many Han in Xiahe, including some cadres, and by a number of Tibetans as well. Inside the temple were three main statues of deities known from Chinese temples in many areas: Erlang with his guardian dog Xiao Tiao; Guandi, the Chinese god of war and one of the most popular Chinese gods;[7] and finally a black, fierce looking deity on a horse, worshipped as the God of Wealth by the Han in Xiahe and as a local mountain deity by the Tibetans. While the Han would bring various sacrifices to this deity, Tibetans would place photographs of the Panchen Lama in front of the statue. The Daoist priest connected to the temple insisted that he was the only Daoist priest in the whole of Gannan prefecture by the mid-1990s, and in addition to traditional rituals within the temple he was often asked to perform rituals in people's homes in cases of sickness and preparation of weddings.

[6] See also Makley 1999.
[7] See Duara 1988.

Han peasants and recent Han immigrants would attend the Chinese temple for special occasions. And in addition Han from the villages would normally also attend Tibetan Buddhist festivals and celebrations of local mountain and other deities. Older Han peasant immigrants often recalled how they had quickly adapted to the Tibetan Buddhist activities after having settled in Xiahe, while at the same time maintaining their customs of worshipping Chinese deities and calling a so-called *yinyang* specialist (*yinyang xiansheng*) for conducting funerary rites.

Most Han peasants living in villages among Tibetans said in interviews that they themselves believed in Buddhism. This included most of the younger people who would, however, often point out that although they, 'in their hearts', believed in Buddhism they did not take part in rituals. In practice most Han peasants seemed to participate in one way or the other in the major Buddhist festivals as well as in local Tibetan worship of mountain deities. During one such occasion in a Tibetan-Han village in 1997, in which I was invited to participate, all men regardless of ethnicity and age took part in the yearly ritual in celebration of the local mountain spirits. In a neighbouring village with only Han inhabitants most men also carried out this ritual.[8] While the Han peasants also took part in all major Buddhist festivals and other activities they would not, unlike their Tibetan neighbours, send a son to the monastery to become a monk. This, they argued, was a special Tibetan custom which they had not adopted, partly because of the problems of language. While the oldest men in the Han peasant families normally understood Tibetan, the old women rarely did and the younger generations hardly ever spoke or understood more than a few words. One old Tibetan living in a village with several Han families said that he knew of no Han who had studied in the Buddhist monasteries: 'Normally, if they want to learn how to "recite scriptures" (*nian jing*) they will go to Linxia to study with a *yinyang* specialist. That is more convenient because they can study in their own language.' Interviews also suggested that even Han peasants who were firm practitioners of Tibetan Buddhism found that sending a healthy son to a monastery would have a too negative impact on the general economy of the family.

[8] Men from the few Christian families were among those who did not participate in this ritual.

On the other hand, the *yinyang* specialists were popular among Han peasants while they were never used by Tibetans. Most Han peasant families would invite a *yinyang* specialist to perform funerary rites, but none of their Tibetan or Hui neighbours would invite neither a *yinyang* specialist nor the Daoist priest for similar occasions. For the Han and Tibetan peasants living together in the same villages this was one of the customs that interviewees themselves emphasised as a marker distinguishing Han from Tibetans. Like other *yinyang* specialists I know of in Yunnan, the ones in Gannan (unlike the Daoist priests) were allowed to marry and have a family. They were normally peasants and their ritual knowledge was transferred from father to son. A *yinyang* specialist mostly performed rituals immediately after somebody's death and again three years later. More rarely he was called upon to help deciding the proper date and partner for a wedding. Unlike the monks who were also often asked to 'recite scriptures' in Han families in Xiahe, the *yinyang* and his assistants charged a fixed price for performing their rituals. By the mid-1990s the price was 15 yuan per person per day (for three days) in addition to food and travel expenses. Normally seven people were needed to perform the proper rituals. For some Han families this was rather expensive because most *yinyang* specialists had to come all the way from Linxia county, and therefore some would rather invite one *yinyang* specialist only and then supply six local (cheaper) Tibetan monks. However, Han peasants in a better economic situation sometimes invited the *yinyang* specialist and all his assistants in addition to seven or eight Tibetan monks to recite and perform funerary rites.

Class, status, time of immigration, age and to a certain extent gender divided the Han in terms of attitudes to and practice of religion. The peasant Han from families that had settled in Xiahe in early periods among local villagers mainly followed local Tibetan traditions while at the same time upholding the custom of calling for a *yinyang* specialist and supporting their own local Daoist temple. Likewise, the few early Han immigrants living for generations among non-Han in the mountains of Sipsong Panna had largely adopted local customs and practices while maintaining and transmitting some traditional Han festivals and beliefs. This was profoundly different from the recent individual migrants in both Xiahe and Sipsong

Panna who would often try to return to their places of origin for major festivals. They did not take active part in major local festivals, though they would often go to just 'enjoy the fun of it' (*kan renao*). They would also, in the case of Xiahe where a Han temple was established, attend this for special occasions. Unlike the state organised migrants they did not perceive their settlement as permanent, even when it might last for many years or eventually become permanent. Mostly their connections to their villages of origin were maintained. They often had close family members there, they had their land intact, and they engaged in relationships with their villages partly based on circulation of labour, money, goods and information. Therefore, unlike the Han peasants settled for generations among local non-Han, their festivals and celebrations also remained first of all connected to their villages of origin rather than to their current place of migration.

While the individual migrants would try to return to their places of origin to celebrate New Year (and more rarely other festivals) with their families, the Han workers in state farms in Sipsong Panna were again a different group. This was due to their settlement within a state organisation which had from the start been of a much more permanent nature. They had settled with their families and would celebrate their traditional festivals within the farm. Most of those who were interviewed pointed out that the local minorities had their customs, festivals and religious beliefs, and that they themselves had nothing to do with those. As they had formed their own societies with large groups of Han within the state farm units—many of them even from the same regions of origin—they naturally continued their traditional celebrations in the new home-place, in practice isolated from the activities of the native inhabitants of the area.

Local Han cadres' attitudes towards the revival of religious activities among the minorities were to a certain extent connected to the economic potential of ethno-tourism in the areas, but at the same time some of them (in Xiahe as well as in Sipsong Panna) expressed personal attitudes towards religious practices and beliefs that went beyond mere economic or political concerns. Many were genuinely concerned that minorities should be allowed to practice their religious beliefs, while upholding the official view that this was only

possible as long as they did not interfere with government policies on, for instance, national unity, education and economic development.[9] But cadres would often themselves take part in local
religious activities and festivals out of personal belief. As one Han
Chinese cadre in Xiahe explained:

> 'I don't believe in religion any more. I study religion as history, but
> I do not believe in it. But I have to say, I feel more at ease when
> I read Buddhist texts. I want to go back and bring sacrifices to
> the grave of my parents. I feel much better, more healthy when
> I….Really, there is no harm in believing a bit!'

This view was shared by quite a few Han cadres, also by some of those
who had been transferred to the minority areas before the reform
period. Likewise, local Tibetan cadres sometimes expressed what
might best be described as a bad conscience about believing in Buddhism when, as one of them said, 'As members of the Communist
Party we are really not supposed to believe in religion or superstition.'

The Tai in Sipsong Panna are Theravada Buddhists and since the
1980s, after long suppression, religious practices especially south of
the Mekong River have flourished. With support from the government and Buddhist organisations, for instance in Thailand, the Tai
have been able to rebuild a number of old temples and monasteries.
When people's income rose from the mid-1980s, many also invested
in new buildings, monasteries and monuments relating to their Buddhist practices. As in Xiahe and many other minority areas, the rebuilding of destroyed temples gained government support from the
1980s, first of all as a recognition of the disastrous effects of the Cultural Revolution and as a means to heal some of the wounds inflicted on the relationship between minorities and Han. For the local
people who had revived and renewed religious practices and other
activities related to their Buddhist monasteries (such as education)
the rebuilding of temples since the 1980s was not first of all the result
of a need or wish to develop tourism. But for local governments in

---

[9] Local sects (such as the *mentu hui* which was widespread in Yunnan and other
Southwest areas in the late 1990s) were for instance forbidden because they were
seen as dangerous for people's well-being and as organised forms of superstition
that undermined the authority of government by being outside the sphere of
legitimate religious organisations.

these areas receiving decreased economic support from the state, beautiful temples were clearly also something to offer urban Chinese visitors with more money and opportunities to travel than ever before in the PRC. For the average visiting tourist in Panna the religious practices of the Tai probably constitute first of all a strong visual encounter with a culture and people different from his own. The more than one million mainly Chinese tourists (about 1.5 million in 1996) who annually visit Panna expect to find—and do find—young boys wearing yellow robes, beautiful temples, and Buddhist celebrations where monks perform exciting rituals. Thus, the commodification of religion has been obvious in areas such as Panna and Xiahe where the income from tourism is an important basis of government revenue and where local cadres, departments and state companies have economic stakes in the tourist industry.

However, although the commercial aspect of religion is significant for powerful political actors on the local scene in many touristic minority areas, and plays an important role in promoting a certain image of minorities and minority areas as lived examples of an exotic past, this in itself does not account for the revival and renewal of religious activities at various levels of society in Sipsong Panna and Xiahe. In some cases religious institutions were able to make use of the tourist potential to increase their income and gain government support, in other cases religious activities were taking place parallel with, rather than integrated with, tourist activities related to the display of religion. The commodified aspects of Buddhism in both Xiahe and Sipsong Panna are clearly directed at attracting tourists and satisfying their immediate demand for entertainment, but many of the Chinese tourists are at the same time attracted to the spiritual aspects of Buddhism. Many bring offers to the Buddhist images, circle the stupas (in Xiahe), and read their destiny in temples on prefabricated notes bought for a few yuan (in Sipsong Panna).

The revival of Theravada Buddhism among the Tai in Sipsong Panna did not lead to, and was not accompanied by, a visible strengthening of religious activities among Han immigrants living permanently in Panna. The Han settlers rarely took part in Buddhist festivals or activities in Panna except as audience or as representatives of state farms or government institutions, and by the late 1990s they had not established Chinese temples or recruited Daoist monks or *yinyang* specialists as in Xiahe. The cities of Panna were dominated by Han immigrants who arrived after the establishment of the PRC, taking part in the Communist modernist projects from the 1950s onwards. They were ideologically imbued with the CCP's view on religion and superstition, and within the state organisations it was for a long time out of the question to engage in activities defined as 'religious' or 'superstitious'. The individual immigrants of the 1980s remained closely connected to their places of origin, which for many were still their main reference for connection with ancestors and the site for important ceremonial celebrations. Smaller festivals were celebrated among immigrants in Panna, but establishing, for instance, a Daoist temple in Jinghong was irrelevant for most of them since that would imply a more final definition of the site as a new home-place.

The future of the state farms is uncertain considering the difficulties they encounter on the rubber market and the decreasing central support for state enterprises. Many employees pointed out in interviews that, in spite of an uncertain employment situation, they envisioned a future where they had to remain in the area because their families were there, their houses were there, their children had grown up there, and they had simply no alternatives. In such a situation, combined with the fact that the local religious activities of the Tai are being strengthened, one could imagine that a number of traditional Chinese religious activities would eventually re-emerge and that new temples in the Han tradition would be established also within Sipsong Panna. So far this has not been prioritised by the vast majority of Han in Panna, either because they are engaged in state organisations and therefore can hardly overstep the political restrictions on government employees, or because they are temporary individual immigrants maintaining close bonds to their place of origin and imaging a day of return. On the other hand, through a common effort initiated by the earliest immigrants, Han in Xiahe have established a public space in the form of a Han temple amidst the predominant Tibetan Buddhist activities. With the second (and third) generation of Han growing up in Panna, experiencing a different kind of connection to the place from their parents, one could imagine that the Han would eventually symbolically 'move in' permanently in Panna by establishing their own temples, common larger-lineage graveyards, ancestor tablets, genealogies and rituals performed in line with common Han traditions by Daoist priests or practitioners with similar skills such as *yinyang* specialists.

Language and education

'If you don't learn Chinese you cannot even find a toilet when you go into town.' (Tibetan grandmother talking about her grandson's education in a village school)

Those Han settlers in border regions who took part in the CCP's modernisation projects—in essence civilising projects—were by and large not expected to learn the local languages of the minorities. They were first of all expected to be in the forefront of propagating and spreading the knowledge of a unifying Chinese national language promoted primarily through the education system and the media. The cadres among the early settlers were encouraged to learn local languages, but only for the earliest pioneers of the CCP in the mid- and late 1940s working to recruit local participants in the revolution was it imperative that they developed competence in local languages and became accustomed to local cultural practices. Many of the workers recruited for state farms only spoke their own local dialects, but their children all attended the state farm schools teaching standard Chinese. Outside the state farms local governments set up special schools, or classes within schools, to recruit minority pupils and in some cases to teach the languages of minorities. At the same time, it was important for the government to build up local education that would satisfy the needs of Han cadres and others who wanted a level of Chinese education for their children to compensate for the disadvantages due to growing up in a remote area with no tradition of Chinese learning. In effect schools, or certain classes within schools, often became divided between those attended by the local minorities and those attended by the Han settlers or children of local cadres hoping to ensure for their children a future with an iron rice bowl.[10]

---

[10] Concerning education of minorities in ethnic minority areas of China see for instance the articles in Postiglione 1999 and Hansen 1999b, see also Bass 1998 on education in Tibet.

It is commonly acknowledged that Han Chinese living in ethnic minority areas tend to have certain advantages with regard to education. The schooling system is based upon the use of the national standard of Chinese language and partly directed at socialising children to become loyal, competent citizens in the PRC with a perception of being part of a national Chinese history that has led to the current leadership of the CCP. According to textbooks, ethnic minorities— construed as a group defined in opposition to a perceived ethnically and culturally homogeneous majority group of Han—did and still do play a role in the creation of a unified nation, the *Zhonghua minzu*. But in the dominant discourse on development in China the national history is carried by Chinese civilisation developed in China proper among Han people, and gradually disseminated into regions considered to be less culturally and economically sophisticated. With the long and persistent tradition of Confucian institutionalised education the Chinese developed an inclination towards school based learning, and even in many rural areas families would struggle to allow at least one son to attend the local Confucian and later the modern school, often in the hope that this would lead to upward social mobility.[11] Recent studies of education in Han rural areas have shown that many peasants are willing to send one or more children to school because they regard it is an opportunity for upward social mobility. As Stig Thoegersen has argued, this was the case even during the Cultural Revolution when school education could be the ticket to a job as driver or worker, considered to be more attractive than being a farmer (Thoegersen 2001).

In Chinese studies of minority education, and of the Han as a *minzu*, this interest in formal schooling has sometimes been presented in essentialising (or racial) terms as an inherent characteristic of the Han people who, compared with many ethnic minorities, were supposed to be more eager to learn, more open towards foreign cultures and at the same time adaptive and capable of assimilating others into their culture. According to the scholar Xu Jieshun, the Han *minzu* was formed by the 'mixing of blood' (*hunxue xingcheng*

---

[11] Concerning Chinese education in the twentieth century, see for instance Cleverley 1991, Elman, Woodside (eds) 1994, Pepper 1996 and the articles in Peterson, Hayhoe, and Lu (eds) 2001. See also Liao 1949 about the Chinese preference for private Confucian schools even after the establishment of new forms of schooling.

de), and it developed through this 'mixing of blood' (*hunxue er fazhan de*) (Xu Jieshun 1994, p. 40).[12] According to Xu, further studies of this historical process of racial mixture in China would show that Chinese civilisation is made up by this constant mixture of peoples and cultures, and this could eventually help prevent Han chauvinism from developing. However, in the same article Xu argues that the Han *minzu* is built upon certain inherent cultural characteristics. Referring to non-Han rulers in Chinese history he writes:

> Whenever any nationality entered the vast ocean of the Han nationality the amalgamative and assimilative force of the Han would cause them to sinicize (*hanhua*) according to a repeated pattern in which the subjugators were subjugated by those they had themselves subjugated. It is precisely because of the self-confidence which stems from this amalgamative and assimilative force that the Han nationality was always open, accommodating and absorbing in the relation with foreign cultures.
> (Xu Jieshun 1994, p. 40)

The myth of a specific power inherent in the nature of the Han people and Han culture serves in effect to naturalise dichotomies between the Han and the non-Han, between the majority and all the minorities. The discursive construction of a Han race is closely connected to the nationalist discourse prevalent in official discourse in China today and, as Barry Sautman has argued, it adds a biologising component to ethnic nationalism, thereby distinguishing the nation even more sharply from its neighbours (Sautman 2001, p. 111).

Within the school system nationalism is most explicitly (though far from exclusively) played out through the various campaigns to strengthen patriotic education as a natural part of formal learning. One aspect of the focus on nationalism as a unifying ideology in China today is reflected in the government's renewed emphasis on standard Chinese as a common, national language and its decreasing attention to the development, or sometimes even the maintenance, of bilingual and other forms of education in minority languages.[13] The urge to speed up modernisation is mostly used as an argument for this trend,

---

[12] For recent studies of racial concepts in China, see Dikötter 1992 and Dikötter 1997a.

[13] Several scholars (who wanted to remain anonymous) concerned with minority education in China, and themselves members of ethnic minorities, have pointed

and implicitly it is understood that minority languages *per se* are less developed and therefore less useful than the Chinese language as modernising tools. This view is reinforced by the fact that participation in higher education and success in many different types of jobs demand fluency in Chinese, and therefore many parents belonging to ethnic minorities (especially those with an education themselves or with positions as cadres) naturally prefer their children to get an education first of all in the national language. Some educators and local cadres working in the education administration have expressed frustration over the past years at what they see as a lack of resources to strengthen education in poor minority areas in general, and at a lack of resources as well as political support to develop means of education that take into consideration local differences of language, history and culture especially. The tendency has been further strengthened by the fact that publishers now have to make money, and books printed in relatively small minority languages rarely become best sellers.[14]

Other local educators argued explicitly in interviews and informal conversation that the time was ripe for China to speed up demands for fluency in standard Chinese, even if it implied a renewed disregard for minority languages. They argued that the CCP's introduction in the early 1950s of special education programmes for ethnic minorities was aimed at facilitating the gradual amalgamation (*ronghe*) of the minorities with the mainstream culture of the Han, directed by the ideology of the CCP. Since this had not yet happened they found it pointless to wait any further, and would rather keep the teaching of minority languages at a minimum and then use all means to strengthen the use of the national language. This view neglected the argument put forward by other educators and teachers

---

out that the amount of material produced and published on the topic of bilingual education has decreased considerably. In many local areas, including some of the towns where my fieldwork was carried out, local teachers and headmasters expressed frustration over decreasing support for local initiatives to improve Chinese language through studies of the mother tongue.

[14] Although some subsidies for publishers publishing in, for instance, the Tibetan language still existed by the late 1990s, government support for publishers is steadily decreasing and publishers mostly have to work on a commercial basis. This has led to rumours of some minority publishing houses selling their ISBN numbers rather than using them for publishing books in minority languages.

who claimed to have very good results from teaching the national language through the mother tongue of minority children, thereby at the same time achieving the goal of increased competence in standard Chinese and supporting the children's fluency in their own language.[15] However, with an increased Han population within areas such as Panna for instance, it had become easier for educators who were against the use of resources to develop education in minority languages and bilingual programmes to promote their arguments.

One should keep in mind that during the Republic era, and later in the PRC, the Chinese governments did not merely establish schools in minority areas in order to promote Chinese learning among non-Han peoples. Schools were also set up to provide schooling for the children of Han government representatives and other Han settlers, including those who had lived for generations in the border regions of the empire. Today, in all areas, even those with schools established specifically to teach through the medium of a local minority language, there are always ordinary Chinese schools as well. And mostly the Chinese language is anyway the basis for continuing into higher forms of education. While most cadres maintained that a minority autonomous area should organise at least some kind of special training in the dominant local ethnic minority language, most agreed that providing proper Chinese state education for children of Han immigrants (especially those organised by the government) was equally important to compensate for eventual losses experienced by these Han.

Han immigrants in the political elite and state farms. With regard to use of language, dialects, level of school education and concern for institutionalised learning, my research among Han settlers in minority areas pointed to a number of marked differences between Han settlers of different periods belonging to different social classes and genders. From the 1960s onwards the state farms in Panna had grown to the degree that they could establish their own schools for children born within the farms. Schools outside state farms were for minority children and Han children whose parents worked as cadres or in other positions outside the state farms. Up till the late 1990s everybody

---

[15] For examples of programmes of bilingual education in China see for instance Upton 1999 and Hansen 2001.

within Panna who had an opinion about education seemed to agree that the state farm schools had managed to develop into the best schools in the area—the criterion being that they were producing the largest number of students able to continue upwards in the education system. In the 1980s some minority parents, mainly Tai parents living near state farms, would therefore pay special fees to have their children enrolled in one of the nearby state farm schools rather than using the ordinary primary or secondary school. The state farm schools were not under the local bureau of education and could themselves find and pay teachers of good quality. When, in 1997, I taught voluntarily for a few weeks in a state farm middle school, students in the senior middle school class were all conscious that they were attending what they described as 'the best middle school in Panna'. They laughed when asked if they thought it would have been useful or interesting to learn something about local Panna history, about the Tai and other minorities in the area, or about the local languages spoken there. These were young people who had all been born and raised in Panna, but they had no perception of being part of a local history, and they did not feel any special kind of social connection with the local Tai or any of the other minorities living there. Together with their parents they had lived all their lives in a small state farm society, largely secluded from the local economic, cultural and social life of the large non-state-farm, non-Han population.

By the late 1990s the state farms were facing an increasing liberalisation of the economy that made it profitable for Chinese companies to import cheaper, and sometimes better, rubber from Southeast Asia. Central government support for further development of the rubber production in Panna was dwindling and the future for the state farms seemed more uncertain than ever. The state farms were no longer able to guarantee work for the so-called second generation and many of them had to look for alternative jobs. The schools which had always been known as some of the best in Panna had fewer resources, and in a new trend some teachers who themselves came from state farms started to prefer jobs in the local (*difang*) schools rather than in the state farm schools.[16] The government's support for the

---

[16] The state farm schools nevertheless still have a very good reputation and in some rural areas they have to limit access of local minority children because too many now apply to have their children enrolled.

special keypoint schools (*zhongdian xuexiao*) since the 1980s had ensured the development of schools, outside state farms, that were recognised to be better than the ordinary ones. Together with the state
farm schools they educated the elite of Panna and attracted mainly
children of cadres, some of them Tai and other minorities (often
with one Han parent) but most of them Han. In 1992 all the representatives of the school's leadership were Han, and so were 92 per
cent of teachers and 60 per cent of students (Hansen 1999b, p. 124).

The local so-called 'minority schools' (*minzu xuexiao*) on the other
hand were of course largely attended by children officially classified
as members of ethnic minorities and a small percentage of Han who
had grown up in the most remote border villages. These schools were
popular not because of their quality or status, but because they provided the students with special economic support. The hierarchy of
different schools at the same levels of education was very obvious and
known to everybody within the area. Thus, most people in the cities
of Panna were conscious of the major differences between minority
schools, ordinary schools, keypoint schools and state farm schools, in
terms of recruitment of students, success with regard to access to
higher levels of education, financial support and local status.

Han cadres and children of Han cadres, as well as employees in various positions within the state farms, mostly emphasised the importance of having established Chinese state schools of high quality for
their children. They all tended to regard education in the state school
system as the most important way for children and young people to
achieve an attractive job, and especially a social position that would
hopefully bring not merely a fixed income but social prestige and
access to social or political resources. Those Han who had come before the reform era as conscious participants in the state's colonising
project regarded the establishment of a new education system not
merely as a necessary means of ensuring state control through the
training of the local ethnic minorities, but also as a necessary service
to the Han settlers who took part in this project. Some state farm
workers pointed out that if they had not moved to the state farm in
the first place their children would have grown up in an ordinary
Chinese rural area which would probably not have provided them
with an equally high quality education system. In this respect, the
state farm workers (much more than the state farm cadres) found

themselves to be privileged, having left their villages and settled in a state organisation, even though this implied moving to the frontiers and leaving behind family members in the villages of origin.

Being an ordinary worker within a rural state farm branch was considered to be hard work, and all those interviewed hoped that their children would find less physically demanding and better paid work. Social upward mobility was behind most interviewed Han workers' wish for their children's future. The Han students in secondary schools in state farms who were interviewed shared the hopes of students and their parents in most other areas of China: they first of all wished to get into a major university. However, compared to their parents they were more open towards the prospects of finding work outside the state sector, for instance in the booming tourist industry or in any kind of larger private company. Going into business was becoming an increasingly accepted career path for cadre children, but this did not diminish their emphasis on the importance of first obtaining as high a level of Chinese state education as possible.

As in Panna, Han cadres in Xiahe would try to send their children to the best possible Chinese schools. With the dual track system of Tibetan and so-called 'ordinary' schools (*putong xuexiao*) Han cadres normally did not doubt where to send their children who did not speak Tibetan, and whose future they hoped would bring desirable positions within the state sector or alternatively in prestigious private companies. The ordinary secondary school in Xiahe had officially 16 per cent Tibetan students, 58 per cent Han and 25 per cent Hui in 1998. Many of the Han, and practically all of the Tibetan, pupils' parents were cadres at various levels, according to one of the leaders of the school. Some of the Tibetan parents pointed to the fact that only this ordinary school could provide their children with the opportunity to study English, which they believed was more important than Tibetan for their children's future careers. Studying English was not possible in the Tibetan schools because of the dual teaching of Chinese and Tibetan, and some regarded this as a great disadvantage. They saw the increased contacts with foreign individuals and institutions as a way to promote the economic development of Xiahe, and they regarded knowledge of English as an entrance to jobs in the tourist industry or outside the local area. For cadres, regardless of ethnicity, there was a strong wish to provide children with a standard Chinese education that would hopefully open doors to a cadre position and bring political elite status, good connections, job security and a relatively pleasant life.

In the Tibetan primary and secondary school (started in 1987) there were, at each level, classes which had Chinese as the main language and others which had Tibetan as the main language. Parents could in principle choose which class they wanted to send their children to, but the majority of Tibetan parents preferred the classes that had Tibetan as their main language. According to one of the leaders of the Tibetan primary school, one reason was that the Tibetans valued Tibetan learning for their children and spoke it as their mother tongue anyway. This was confirmed by some Tibetan parents who had deliberately sent their children to the Tibetan classes. At the same time comments by other Han school administrators suggested widespread perceptions of the Tibetans parents (and implicitly *not* the Han parents) as being 'traditional' and 'not open towards the outside'. This characteristic was based on their preference for classes conducted in their own language rather than the national one. The interviewee quoted below explained the rather clear-cut ethnic division between schools in Xiahe in a way which was not uncommon among educators:

'It is normally the head of the family (*jiazhang*) who determines which school—the Tibetan or the ordinary—children enrol in. The Han nearly always prefer the ordinary school. The Tibetan commoners (*laobaixing*) normally prefer the Tibetan schools. They prefer their children to study the language of their own ethnic group. Those whose minds are relatively open also have an interest in things from outside (*wailai de dongxi*). They want to send their children to the ordinary school.'

Since too many Tibetan parents wanted their children to attend the classes that used Tibetan as the main language, the school insisted on dividing children more or less equally between the two types of classes. Consequently, those Tibetan children who were best in Chinese were placed in the classes that had Chinese as the main language of instruction. In the 'ordinary' schools, on the other hand, no Tibetan was taught at all. They were, like the ordinary schools in Panna, established partly with the purpose of providing Han settlers with the opportunity to secure for their offspring, growing up in a frontier minority area, an ordinary Chinese education. In Xiahe as in other ethnic minority areas profound knowledge of Chinese and some degree of education in a state school were often essential even when looking for local jobs as drivers, postmen and other local service jobs, and though this was a Tibetan area the working language within the administration was in practice mostly Chinese.

The recent individual Han immigrants. The educational situation for the earliest Han peasant settlers and their descendants in rural villages, as well as for the children of the numerous recent individual immigrants and temporary residents, differed in important ways from that of the Han in state farms or in cadre positions in the cities. Simply being Han did not provide them with any clear-cut advantages in terms of education within the minority area. The majority of recent economic migrants in Panna had no permanent residence permits and their children had no right to attend the schools in Panna. Most interviewed parents had their children with them when they were very young, but sent them back to the grandparents in their villages of origin when they reached school age. Quite a few had more than the one or two children allowed.[17] They would sometimes pay relatively large sums of money to guarantee a household registration (*hukou*) for at least one child in Panna, and then pay to have him (it was mostly a son) enrolled in one of the better schools in a state farm. This was especially common among peasants from Hunan who had distant relatives who had settled in one of the state farms in the 1960s or 70s, like this woman:

> 'Living conditions here are really better than at home. At home we were peasants, here we make money. The state farms around us treat us well. We are not planning to return for good to Qidong. As long as they [*sic*] allow us to continue this work we stay. We [the woman and her husband] have never been to school for more than a few years. Therefore, my children have to go to school. We save money for their education. Through our contacts with the state farm we have managed to have all our three children enrolled in the primary and secondary state farm schools. This costs

[17] In most areas peasants were allowed two children if the first was a girl.

us all in all more than 1,500 yuan per semester. For our oldest son [in first year of senior secondary school] we only have to pay 200 yuan per semester because we have already bought him a residence permit [*hukou*] for 3,000 yuan. The state farm schools are the best here. In the other schools the children are really naughty [*tiaopi*] and the quality is not good. The administration in the state farm schools is much better. We are willing to pay quite a lot for our oldest son's education. Hopefully he will then manage to get into a university. We will send him back to Hunan this year to continue his education, because our son says that the secondary school in Qidong is better than here.' (40-year-old woman from Hunan with three children)

Some interviewed parents had fled their home towns because they had given birth to more children than allowed and some had therefore lost their houses and the right to use the land they had contracted. These parents were more inclined to settle long-term or even permanently in the border region, and therefore also to find ways to have their children enrolled either in one of the ordinary local schools or in a state farm school. Like the interviewee above, many of the recent immigrants had strong opinions about the need for educating their children, and many were convinced that it was a good investment for a family to secure one child's education. When asked what saved capital would eventually be spend on, most people emphasised education for at least one child (either the son or the one considered to be brightest), weddings of children, and housing. But few of them were willing, or able, to pay the necessary amount of money to try to secure an education beyond primary or junior secondary school within the minority area for several children. Therefore, the majority of the recent immigrants either sent their children back to their grandparents when they reached school age, or did not send them to school at all. Their children were rarely going to school or kindergarten with local minority children, and they only naturally played with them when living physically very close to minority families with children. For the parents who had migrated to the minority areas in the reform period and settled temporarily (often not knowing themselves how long they would eventually stay) it was first of all their own attitudes towards their children's education, their possibilities (financial and others) of accessing the local schools in the area, and their relationship with relatives and authorities in their places of origin that determined if and where their children would attend school.

Studies have shown that school attendance among children of Han immigrants in large metropoles is remarkably lower than among children officially inhabiting the cities. In 1995 only 40 per cent of immigrant children in Beijing between five and twelve years were enrolled in school compared to 100 per cent of the native Beijing children of the same age group (Solinger 1999, p. 266). In Xiahe and Panna I found no specific statistics on school attendance of recent peasant immigrants, and since most did not keep their children with them after school age, local authorities found it both difficult and irrelevant to make estimates of this. The problem of limited schooling among peasant immigrants' children in the large cities has been debated in recent years among Chinese educators and local authorities, and some initiatives have been taken to establish new schools especially for immigrant children growing up in cities with large concentrations of rural immigrants. Still, many parents have problems financing their children's schooling, and some people within the cities have raised objections against special schools for immigrant peasant children, because they help to legitimise unauthorised settlement in the cities. Others have argued for the need to further raise the educational level of children of peasant immigrants in cities.[18] Among recent individual Han immigrants in Xiahe and Panna, there were no collective initiatives to establish special schools for their children, neither did local educators pay much attention to this issue. They did not feel that this was their responsibility since most immigrants would anyway send their children back home to attend school. In the longer run, if more people eventually decide to stay permanently in the minority areas one might expect that more immigrants will start to raise demands for easier access to local schools for their children.

Descendants of the earliest peasant immigrants. Like the children of recent individual immigrants, the descendants of the earliest peasant Han immigrants in villages in Panna and Xiahe were not particularly privileged with regard to local education. Like other people in the

[18] See for instance Deng Ke 2001.

rural areas of Panna and Xiahe they faced relatively poor conditions in schools and the problems of recruiting, and especially keeping, teachers in villages. Nevertheless, many rural Han settlers and their descendants demonstrated a concern for formal learning for at least one of their children which suggested that the official Chinese school—regardless of its actual content of education—was accepted as a main springboard for finding jobs outside agriculture. In villages in Xiahe where Han and Tibetans lived together, largely similar perceptions of formal Chinese education were expressed by both Han and Tibetan peasants who all lived close to the county capital and were unable to maintain a living for their entire families on the basis of income from agriculture and possible part-time herding alone. With the development of tourism and increased trade, several Tibetan peasants interviewed found that a profound knowledge of Chinese was essential to succeed in obtaining a more permanent attractive job outside agriculture. Formal Chinese state education was brought forward as one attractive option for eventually securing a job and income for children. The same views were emphasised by Han peasants interviewed in Xiahe. Nevertheless, the actual level of education among these peasants and their children was rather low and few had finished education beyond junior secondary school.

In an ethnically mixed Tibetan-Han village surveyed (River Village), the majority of Tibetans and Han belonging to the oldest generation (between fifty and seventy years old) had not been to school at all. People in the village between thirty and fifty years old had at least some years of primary school, and the youngest generation had nearly all finished six years of primary school. Several had continued into or finished junior secondary school, but only a couple of people had an education beyond that level. Boys generally stayed longest in school. The oldest Han in the village nearly all spoke fluent Tibetan, the next generation in Han families spoke Tibetan well enough to manage communication about basic issues with their Tibetan neighbours, but the youngest generation hardly spoke any Tibetan at all.[19] The Tibetan children all spoke Chinese as well as Tibetan. This was

---

[19] This information is largely based on accounts by my different assistants who were Tibetan and, unlike myself, capable of judging levels of spoken Tibetan among interviewees.

a village with predominantly Han peasant families and it was therefore not surprising that the local Chinese dialect was the main language among villagers. In other Tibetan-Han villages, the Tibetan language was spoken by Tibetans while Chinese was also commonly used in communication between Tibetans, Han and Hui. Bilingual competence was very widespread among Tibetan peasants, especially the younger generations, and a number of teachers and cadres working with education in Xiahe told that Chinese was becoming increasingly important as a mean of communication among Tibetan peasants also. This was attributed to the fact that the main language of career-wise success was Chinese, and to the demands for Chinese speaking employees in the tourist industry and trade.

Although a number of peasants, both Tibetan and Han, argued that some kind of schooling and a profound knowledge of the Chinese language were important for children, many parents found schooling beyond primary school too expensive. When paying several hundred yuan per semester for a child in junior secondary school most parents and grandparents wanted value for the money in terms of continued education and ultimately a job outside agriculture. Thus, education in state schools was often first of all evaluated on the basis of the direct job-wise advantages it would bring. In conversations with members of Tibetan peasant families it was striking how their expressed views on education, and their perceptions of the advantages and disadvantages of spending money on it, resembled those of their neighbouring Han peasants. Money was wasted and face was lost for both child and parents if education did not bring about a job:

> A [young, Chinese educated Tibetan man from peasant family]: 'If you have been three years to junior secondary school and you then don't manage to continue into senior secondary or specialised secondary school, you just have to return home and become a peasant. Then people talk about you! They say, "ayah...this person...so many years in school and now anyway a peasant!" That is really tough on those who don't manage to continue. People say all kinds of things and you feel you have wasted the money of your family. Not only the money spent on schooling, but you have also not been making money for the family during all those years you have been at school.'

   B [old Tibetan from a peasant family previously with long Buddhist training]: 'Many children do not like to go to school. Many don't want to continue into junior or senior secondary school precisely because they are afraid what people will say about them if they do not manage to continue further. They are afraid because they know that they will feel ashamed. On the other hand, if you do manage to continue—especially into higher education—everybody thinks you are really good, really smart, they think that your family is lucky. So the burden on the children here is really very heavy and few children like to go to school.'

While similar views were expressed by Tibetans and Han alike in River Village and among Han and Tibetans from other villages as well, one important aspect distinguished Han peasants from Tibetan ones: although many of the Han in the villages were Buddhists like the Tibetans and participated in the same rituals and celebrations, they would never send a son to one of the local monasteries to become a monk. Unlike the Tibetans, they saw participation in the Chinese state education system (and to a lesser degree apprenticeship) as the only institutionalised way to promote a future outside agriculture for children. Becoming a monk or nun in a local Tibetan monastery was considered not merely a form of religious training and learning, but an act defining 'Tibetanness'. As explained by several older Han who considered themselves Buddhists within the same tradition as their Tibetan friends and neighbours, the monastic education was in the Tibetan language and first of all meant for Tibetans. It was respected as an important form of learning, and monks were highly regarded as religious specialists and people with a high level of knowledge and learning. But sending a son (or a daughter) to a Tibetan monastery was considered to be 'normal' for Tibetans only, and very unusual for the Han. Monastic education was too closely connected to Tibetan language, script, tradition and identity to become a natural choice for Han parents considering their own and their offspring's future, even when they were themselves declared Buddhists sharing the customs and practices of their fellow Tibetan villagers.

Differential policies for Han and minorities

As pointed out by Barry Sautman, the PRC 'has one of the oldest and largest programmes of state-sponsored preferential policies (*youhui zhengce*) for ethnic minorities' (Sautman 1999, p. 173). The main aim has been to narrow the social and economic gap between Han and minority areas and help prevent ethnic conflicts. In addition to policies granting financial subsidies, exemption from tariffs for some imported goods, and liberal investment laws, a number of other preferential policies directly influence major aspects of the lives of minority individuals: '....preferential policies for family planning (exemption from minimum marriage age and one-child strictures), education (preferential admissions, lowered school fees, boarding schools, remedial programs), employment (extra consideration in hiring and promotion of cadres), business development (special loans and grants, exemptions from some taxes) and political representation' (ibid. p. 174). In the various provinces and autonomous regions, and at lower administrative levels in minority autonomous prefectures and counties, there are a number of specific and different policies all within the definition of preferential policies for the fifty-five officially recognised ethnic minorities.[20]

Preferential policies have been a fact throughout the period of the PRC and there seems, among many Han, to be a widespread understanding, or at least acceptance, of why the government has insisted on these policies—a conviction that the areas inhabited by minorities are backward, that the people belonging to ethnic minorities need special help, and that preferential policies are therefore a sign of the willingness not merely of the Communist Party, but also of all the Han, to assist in their development and modernisation. At the same time, as Sautman points out, there is 'anecdotal evidence' that preferential admissions into higher education for minorities are not only envied, but also resented by many Han (Sautman 1999, p. 194). Also, William R. Jankowiak has pointed out that in the city of Huhhot where Han outnumbers Mongols by about twelve to one, the entitlement programme has provoked resentment among the Han population against the Mongols and, indirectly, against the government (Jankowiak 1993, p. 37). In areas where the living conditions of many rural Han were clearly more or less similar to those of

---

[20] Some local areas also practice preferential policies towards ethnic groups that are not officially recognised. In Lijiang, for instance, the Mosuo who are officially classified as Naxi are sometimes granted extra points when entering local secondary schools, not because they belong to the Naxi nationality but because they are acknowledged as 'Mosuo people' (*Mosuo ren*).

the minorities I have also heard Han people argue that the policies of preferential treatment, especially in education, were unfair. However, Sautman seems to be right when suggesting that one major reason why resentment has not been strong enough to manifest itself in public discourse is the fact that at least in education the policies do not challenge the actual opportunities of Han in general. Contrary to the findings of Sautman and Jankowiak, my research in minority areas suggested that in fact only a few Han immigrants rejected, or had any strong opinions about, the preferential policies for ethnic minorities.

Among interviewed Han belonging to the class of state employees, and living in ethnic minority areas as a result of their parents' participation in one of the state's modernisation projects, the preferential policies with regard to education were largely seen as directly advantageous to themselves. The children of early Communist pioneers were the only Han who actually directly benefited from the preferential policies, because of the rules that also provided extra points in examination for those Han who had grown up in a border area, especially with parents who had resettled through their participation in a state sponsored project. Children of cadres or workers who had been in the area for more than thirty years, as well as children in state farms, could be allowed into a college for minorities. Their parents' status as state employees in the border area or as 'supporters of the borderland' would sometimes be positively considered in connection with eventual job distribution after graduation. These rules did not apply for children of later immigrants or of individual immigrants not organised by the state.

In mountain villages with early Han settlers in Panna (the people locally known as the 'mountain Han') those who were concerned about their children's education would normally take care to register them as minority rather than Han children. This was no problem because often children either had one parent who was a minority member or was registered as such, or could trace other relatives who belonged to one of the minorities from their villages. Regarding oneself as Han but being registered as a minority person was no problem for those interviewed in this group. They were first of all concerned with the eventual advantages of being registered as belonging to a minority. It was a matter of practical consideration, and the preferential treatment in education was presented as one important reason for this. However, most of my interviewees belonging to the Han living in mountain villages in Panna happened to be people who had themselves succeeded in the education system, and they were therefore probably more concerned with the policies of education than other people from their villages. Like this woman, they all agreed that it was a matter of practicality to be classified as a minority person:

> 'Maybe the Han are a bit more clever than the Aini [local name for the Akha]....or maybe it was because we all spoke Chinese at home...In any case, more children from our Han village [with inhabitants mostly registered as Lahu] than from the Aini village nearby continued in school. We Han were also poor, but we always lived a bit better than the Aini who went to our school. Our village is completely Han, but we call ourselves Lahu. This is an advantage here, for instance with regard to education.' (Female administrator, born 1962 in a Han-Lahu village in the mountains of Panna)

As in Panna, all Han I encountered in Xiahe who were married to minority people (normally Han men married to Tibetan women) had registered their children as Tibetan. They, similarly, argued that the main reason was the preferential treatment with regard to either education or birth control. In Xiahe in the late 1990s, while Han peasants were allowed to have two children like the Tibetan and Hui peasants (herdsmen were allowed to have three), other Han registered in the towns were only allowed one child. Especially in the county of Zhuoni (also within the prefecture of Gannan) where there have been larger Han settlements for a long time, many Han managed to register as Tibetans. One Han interviewee had arrived in Xiahe in the mid-1950s and married a Han woman from Zhuoni. The wife's Han grandfather had come during the Qing Dynasty as a trader and he and his children had married other Han. However, through the generations they had lived among Tibetans, and the family had largely adopted local Tibetan customs and language. The interviewed couple were originally both registered as Han, and so were their children. However, by the mid-1980s the son of the couple failed to pass the university exam. Had he been a Tibetan at the time he would have received extra points owing to the policy of preferential treatment and passed. The Han father therefore tried, and eventually managed, to reregister all the couple's children as Tibetans, arguing that their mother for all practical purposes was Tibetan: her family had lived for generations in a Tibetan domi-nated village and had adopted Tibetan traditions. The following year, thanks to his new status as a Tibetan, the son managed to pass the exam. As the happy father explained: '*All* cadres who had this opportunity, for instance if they were married to a Han from the ru-ral areas of Zhuoni, would have done this.'

The individual Han immigrants of the reform period obviously did not have the choice of registering their children as minority members, but they nevertheless mostly expressed indifference to the policy of preferential treatment for minorities in education. Their children would never gain any advantages from preferential admis-sion rules because they were Han whose parents had not migrated as Communist pioneers or in connection with the state's modernisa-tion projects, and anyway interviewees in this group were mostly not aware that preferential policies in some cases benefited Han in mi-nority areas. When told about the policy, they would mostly remark that of course this special policy was specifically created for the Han cadres' children and had therefore nothing to do with themselves. Several commented that since the government had decided upon the special policies for minorities these were probably necessary and they themselves were not very concerned about it anyway. Thus the Han living within the minority areas were generally not among those who complained about, or envied, the preferential policies re-garding education for minorities. Few saw the policies as threatening to themselves and their own possibilities in education, and many did not bother about these policies at all. The few who expressed resent-ment were mostly adult children of early Han immigrants who had not managed to enrol in the higher education they had hoped for, and felt that had they been members of minorities they might have been given other opportunities both in education and with regard to job distribution.

Concerning birth control there are considerable variations in the ways in which the preferential policies have been applied to mino-rities in different areas. Both policies and practices change rather quickly, depending partly on the evaluation by higher administrative organs of the work of local birth control committees, partly on local

policies. Committees carrying out the population control programmes are under very strong pressure to present figures to the provincial government that positively demonstrate their ability to secure
low birth rates and late births, and success in implementing sterilisa-
tions or promoting the use of other contraceptive methods. Especially in the late 1990s, policies towards minorities were strengthened
after years of more liberal practices with regard to birth control.
Nevertheless, it is not uncommon to encounter areas where three
children are accepted, for instance for nomads, and often policies
depend not merely on ethnicity but on social position and rural-
urban distinctions with regard to household registration.

It is common that peasants in minority areas may have two children regardless of ethnicity, while cadres may have two if they belong to a minority and one if they are Han. In Xiahe and Panna, for
instance, the policy is practiced this way and in addition the Tibetan
nomads in Xiahe may have three children. In any case, Han living
within ethnic minority areas are directly faced with the fact that
people living within the same region, and sometimes having the
same kind of jobs, are treated differently with regard to birth control
because of their ethnic identification. For Han people living in the
central and eastern parts of China, the preferential policies with regard to minorities' birth rates might be a somewhat distant matter—
a policy designed for political reasons for peoples living on far away
borders, whom most would never come into direct contact with.
Among Han living in ethnic minority areas the situation is different
because they live within the areas where differential policies are
practiced. Considering the dissatisfaction with the one- or two-child
policy often expressed by Han peasants and immigrants in the two
minority areas, one might have expected this to result in resentment
and envy directed towards the local minorities. This, however, was
only rarely the case among the Han within the minority areas.

The interviewed Han members of the local political and educational elite tended to paraphrase official arguments for preferential
policies, and some explained that leniency with regard to birth control was a sign of the Party's (and the Han's) understanding of the
special situation of the minorities. Some also found it a necessity to
avoid ethnic conflict. More common was the view that peasants and
minorities were people who lived in rural areas where it was more

essential to have more children and only a long-term modernisation of China and people's minds would lead to changes that could ensure lower birth rates. Therefore, in the meantime, the government just had to adapt to some demands from the rural population. The general acceptance among cadres of the more lenient population policies for minorities did not lead them to resent Han cadres who attempted to be registered as minority members themselves. This was anyway normally done for educational reasons, and not to have more children, and it rarely resulted in moral indignation on the part of those who did not have this opportunity. It was commonly accepted among interviewees from this group that blood relationship, even when distant, could be used as the determinant of ethnic classification—if, for instance, a grandmother had been a non-Han this was an acceptable reason to have grandchildren and great-grand-children reclassified as minority members.

The recent Han economic immigrants were rarely able to prove a blood relationship with an ethnic minority person that would qualify for having more than one or two children, and they were themselves the immigrants most likely to break rules of birth control. On the basis of rules from their provinces of origin where they had their household registration, the recent peasant Han immigrants in Panna and Xiahe were mostly allowed two children when the first-born was a girl. However, it was much more difficult for the authorities to control people who travelled than peasants who remained within their villages, and it was not uncommon to meet recent Han immigrants in the two areas with three, four or even more children. As mentioned above, other locals and cadres referred to these immigrants somewhat derogatorily as the 'moving guerrilla of people having too many children'. Some interviewees among the recent settlers had fled their villages because they had lost their houses and had their land confiscated when they gave birth to a fourth or fifth child. In Panna they were able to resettle, start a private shop if they had some capital, maybe pay for one or more children's schooling and rebuild a home. Obviously not all of them had this opportunity, and some would leave one or two of the oldest children at home with the grandparents, bringing only the smallest ones to their new home-place.

Many of the recent immigrants were very dissatisfied with the policies of population control, but they nevertheless rarely directed their resentment against the minorities and the special policies applied to them. Minorities were anyway also restricted with regard to the number of children allowed, and there seemed among the many recent immigrants to be a widespread feeling that policies towards minorities were something that did not really concern them. They would like to have fewer restrictions on births and movement especially, but how minorities were eventually treated was not considered to be any of their business. The majority of recent immigrants interviewed did not have an excessive number of children, although they mostly said they would have liked to have more if restrictions were lifted. The topic of children was sometimes a sensitive one in discussion with unregistered immigrants in particular. I will certainly not rule out the possibility that some interviewees did not tell me the correct number of children in their family, fearing that I might have connections with local authorities, fearing that neighbours were listening to the interviews, or simply because they preferred not to tell anyone that they had broken rules of birth control.

In Panna by the late 1990s birth control was rather strict and many Han immigrants were controlled by the authorities from their place of origin. Since so many of the recent peasant immigrants had come from the same two counties in Hunan, the local birth control administrations from Hunan were to some extent able to enforce their policies on their inhabitants, even though they had physically moved to Panna. Staff from the birth control administrations in Qidong and Liling in Hunan travelled to Panna every three months to perform check-ups on women. It was relatively easy for the authorities from these counties in Hunan to find the relevant women, because some families had temporary registration in Panna and many individual immigrants from the same counties of Hunan lived together within smaller areas of Jinghong. Rules also demanded that the women returned back to their county of origin to meet the birth control authorities once a year, but nothing serious was seemingly done to enforce this policy. Considering the level of control, many interviewed recent immigrants found that the price to pay for having more children than allowed was too high—losing schooling opportunities, having to pay fines, in some cases loosing certain local positions:

> 'You can still get around the birth control if you really want to, but the price is high. In the cities many now prefer to have a daughter

because they are more obedient, but in the countryside people still want a son. Before people would talk really nasty about you if you did not have a son, but they do not dare to do that now. Birth control is very strict now, so nobody dares to talk badly to someone who has got two daughters.' (21-year-old woman from Jiangxi, newly wed and with no children)

Among recent immigrants, as well as among local peasants, resentment against the policy of birth control, including the many campaigns to enforce compliance with the rules, was widespread. Discussions often arose around this topic, sometimes sparked by the fact that my own two children came with me during some fieldwork periods. But only very rarely did resentment turn to expressions of envy of minorities. Envy was rather directed towards me as a foreign woman who was allowed to make my own decision on a possible third and fourth child and even get financial support from the state for this. At the same time there was also among many recent immigrants a general consensus about the fact that China was a developing country with scarce resources, not least considering the growing size of the population. Some therefore argued that restrictions were necessary, but that the financial restraints on peasants in general should be resolved at the same time.

Through focus on the spatial organisation of Han immigrants' living quarters, their practices of religion within the ethnic minority areas, their engagement in state education and their perceptions of the preferential policies for minorities that they encountered through their migration, it became clearer how Han immigrants living in ethnic minority areas had different ways of interacting with the local minorities and of adapting to life in their new home place. This was largely a result of the differences in social status, occupation, and time and reason for migration among the individuals belonging to the heterogeneous group of Han immigrants in the two areas researched. Generally, close social contacts between immigrants and locals across lines of ethnicity—partly drawn and hardened through the state's own classification and its preferential policies—were limited, with the descendants of the earliest rural Han immigrants as the main exception.

Unsurprisingly, Han peasants and their descendants who had settled generations before among non-Han peasants in villages in Xiahe and Panna had developed often close relationships with non-Han people. As I shall examine further later on, they sometimes married minority members and adopted local religious traditions and customs. And they defined themselves as Han without emphasising strong feelings of unity with the Han immigrants who came later after the 1950s as participants in the Communist government's modernisation and civilisation projects. The reasons for the earliest immigrants' different approaches towards the local native population were relatively obvious. They had not come in larger groups of Han with a pre-defined political and ideological purpose behind their resettlement. Neither had they (like the immigrants of the reform period) come at a time when Han people, the Chinese language, standard state education and the Communist political system were already well established in the areas.

The later government-organised immigrants' attitudes towards change and towards minorities' cultural practices were largely formed by the perceived ideological importance of their own mission in the area. They were first of all expected to transform the areas they came to, and not to be thoroughly changed themselves. They were to be in the forefront of the Communist Party's modernising and civilising project, and as such they can perhaps best be understood as participants in an internal colonisation project. Their ways of settling in often secluded communities, their ways of establishing control over local resources and defining the language and education system of success, were largely similar to those of other colonisers around the world. The Han working in state farms and administration knew they had been resettled permanently, but owing to their special political mission, nevertheless they would normally neither participate actively in local minorities' celebrations and festivals, nor return to their areas of origin to participate in similar celebrations in the places of origin.

The recent individual immigrants, arriving in a time of economic liberalisation, were able to benefit from many of the changes that the minority areas had undergone since the arrival of the first state-organised Han immigrants after the 1950s. They arrived in areas that were not too unfamiliar for them because they were able to find within the areas largely similar educational programmes, TV stations and festivals, and forms of administration that they were used to. Furthermore, they arrived in a linguistic environment where Chinese was already dominant in the towns and cities where they mostly set-tled. They mainly interacted with the local non-Han population on the markets and in business relationships, but their children rarely played with minority children and they were mostly sent back to their places of origin when starting school. While peasant Han im-migrants of earlier periods had adopted local religious customs and at the same time established (in the case of Xiahe) their own temples within Chinese tradition, the recent immigrants would still ideally return to their villages of origin during major festivals and would just participate in minorities' festivals and celebrations 'for the fun of it'. To most of them the minority area was—at least in their imagi-nation—not their final destination but only their place of living as long as it provided the desired economic improvement.

4

HAN FAMILIES AND IMAGES OF HOME

"'Home", we suggest as a working definition, "is where one best knows oneself"—where "best" means "most", even if not always "happiest". Here, in sum, is an ambiguous and fluid but yet ubiquitous notion, apposite for a charting of the ambiguities and fluidities, the migrancies and paradoxes, of identity in the world today.' (Rapport and Dawson 1998b, p. 9)

In a world where more and more people are travelling and migrating—and where an even larger number of people are aware of *other* people's opportunities of travelling and migrating—research into concepts of home, connection to a 'home place', transnationalism and diaspora has redirected our attention from culture and people as rooted in particular places and times to the various ways in which multiple homes, attachments and 'native places' are narrated and constructed.[1] Notions of home as microcosmic communities, as the stable physical centre of family members' universe, and as a safe, familiar place (whether house, village, region or nation) that one may leave and eventually return to, are now described as being anachronistic (Rapport and Dawson 1998b, pp. 6–7). The relationship between movement and home has changed:

> Increasingly, one is seen as moving between homes, erstwhile to current; or as moving between multiple homes (from one compressed socio-cultural environment to another); or as being at home in continuous movement (amongst creolized cultural forms); and so one's home as movement *per se*. (Rapport and Dawson 1998a, p. 27)

[1] For recent studies of Chinese transnationalism and diaspora see for instance the articles in Ong 1996 and Benton and Pieke 1998.

However, as pointed out by Karen Fog Olwig, most people hardly regard home first of all as an abstract discursive place, seeing it rather as a concrete place of mutual relations of social exchange:

> Thus it may be useful to distinguish between home as a locus involving specific relations of social and economic rights and obligations, and home as a more abstract entity that is primarily expressed through various types of narratives and other forms of symbolic interchange. These two aspects of home mutually reinforce and implicate one another, so that 'home' will not exist in the form of a concrete set of socio-economic rights and obligations if it does not receive some sort of recognition and validation through narratives and other kinds of symbolic expression among interacting individuals. Similarly, the social and economic practices of home will have an important bearing on the kinds of narratives of home that will be related by the individuals involved. (Olwig 1998, p. 235).

This interrelationship between home as narrative and home as social practice was significant for understanding the ways in which Han settlers from various regions, with different migration histories and belonging to different social classes, themselves recounted and explained certain observable social practices related to family, home and relatives in their 'old home' (*laojia*). For the Han settlers, as discussed in chapter 3, the minority area was in some aspects obviously far from home, while it was also relatively 'near' because it was part of a well-known political system, promoting at the official level the same kind of education, language, morality and economic system that they were used to. The minority area was probably not where they 'knew themselves best'. However, since they were not forced to adapt to a profoundly new political and cultural system, and since they were mostly able to keep contact with family members in other parts of the country and their areas of origin, they rarely expressed feelings of 'being lost' in the new area, or of being 'out of home'. Still, 'home' in the minority area often meant something different from 'home' in their place of origin as they imagined it. All Han migrants regardless of social position were conscious of having moved to another place within their own country—a place that was often regarded as remote, both in terms of geographical distance from the political centre and migrants' own places of origin, and in terms of cultural practices, history and the economy.

Recent studies of migration have questioned conventional ways of perceiving of migration in terms of an opposition between 'here' and 'there' (as a movement from one fixed entity to the other), and have suggested instead regarding movement as 'a mode of being in the world' (Carter 1992, p. 101).[2] And as Nigel Rapport and Andrew Dawson have shown,

> A world of movement 'can be understood in terms of actual physical motion around the globe and also as an imagination: an awareness of movement as a potentiality and a vicarious knowledge of movement as a phenomenon of overriding impingement.' (Rapport and Dawson 1998b, p. 4)

For many of the migrants in my study, moving from one place to another in a continuing search for working opportunities could possibly be described as a 'mode of being in the world', but not an unproblematic one or one that was merely the result of free choice. Many migrants expressed their experience of resettlement in terms of a contract between leaving the 'old home' (*laojia*) and arriving in the 'present place of living' (*xianzai zhu de difang*), even when conscious of the fact that this 'present place of living' might change again. They had sometimes lived in several places in addition to their places of origin, and they were concerned with what they themselves saw as the 'essence' or 'characteristics' of those various places. Essence—defined as a natural property of a given entity that through a process of transcendence becomes a pure form—is a social construction (see Lavie and Swedenburg 1996a, pp. 12–13). But a social construction can become essentialised, and many of the Han migrants expressed concepts of their 'old home', and to a lesser extent of their 'Han-ness', in terms of roots, ancestors and, sometimes, nostalgia connected to their 'old home'. This does not mean that they would necessarily actually return to the 'old home' later, or even that they would like to do so.

Studies of Chinese culture and Chinese people abroad have often ascribed to the Chinese strong emotional attachments to one's place

[2] See also studies such as, for instance, Chambers 1994, Lavie and Swedenburg 1996b and Rapport and Dawson 1998c.

of origin—attachments that have also manifested themselves in organisations based on common regional affiliation.[3] Attachment to place of origin was to some extent also expressed orally and in actions by Han settlers in the minority areas. However, the ways in which Han settlers represented themselves and their connections to their places of origin suggested that their own social strategies, related especially to economy, education and power, were at least as important for their relations to local area and place of origin as some kind of primordially inscribed rooting in a certain region. Nevertheless, especially when strategies of accumulating capital (social, cultural, educational or economic) failed, migrants tended to emphasise, and attempt to make use of, connections related to place of origin.

In practically all interviews with Han immigrants the topics of old home, place of origin and family relations were brought up. Often discussions around the topic of home developed as a result of interviewees' interest in knowing more about me as a foreign researcher and traveller (where was my home, where did I come from, where had I been, where would I eventually return to, when and why). The degree of intensity of discussions about the topic of home and family (often among various interviewees rather than as responses to interview questions) indicated how important this topic had become, both for those Han who had been resettled in the Maoist era and for those who had been moving around between several different locations, with or without their closest family members, since the mid-1980s. Furthermore, people employed in special offices in the state farms and government collected personal memories of migration and wrote historic accounts of Han settlement in the minority area. They thereby participated in the construction of a set of authoritative narratives of Han settlements in the border areas, providing settlers with a sanctified version of the reasons, goals and importance of their own migration. These (often internal) publications gave meaning to resettlement and thereby also created certain images of how 'new' and 'old' homes were constituted.

While this is discussed in more detail in Chapter 6, this chapter focuses on the ways in which home, family and ancestors were

---

[3] Concerning studies related to Chinese attachment to place, see for instance Skinner 1977, Tu Wei-ming 1991, Wang L. Ling-chi 1991. For a recent study of Chinese clan associations see for instance Brøgger 2000.

represented by Han settlers in interviews, and how these discursive constructions of home were inseparable from the ways in which social relations of home and family were played out in daily life.

Marriage as an ideal and in practice

Examples from the Han-Tibetan River Village in Xiahe illustrate how peasant Han settlers since the 1930s in a Tibetan area have expanded their families within the villages, and employed various strategies to continue their lineages (see map, p. 127). River Village was established in the late 1930s by four Han families of different lineages, all escaping from the Muslim uprisings in neighbouring Linxia. The Yang, Yao, Ka and He families settled down, built houses and rented land from Labrang monastery. More Han families moved in shortly afterwards, and by the late 1990s there were twenty mainly Han households made up of nine different Chinese family names. Six Tibetan families had become part of the village when, in the late 1970s, they moved downhill from another Tibetan village that was part of the same production team as River Village (explained in Chapter 2). When talking about different households and families within the village, villagers normally distinguished between Tibetan and Han families—although intermarriage was not unusual in both the Han lineages and the Tibetan households. If a Han was married to a Tibetan, children would normally have a Han and a Tibetan name, the lineage name remaining Chinese. Some children of Tibetan parents in other villages of Xiahe were known to have a Chinese as well as a Tibetan name. One reason for this was that people would sometimes ask the nurse or doctor who received the child at birth to provide it with a name. Since most medical workers were Han, they would normally provide a Chinese name. If the baby cried and was not feeling too well within a day or so after naming, some would ask a Tibetan monk, or in the case of the Han sometimes a Daoist one, to provide another name more appropriate for the child. A Tibetan monk would then provide a Tibetan name, while a Han Daoist monk would suggest a Chinese name.

The family name (*xing*) remained very important for all Han families. Both narratives of family and strategies of marriage underlined the importance of having at least one male descendant to continue

Map 1: Households in River Village, Xiahe

Yang: empty house for youngest son when family is to be split	Ka: 4 people, all Han	Bai: 6 people, all Han	Ka: 9 people all Han	He: 3 people, all Han
Qi: 6 people, all Han	Li + Yang 6 people, all Han	Tao: 6 people, all Han	Tao: 6 people, all Han	Ka: 5 people, all Han
Ka: 7 people, all Han	Tao: 7 people, all Han	Yang: 9 people, all Han, preparing to split	Ma (+ Shang): 5 people, all Han	Yang: 3 people, all Han
Ka: 8 people, all Han	Ka: 5 people, all Han	Tao: 4 people, all Han	Ma: 6 people, all Han	Tao + Tibetan wife: one Tibetan child
Ka + Tibetan wife: 4 people including two Tibetan children	Shang: 5 people, all Han	Yang: 4 people, all Han	Tibetan family: 5 people, all Tibetans	Tibetan family + Han son-in-law: 5 people, children Tibetan
Tibetan family's empty house	Tibetan family: 8 people	Tibetan family + one Han man: 6 people, all children Tibetan		

the lineage, honour the ancestors, and provide for the older generation. Continuing one's family name through sons in immigrant villages composed of several surname groups was essential, not merely
for practical reasons, but because it constituted a central aspect of the
very identification as Han.[4] The practices related to the continuance
of surname groups also helped to explain why Han families especially were expanding within the village.

An example of this was the Ka family which was one of the first
to settle down in River Village. The name Ka is not a common Chinese name, and according to family history it originated from an ancestor who had married a Tibetan woman and, for some reason
unknown or unspoken of, changed his own family name into Ka,
thereby establishing a Ka lineage. The first Ka couple in Xiahe had
eight sons of whom two had remained in River Village and continued the lineage there. The only one remaining of these (two) sons
was Old Ka who recalled fleeing Muslim uprisings to Xiahe with his
parents when he was ten years old in 1938. They got permission
from the Labrang monastery to settle down and built a house, and
after three years they started to pay part of their crops and income as
tax to the monastery. Thus the family had re-established a way of
living providing them with what Old Ka thought was a fairly good
income at the time, and like many other immigrant Han families
from that time they did not move on. By the late 1990s the Ka families had split several times (*fen jia*) according to common practice
among Han peasants, and seven households in River Village were
part of the Ka lineage. In all 42 adults and children lived in the Ka
houses of River Village, all of them regarded as members of the Ka
lineage. Proper spouses for Ka sons and daughters were normally
found among other Han in Gannan, or among Han families in
neighbouring Linxia, but in the cases where spouses were Tibetan
children would still be part of the Ka surname group.[5]

---

[4] See Ebrey 1996 for an historic overview of the importance of surnames for the
identification as Chinese or Han.

[5] As discussed by Patricia Ebrey, 'Chinese were never preoccupied with notions of
creoles or half-breeds. One Han Chinese migrant in the Han, Tang, or Song
dynasty could be enough to allow thousands or tens of thousands of patrilineal
descendants to lay claim to Chinese ancestry and thus Chinese identity.' (Ebrey
1996, pp. 33–4).

The graves of the oldest Ka were placed in the mountains nearby where they could be properly attended to, and there had apparently been no consideration of moving back to Linxia where their ances-tors had come from and where they also had ancestral graves. The main considerations of the adults had been to provide themselves and their children with the necessary means of living, and the village in Xiahe had given them this opportunity. During most of the period between the late 1950s and the 1970s moving had in any case not been an option, and after the start of the reform period previous col-lective land was divided between private households, initially making it advantageous to stay and till the new private crops. However, with the expansion of the Ka family within River Village, land had already been divided between several sons and each household was therefore depending on alternative means of income as well. For that reason mainly, the option of migrating more permanently to other places was being considered by some of the younger men, but since competi-tion in the larger cities was known to be fierce and they were often needed in the fields, most chose instead to supplement their income by working in part-time odd jobs (*dagong*[6]) in the neighbouring areas.

In River Village and other ethnically diverse villages in Xiahe as well as in Panna, a number of intermarriages between Han and non-Han took place, mostly between Han men and non-Han women. One of the Ka households, for instance, was established in the 1980s when a nephew from Linxia became a widower with a child. The Old Ka then negotiated marriage with a Tibetan family within the village whose daughter had divorced and also had a child of her own. She was considered rather old for remarrying and the match be-tween the two was therefore described as 'a proper one'. The concept of a proper match normally meant a marriage between social and economic equals and to some extent also included considerations of ethnicity.[7] In particular many older interviewees liked to talk about the topic of a 'proper marriage'. They had all had to consider the marriages of their children, which were rarely decided upon without

---

[6] A term difficult to translate as it implies all kinds of unskilled labour. The term 'odd jobs' is borrowed from Solinger who uses it to distinguish from definite working positions (*gongzuo*) (Solinger 1999, p. 245).

[7] One of the common Chinese terms used by interviewees to express a proper match was *mendang hudui*, 'proper family and suitable background'.

intense negotiations with parents, among families or sometimes with a matchmaker engaging in the direct introduction and negotiation. When I asked villagers in the Xiahe area why Han men were more likely to marry non-Han women than the other way around, quite a few Han peasants (men and women) insisted that Han women either were afraid of the Tibetans' cows or refused to milk them. Milking cows, they insisted, was an activity which Tibetan men expected from their wives. This was taken as an indisputable fact, unnecessary to discuss further and simply marking what was perceived as an essential cultural difference hard to overcome.

Marriages between Hui and non-Hui were in general very rare and this was always explained by differences in religion and diet. Dramatic stories travelled among Han and Tibetans about local Hui women who had wanted to marry Han men, and therefore had to flee with the result that they were hunted down by angry family members seeking revenge.[8] These stories tended to highlight histories of conflicts between Han and Hui in the area, while in fact most current encounters in Xiahe between Hui and other groups were not particularly marked by ethnic or political hostility. In Han and Tibetan narratives of ethnic and cultural differences between Han, Hui and Tibetans, it was common to emphasise the closer relationship between Tibetans and Han than between the Hui and both Tibetans and Han. In the case of Tibetans and Han, in spite of narratives of cultural differences (food and cooking, clothing, language, to some extent religion), ideas of 'the perfect match' seemed first of all to be derived from, and developed in relationship with, social strategies and considerations of how the family could best strengthen its social and economic potential.

It was often difficult to assess what role ethnicity actually played in decisions on marriage. This was partly due to the methodological problems of interviewing. It became quite clear to me that interview questions sometimes indirectly demanded that people confronted the issue of ethnicity. A very evident example is a situation where

---

[8] My interviews and fieldwork in Xiahe concentrated on the Han and to a certain extent Tibetans. I only did systematic surveys and interviews with a smaller number of Hui people. These have therefore not been included to any large extent in this work, and the limited data presented on the Hui should be regarded as preliminary.

one asks Han peasants why Han women hardly ever marry Tibetan men. The framing of the question already suggests an explanation based on ethnicity, and people may therefore try to respond by turning to narratives of ethnic self and others. However, the concrete examples of marriages among villagers suggested that considerations were often first of all based on social and economic issues, and these were then in practice often inseparable from ethnicity. When questions were not referring to ethnicity, but simply asked what constituted a good match or why and how a certain marriage had been arranged or decided upon, people in the villages where Han and Tibetans lived together rarely brought up the issue of ethnicity. Instead, practical considerations relating to lineage, economic circumstances and care-taking in combination with personal relationships were stressed, not only when describing marriages already sealed but also when discussing marriages being planned or anticipated. These considerations often resulted either in Han marrying other Han, or in Han men marrying Tibetan women.

Women who moved out of the family after marriage, as most Han women did, had to adapt to the lives of their in-laws, which was often not easy. Interviewees among Han peasants often pointed out that it was important for a daughter to know how to keep the house, how to cook the right food and so forth, and that this might be even more difficult if moving to a Tibetan family. All were here referring to peasant Tibetan families as nobody even considered the possibility of marrying into a Tibetan nomad family. At the same time, and seemingly just as important, many of the Han interviewees emphasised that daughters marrying out of the house would generally obtain a better economic and social status if going to a Han village in neighbouring Linxia, or to another place with a better developed economy than a village in Xiahe.

A woman was preferably to marry a man of a somewhat higher social status or at least at the same level as herself, and in this respect Tibetan partners often came out unfavourably since they were more unlikely to have, for instance, a Chinese education beyond primary or junior secondary school. Social and economic conditions, as well as a wide range of cultural practices, differed profoundly between most peasants and cadres or between nomads and settlers regardless of ethnicity, and these were distinctions of major importance to most people considering marriage for themselves or their children. Marriages between peasant men and women with jobs in the state sector were extremely rare regardless of ethnicity. At the same time, most interviewed members of the families in River Village could easily, and without much thinking, provide a list of issues that would force them to accept a not-so-attractive spouse for their children: previous divorce, high age (near-thirty for women), poverty of the family, lack of labour in the household, poor education (especially for sons). Interestingly, compared with those Han who lived in ethnically mixed villages of Xiahe, interviewed Han from the only all-Han village were generally more explicit and outspoken in their objections to Han-Tibetan intermarriage, and they tended more towards framing of explanations of certain marriage choices in a language of ethnicity.

In addition to the social and economic considerations continuance of the lineage remained an important issue for all Han families. This was most evident in cases where a family, for lack of sons, risked breaking the continuance of its lineage. A common solution in such a situation was to find a son-in-law willing to move in with the daughter's family (*zhao xu*). This was not considered too difficult since quite a few peasant families with several sons found the marriages of sons to be an economic burden. When the daughter-in-law moved into the house of her husband, the husband's family had to pay considerably more to the wife's family than in cases where the son moved to the woman's house. The first Xiao family to settle in River Village only had daughters and they had therefore arranged to have one son-in-law move in with them. He had the family name Ma, and in order to continue the line of both the Xiao and the Ma ancestors, the second son of the Xiao-Ma couple, unlike their other children, was given the mother's family name Xiao. When the family split up, the son with the name of Xiao got his own house and settled there with his mother. In this way one branch of the Xiao lineage was continued in a new household. Another example was the Li-Yang family. Mr Li had been alone without parents and with no family in Xiahe. He had originally come to look for work and was introduced to Mrs Yang who had also lost her parents and her husband, and lived alone with her three daughters. Li and Yang married and had one son together. Since the father had brothers who continued the Li lineage, the son was called Yang after the mother whose family name would otherwise not have been continued. This pointed to very flexible practices of family and lineage.

When Tibetan women in River Village intermarried with Han men and moved to their homes children were commonly raised and named as Han. However, several cases of intermarriage between Tibetans and Han showed that when a Han man moved into a Tibetan wife's family, children were mainly raised as Tibetans, speaking Tibetan and having Tibetan names. In one such Tibetan family the oldest person in the house was a Tibetan women over sixty years old who had come from Qinghai in the mid-1970s, fleeing some kind of problem that was not spoken of. The woman had three daughters, but only one had lived with her mother in River Village when land was distributed in 1981–2. The family was therefore poor. Through introduction the daughter married a Han man (poor and with no relatives himself) with the family name of Xu. The two children of the Han-Tibetan couple were given Tibetan as well as Han names, but in practice they did not use the Xu family name much. They were registered as Tibetans (as always in cases of mixed marriages) and spoke Tibetan very well, and it seemed unlikely that the family would continue the custom of ancestor worship or be concerned about the contribution of their Chinese family name.

The examples of family strategies in a mixed Han-Tibetan village strongly suggested that generally considerations of continuance of lineage were important for Han families, but also that this could be organised relatively easily even when couples had no sons. Family policies allowing only two children for rural couples in Xiahe (regardless of ethnicity) had been strongly enforced since the mid-1990s, and in the coming years this will most likely strengthen both traditional and new strategies for continuing patrilineal surname groups even without sons born into the family. According to many older interviewees, attitudes towards sons-in-law who moved in with their wives had become more positive, with people realising that the strict birth control system would definitely prevent an increasing number of Han families from having sons.

For interviewed families in rural villages in Xiahe, considerations of economic and social position were significant and practically always taken into account when marriages were planned. Equally important, many interviewees stressed, was that a peaceful family life could only be assured if children found spouses whom they got along with and who treated the family and the spouse properly. Therefore, marriages were normally arranged in agreement with, or at the suggestion of, the young people involved. Thus, while ethnic affiliation to a certain extent mattered when people looked for marriage partners for themselves or their children, this was in fact not merely a matter of considering ethnicity but as much a matter of finding partners with a suitable social and economic status and position. Peasants tended to marry other peasants, and especially in mixed Han-Tibetan villages, ethnic borders were flexible and not perceived as hard or uncrossable. Nomads married other nomads (which in itself excluded marriage with Han, since all nomads were Tibetan), female cadres married male cadres or men with an education, while men with education and jobs in the state sector often married women in sectors considered to be of a somewhat lower status. Since the Han in general tended to have higher education than most Tibetans, and were educated in ordinary Chinese schools which provided more opportunities for continued education and jobs, this strengthened the tendency for educated Han to marry other educated Han.

Generally, interviewed Han and Tibetans tended to have very strong and clear notions of a hierarchical division of occupations, household registrations, and places of living. Peasants tended to be regarded as a relatively low social group both by cadres and by other people working in state sector, by businessmen, and by Tibetan nomads. On the other hand, small-scale traders and people working in construction, service jobs and transport often had peasant backgrounds themselves and expressed no special negative attitudes towards marrying a peasant. They sometimes saw it as an advantage because of the assumed higher degree of economic security brought by the combination of having access to land with having the opportunity to make money outside the agricultural sector.

As in the case of Han villagers in Xiahe, narratives of partnership and marriage among people working in state farms in Panna, and among Han cadres in both Panna and Xiahe, tended also to focus on the combination of social/economic compatibility between partners and mutual understanding and sympathy between them. In cases of ethnic intermarriage among cadres the couple had normally received the same education, and had met in an educational institution. In practice intermarriage across ethnic lines was very rare in state farms where Han people tended to introduce each other, or other family members, to other Han as potential partners. In the initial period of the state farms in Panna contacts between the first generations of employees in state farms and the local minorities were not close, and there were such disparities of language, customs, religion and social status that intermarriage was practically never considered an option. Most workers from Hunan had spouses from Hunan, and also cadres in state farms tended to marry Han women from their own places of origin. In the mid-1950s some state farms arranged themselves to bring in single Han women as workers who could potentially marry single Han men. This was a conscious strategy of the leadership to make life more bearable for the immigrant state farm workers and secure a more stable working force. As one cadre in a state farm explained:

> 'After 1956 those who recruited the workers [for the state farms] took care that the number of men and women was relatively bal-anced. This was because they took into consideration that most workers were young people and had not yet married. To create a stable working situation in the borders, they needed to find spouses within the same area. It was difficult to leave your home and go to a place where you were not accustomed to life. If you would then even marry somebody who was not from your own area you would encounter all kinds of problems because your ways of living would be very different. So they [the state farms] deliberately took care that both men and women were recruited.' (Cadre in state farm)

Today, among the younger generation in state farms a few men have married local Tai or other minority women, but the majority of the second generation have married other Han from state farms, or in some cases other Han from their parents' place of origin. Thus the expansion of the Han population in both Panna and Xiahe has not only been a result of increased immigration, but also a conse-quence of the strong inclination of Han settlers to marry other Han.

Their children have been registered as Han, speak the dialect of their parents and/or standard Chinese, have Han names, and have household registration in the minority area. Many interviewed families in state farms had started out with one male signing up in the 1950s to go to the borders and had gradually expanded to more than 30 members including children, children-in-law, grandchildren and relatives whom they had later helped to come as individual settlers.

Regional attachments, identities and stereotypes

> —'Do you have friends from other places than Hunan?'
> —'Ayah, we are so many people from Hunan here that it is really not necessary....You know, where there is a road there are Japanese cars, where there are people there are Hunanese.' (Hunanese worker in Panna)

In Panna as well as in Xiahe one finds Han individuals and families from a large number of different regions in China. Regional attachments and identities of Han settlers mostly manifested themselves in the mutual networks established to help people from home regions find jobs, housing and sometimes spouses in the new place of temporary or permanent settlement, and in different types of cooperation related to trade and transport. As discussed for instance by Myron L. Cohen, traditional place of origin was one of the 'major ascribed statuses' in Chinese society and one dimension of being Chinese was to have an origin from somewhere in China (Cohen 1994, p. 96). This has also been testified in numerous works on Chinese regional attachment and networking in other places.[9] Although cooperation between Han immigrants in the minority areas was to a certain extent based on regional identities it did not exclude other networks based on, for instance, neighbourhood in the new area, common trade and occupation, or personal relationships. In a pattern known from other immigrant communities, regionally based networks (as discussed in chapter 2) were often established around

[9] Some important studies of the significance of native place in Chinese identity processes and livelihood strategies include Ho 1954, Skinner 1976, Rowe 1984, Rowe 1989, Honig 1992 and Zhang 2001.

one common trade (clothes-sellers from Zhejiang, tricycle taxi drivers from Jiangxi, restaurant owners from Sichuan, etc.)

One special aspect of regional networking among immigrants in Panna was related to the policy of recruiting state farm employees from specific areas of one province, Hunan. Since the vast majority of state farm employees before the 1970s had come from Qidong, Liling and to a smaller extent Shaoyang in Hunan Province, the Hunanese from these particular areas formed the majority of Han settlers in the mid- and late 1990s. In these immigrants' narratives of home, the county of origin was often ascribed major importance, and one of the striking elements in their and other Han immigrants' narratives of home was the stereotyped descriptions of Han immigrants from other places of origin.

Stereotyped descriptions of Han from different regions can be heard all over China, but as with other kinds of stereotypes based on region or ethnicity one can only approach an understanding of their actual implications and consequences when they are situated in their specific historical, social and political context. The most comprehensive study so far of Han prejudice against another group of Han in China is probably Emily Honig's study of Subei people in Shanghai.[10] Although Honig warns against reducing ethnicity to class, she convincingly shows that in the case of the Subei people class overlapped with ethnicity, thereby enforcing the discrimination by Shanghai people against the Subei people. Furthermore she argues that 'Since the status of Subei people, unlike that of the working class or national minorities after 1949, has never been a political issue almost no sensitivity, embarrassment, or shame censored people's derogatory comments' (Honig 1992, p. 17). Among the Han from different regions living within the researched minority areas a lot of stereotyped descriptions of Chinese from different regions and provinces, and of northerners and southerners, were expressed in interviews and informal conversations. But Han stereotypes of other Han from different regions, all living within the same minority area, differed from the Shanghai people's attitudes towards Subei people in some important ways: regional prejudice expressed in stereotyped descriptions and remarks normally did not overlap with prejudice against certain

[10] Honig 1992.

social groups or classes; and prejudice was mostly not based on historical experiences of unequal interaction between the people from the different regions.

As suggested by the few examples below of regional stereotypes expressed by Han in Panna and Xiahe, many Han (like the Shanghai people in Honig's study) were straightforward in descriptions of Han from other regions. They tended to focus on what they perceived as physical, objective differences, and stereotyped descriptions normally served to affirm people's own position positively in opposition to the negatively perceived Other. Interestingly, in some cases, as shown in the first example, people also used their own regional attachment rather than their identification as Han to construct a definite difference between themselves and the ethnic minorities, thereby indirectly creating a distance from Han from other regions of China:

> 'Finally, you have to be clever to do business. The people from back home [in Hunan] are rather clever, and the cultural and educational level (*suzhi*) of the locals here is rather low. Their brains (*danao*) are ten to twenty years behind those of the people in the interior. So all in all this is a good place for us to do business. The level of education (*wenhua*) in Hunan is generally speaking good. And the brains of the people in Hunan are rather active (*Hunanren de naozi hen huoyue*).' (Hunanese shopkeeper)

Other common examples of expressions of stereotypes focused on comparisons between Han from different provinces:

> 'We Sichuan people are everywhere. We really have a high level of technical knowledge and education. Definitely much higher than those from Hunan. Sichuan people are the most hardworking, they can stand hardship and their cultural and educational level is really high.' (Sichuan restaurant owner)
>
> A: 'The people from Guangdong happen to be the most clever ones. They can really do business and make money.'
>
> B: 'Really, the Sichuan people are the best, I am not lying, they have just not been used to doing business for so long. Just wait a while and the Sichuan people will be better than those from Guangdong. The Hunanese of course are quite simple people.' (Guangdong small businessman and Sichuan private shop owner)

'People from Jiangxi are the most stupid, why else would they be driving the tricycles? They are not able to do anything else.' (Sichuan owner of small workshop)

Since people were expressing these views within a minority area one might have expected, as suggested by Honig, that their descriptions of the minorities living within the same area would be more careful and restrained, considering the political sensitivity of the issue of 'great Han chauvinism' against minorities. This, however, was not the case—rather the contrary. Many of the derogatory expressions used to describe Han from other areas of China were readily repeated when Han from different regions talked about local non-Han, and stronger derogatory expressions were used much more frequently to describe the local ethnic minorities than to describe Han from other regions.

Although they were sometimes rather extreme in their expression, I understood most of the derogatory descriptions of stereotyped Han from other provinces to be in effect harmless as compared to stereotyped images of the local ethnic minorities (discussed in detail in Chapter 6). The reason was first of all that the stereotyped and sometimes offensive expressions by Han regarding Han from other provinces or local areas were not part of a larger, hegemonic discourse on a perceived objective hierarchy of social, economic and historical inequality between Han from the different areas. Official discourse on ethnic groups and minority cultures tended to enforce feelings of communality among Han in minority areas who all shared experiences of migration and who were all, regardless of region of origin, to some extent represented in official discourse as participants in a grand modernisation project benefiting the local minority area and the nation as a whole. Stereotyped focus on discrepancies among Han immigrants, based on region (food, language, customs, identity...), was always superseded, or at least challenged, by a much stronger and more coherent discourse focusing on the unity of the Han as an immigrant majority helping to develop those who were represented as slow-coming non-Han in the modernisation process. In addition, geographically based stereotypes and prejudices by Han about other Han living within the same minority area were (with some important exceptions that I shall return to) expressed by people who were relatively equal in terms of class and position and who did not possess unequal degrees of access to power. Thus in most instances popular stereotypes of Han from different regions were not supported by official discourse, nor did they derive from, or have any direct consequences for, the ways in which local policies were formulated and practiced.

In the examples above, provinces were used as the basis for definition of regional belonging. However, in Panna relations between people from two different areas within the province of Hunan—namely Qidong and Liling—were special in a number of ways, deriving from the fact that most people in state farms since the late 1950s had been recruited from these two areas. In 1959 approximately 20,000 workers had been recruited from Liling to 'support the borderlands' and go to Panna, Honghe, Simao, Dehong and a few other places in Yunnan. One year later about 40,000 people came from Qidong. Quite a few of the earlier Liling settlers became cadres and leaders at different levels when the state farms developed further and more new workers were recruited. In the case of Qidong and Liling regional identities of Han immigrants in fact often overlapped with class because most workers in state farms were from Qidong (or from Shaoyang in Hunan) and most cadres were from Liling. The two counties were not far from each other within Hunan, but people from the two counties spoke different dialects and had variations of customs and a certain degree of regional identity based on attachment to the specific counties.[11] At the same time people from the two regions had become united in the area of migration as employees in state farms, as 'Hunan people', and as members of 'the Han' often praised in the media and publications as people settled to support the borderlands. They were united, according to official discourse, as people who had sacrificed themselves to participate in the establishment of the state farms and the development of a poor and remote minority area.

However, during the process of doing interviews in state farms I became aware of the importance many people attached to the pattern of class distinction between people from Qidong and from Liling. In some interview situations this class and regional distinction

---

[11] Information about relations between people from Liling and Qidong is based only on fieldwork in Panna. I ought to have included fieldwork in Hunan as well, but in spite of several attempts I never managed to get a research permit for doing this and therefore decided to limit fieldwork to the minority areas.

within the state farms became almost painfully explicit. In one such case, my assistant and I had gone to a rural branch of a state farm and asked for permission to do interviews with cadres, leaders and ordinary workers. This was unusual because we normally just walked around talking to workers in the neighbourhood of state farms, and were then simply introduced by them to other relatives and family members. In this particular state farm branch, however, the Party secretary was feeling uneasy about our research topic and, at the same time, wanted to help us without risking to create any trouble for himself or others in the state farm afterwards. He therefore insisted upon organising interviews with workers for us. The Party secretary first called upon a middle-aged worker who was brought into the room where my local assistant, the Party secretary and myself were present.

We were seated at a table on ordinary chairs, while the worker was seated by himself on a couch, with the result that he had to look upwards to talk to us, thereby facing a row of three people questioning him. He was instructed by the Party secretary to answer all our questions as honestly as he could. We tried to make the situation a bit more relaxed, but that quickly proved impossible under the circumstances. The worker clearly, and understandably, felt extremely uncomfortable. When approaching the worker, the Party secretary changed his voice, his vocabulary and his body language in ways that emphasised the unmistakable difference in status and position. He spoke to him as to a child, was very patronising and did not hesitate to explain to us, that workers in state farms were '*hen pusu*', that is, 'simple and plain'. In this way he emphasised how he regarded workers as children, or as adults conceived to be naive and non-pretentious, but implicitly also simple-minded and unsophisticated. We felt obliged to ask a few questions, and the worker politely answered in very short sentences while always looking at the Party secretary as if searching for clues that he was indeed providing the correct answers. Needless to say, we politely but firmly refused more organised interviews with workers and continued by interviewing cadres whom the Party secretary felt were able to talk to us without his supervision.

Within this particular state farm nearly 70 per cent of employees had come from Qidong in Hunan like the 'interviewed' worker. The cadres and party leaders were almost all from Liling in Hunan. Most of them had also spouses from Liling and many expressed a strong consciousness of a regional identity connected to their current status and class. In the words of one of the leaders from Liling,

> 'There were so many people from Liling in Hunan who became cadres and all kinds of leaders. It is not like the people from Qidong [lowered his voice to a near whisper]: their level of education [*wenhua*] is lower, their "quality" [*suzhi*] is also somewhat low [*cha yidianr*]. We Liling people are of a rather high "quality" [*suzhi bijiao gao*] and our level of education is also rather high [*wenhua shuiping ye bijiao gao*]'.[12]

Commonly heard comments about people from Qidong were that they were simple, poorly educated, did not like to have contact with people from other places, and often cheated their customers. On the other hand, it was not uncommon to hear people from Qidong comment that people from Liling were arrogant, corrupt and willing to do anything to get a powerful position. This was clearly connected with differences in current status and occupation, but in the local discourse on differences between Han from Qidong and Liling it was often regional identity that became the focus in the stereotyped descriptions.

From the perspective of cooperation and relations between Han Chinese all living as settlers within the minority areas there were obviously divisions in terms of occupation, level of income, status and access to power, as well as regional identity. At the same time the common experience of being a Han immigrant in an ethnic minority area and, probably more important, the multi-levelled official discourse on the unity of the Han and the common mission of Han settlers superseded to a certain extent, and in certain situations, the cleavages between different social, regional and occupational groups of Han. This was also related to the ways in which images of the 'Han settler' were created through social memory and local history, as part of that discourse to which I return in Chapter 6. Stereotypes of Han from other places and preferred networks of Han from the

---

[12] As mentioned before, the term *suzhi* (as commonly used by interviewees) often refers to level of education. However, it also often connotes something more than mere education. In this case it was clearly used to add something extra and unspecified to the argument referring to educational level, something related to ideas of being civilised and proper and having correct moral behaviour.

same regions were features of Han interactions in the minority area, but regional stereotypes were not supported by or derived from a general discourse on inequality or historical experiences of unequal interaction, and they were not transformed into discriminatory policies. Other, more important cleavages between people sharing an identification as Han, and sharing the experience of having settled in an ethnic minority area, were based on class, status, access to power and (as explored further in Chapter 5) perceptions of what actually constituted a 'Han settler'.

Multiple homes—stay or return?

All Han immigrants used the term *laojia*, home or native place, in the common Chinese way, namely to refer to the place where ancestors and thereby oneself originated from, even if one was not born there and had never been there. Often people who had never visited their parents' places of origin and whose parents had maybe moved away from this place at a young age, sometimes without ever returning there, would nevertheless refer to a specific place of paternal ancestral attachment, *laojia*, when asked where they came from. It was common for Han of the second generation in the minority areas to answer a question about origin by saying that 'my *laojia* is in Hunan, but I was born here in Panna'. Through stories of lineage and clan, of ancestors and origin, the *laojia* was something most descendants of immigrants in the minority areas could account for and abstractly relate to. Since the minority areas were in effect also places of encounter between Han immigrants from various places of China, conversations among them were often initiated around the topic of home and place of origin. This often served as the basis for further acquaintance, connections and friendship. Common dialect, food habits, knowledge of certain people, and stories from a common province or county of origin could often bring people previously unknown to each other closer within a rather short time span. Han immigrants with family connections in similar places of origin often—though far from always—engaged in special relationships based on mutual exchange. Often ways of expressing ideas of home and attachment were derived from, and developed in interrelationship with, social strategies to accumulate social or economic capital.

For immigrants who came from rural areas of China, and who had been peasants leasing land in their villages, the possibility of accumulating economic capital was the most important factor in decisions about movement or resettlement. Many explained that they would go where there were opportunities for making money, regardless of chances of gaining official household registration, and regardless of distance from their original villages. Many had already been working and living for long periods in other parts of China before coming to the border area, either alone or with their spouses and children below school age. Except for those who were trying to escape fines or destruction of their houses and confiscation of land due to an excessive number of births in their original villages, interviewed peasant migrants told me that they were able to return 'home' if they wanted to. Many still had land, family members and a house there, and many anticipated that they would eventually return when they felt too old to continue working long hours in often physically demanding occupations. However, land in their villages was scarce and barely enough to feed a family, and they were therefore always searching for places that were in the process of developing new opportunities for work in the private sector. Tourist areas in minority border regions, such as Panna and to some extent Xiahe, were considered by many to be ideal because competition was not as fierce as in the large cities. Han entrepreneurs often preferred Han workers, and they were generally received better than in the large cities where many recalled having been treated as stupid, dirty and uneducated peasants by urban inhabitants:

> 'It is hard work here but people are more friendly [in Panna] than in Guangdong. I was treated really badly in my job there. Here at least we have the freedom to decide when we want to drive the tricycle. Our host [a Tai who rented out eleven rooms to eleven families under his own house] is quite good. He is friendly and lets us decide who rents the rooms. He also only wants people from our home place because that makes it much more convenient and safe to live here. Of course many people look down on us who drive tricycles, and some try to run away from their bill, but most people are quite friendly here.' (Peasant immigrant from Jiangxi with previous experiences as a worker in Guangdong)

Most of the peasant immigrants would stay as long as they made money and had no better alternatives. With the increased competition among an ever increasing number of individual immigrants in Jinghong city in Panna during the 1990s, many migrants decided to go to other places within Panna (mainly other county capitals) that were developing into tourist attractions and were expanding trade but were still not as well known and popular among immigrants as Jinghong. Others even crossed the borders and went to Thailand or Burma. Han peasant migrants in Xiahe tended to come from places within the province of Gansu, and they also circulated between different places when they found it opportune for increasing their income. Small-scale salesmen selling all kinds of things on the street, for instance, would stay for some days in Xiahe and then circulate between other towns nearby.

Relations with children were often of paramount importance for the ways in which people presented their own ideas of home. When interviews and talks evolved around the topic of where and what home was, those who had children would very often bring this in as a factor of major importance. This was also partly because I sometimes took my own children during fieldwork and it therefore often felt natural to talk about children. I was always asked a lot of questions about my children, about travelling and moving as a mother, by the interviewees who were themselves experienced movers and travellers. Through this, different views of what constitutes home were almost naturally exchanged as well. Many of the peasant immigrants in Panna were living for years away from their children and only saw them once a year or every second year for New Year. They lived in smaller and more primitive houses or rooms in the minority area than they were used to at home, and many did not find it convenient to raise their children under such conditions. They stayed themselves in the minority area with the main purpose of making money for the family, and that implied very long working hours and as low costs locally as possible. People explained that they saved money for children's education, for their marriage, for when they would themselves get old and be unable to work, for the older people at home, and for maintaining their house back home—the order of the answers reflecting the most common priorities mentioned by interviewees. Even those who did not have children would explain that they were saving for future children's education.

It was, however, almost impossible to determine how much money people were really saving and, especially, how savings were actually spent. But the living style and local consumption of peasant immigrants testified to explanations by people of how important it was for many not to spend money locally, but to save it or send it back to children and relatives at home. In particular the Han immigrants in Panna from other provinces than Yunnan lived under housing conditions that were more simple and much cheaper to maintain than they were used to in their home towns and villages. People had often brought photos of their houses and family members from their original villages, and many told stories of the sacrifices they felt they were making in order to add to the low income from agriculture in their villages of origin.

Sacrifice and notions of Home: the Zhang family from Qidong in Hunan. On the fields outside a Tai village in Panna several Han immigrants had rented land from local Tai peasants. Much of the land was very dry owing to common droughts, and the Tai preferred to rent it to Han peasants rather than cultivate it themselves. The Zhang couple had left their village in Hunan three years before when a distant relative of Mrs Zhang in one of the state farms had agreed to introduce them to some Tai villagers who were interested in leasing their land. Approximately two-thirds of the land in the Tai village was rented to Han peasants. Mrs Zhang had rented 7 *mu* of land for 200 yuan per year and she and her husband grew vegetables which they sold at the local market every morning. The first year they had made 6–7,000 yuan, but the second year they lost most because of a lack of water. They had to borrow money from an uncle, and only when this was paid back did they start to make money for themselves.

Mrs Zhang was born in 1962 and by 1997 the couple had two children, a girl of fourteen and a boy of ten. Both were with their grandparents in Hunan. Mrs Zhang showed pictures of them, saying that she had not seen them for two years, because it took six days to travel back to the village in Qidong, except during New Year when special buses were organised from Jinghong for the numerous Hunanese migrants going back to Qidong or Liling for the holiday. However, during the New Year season it was particularly profitable to sell vegetables locally, and the Zhang couple therefore did not dare to leave in this period and lose this opportunity for income. The Zhangs were living in a very simple bamboo hut built directly on the fields they rented. The hut was 2 × 2 metres. and there was room for one bed, a few stools and a place for washing. They cooked outside under a roof, had no electricity and fetched water from the river. A younger brother of Mrs Zhang had joined them with his new wife, a woman of Wa nationality from Lancang in Yunnan. The hut was therefore extremely crowded but everyone helped to make an income from the fields. For Mrs Zhang these were choices made in a situation where considerations of economy and the future well-being of the family were in the forefront, but where working conditions after all also played a role, as shown in this abstract of an interview with her:

'Nearly all young people from our village in Qidong have left to find work in other places. First we tried to work in Guangdong. Our son was only two years old then so we went home every six months. Most peasants from Qidong who do not have relatives or friends in Panna go to Guangdong to work in factories or construction. I worked in a clothes factory for three years and I did not see the sun. It was so hard. Later an uncle from a state farm helped us to come here. At least, being a peasant you get to see the sun. You have more freedom. If I was in that factory now I would not have been allowed to take time to talk to you. [...] Of course it is tough to be away from my children. I look at their picture every day and I know they have already changed a lot. My family has no telephone. We send money back to them. School is expensive, but the quality of schooling is better in Hunan than here. I want my children to go to school. I don't want them to be peasants and I don't want them to work in a factory. They should have a better life. It is so difficult to live here. At home we had a real house. Much bigger than this and with a TV. We had electricity. We could watch TV in the evenings. Here we live very primitively. But when we have made enough money here we will go home [*hui jia*]. My home is in Qidong. Not here. This is just the place where we live for the time being [*xianzai zhu de difang*].'

Often home was, or rather gradually became, the place where children were, and where one expected or presumed that they would settle permanently. For Mrs Zhang it was unthinkable that her hut on the rented fields in Panna would become her 'home', even if it turned out to be her permanent settlement for many years to come. She emphasised many times that her children were growing up in Qidong, went to school there and would probably find work if not in Qidong then at least within Hunan. She and her husband would then be able to return and eventually they would be united as a family. 'Home' would be re-established. The narrative of home was focused on the village of origin where the children still were, while home as the locus of daily social and economic activities was in the minority area. In this respect Mrs Zhang expressed views that were shared by many of the interviewed recent immigrants from outside Yunnan whose children were left with their grandparents or other family members in the parents' village:

> 'My oldest child is doing very well at school [in Hunan]. I don't want to take her here. I am afraid they won't get used to the life here. It is so different from back home. I don't know anything about how schools are here—if they are better or worse. I only know that she is doing well at school and I do not want to move her from that…to a place she can maybe not get used to.'

The future for the children of Mrs Zhang, and many other parents recently settled in the minority areas, was regarded as being not in the minority area but back 'home' where they came from and where the parents 'best knew themselves', to use Rapport's definition of home. Consequently 'home' was not merely connected to ancestors and the lineage's place of origin, but just as much to the expected and actual residence of descendants.

Stories of low living standards in the minority area as compared with villages in Han areas of China were common among immigrants. At the same time there were contrasting accounts from those Han in Panna who had migrated from very poor areas within Yunnan Province. Their experiences of poverty clearly influenced their own conceptions of home. A number of Han from the Hani Autonomous County of Mojiang not far from Panna were keen to find work and settle permanently with their families in the more economically developed Panna. They were used to poor living conditions and few opportunities of finding work, but in Panna many of them had experience of their ethnic affiliation as Han helping them when looking for jobs. Some were specifically recruited by Han entrepreneurs preferring Han labour from areas so poor that even primitive living conditions in Panna were considered an improvement:

'For the rural enterprises here [e.g. contracted rubber plantations, sugar processing, enterprises in tourist industry] we get most of our workers from poor places outside of Panna. Most are Han from Mojiang or Jingdong where people are poor. We deliberately go to poor areas to keep our costs down. We rarely recruit from minority areas such as Lancang or Ximeng because there the problems are the same as in Panna: the minority people cannot eat bitterness and when we have anyway tried to hire a few, they quickly leave again. They are not stable. Sometimes the Han workers come to look for work, at other times we go there to look for them. Mostly we ask couples to come because they are more stable. When they come here they have nothing. Just a backpack and nothing else. They stay because they make more money here than they were able to at home. We do just as private companies in Taiwan, Hong Kong and Guangzhou do: we find workers in areas where the costs are low. About 80 per cent of the workers stay here, and after some time we can help them get a household registration in Panna. They really want a household registration in Panna.' (Han entrepreneur from the second generation in a state farm, with a leadership position in administration related to rural enterprises)

By the 1990s, the household registration system (*hukou zhidu*) was so flexible that peasants in practice were able to move around and settle more or less permanently in cities without being registered. But the matter of children's future opportunities, and the family's maintenance of land entitlement for extra security and income in the village of origin, remained important issues for recent immigrants, and therefore the question of household registration was still a significant one. Recruited workers from very poor areas who found work in enterprises such as the one described above were often interested in staying with their families in the area where they found working opportunities more plentiful than in their villages. Many of the recent individual immigrants, who did not have an enterprise backing permanent settlement, still expressed interest in potentially staying permanently if they would be able more easily to change their household registration while continuing to make money in the area. Thus, more immigrants would probably settle permanently with their families if the household registration system were eventually abolished (as might be expected), if their children were allowed to attend the local schools on equal footing with local children and, not least, if they were able to freely sell the land in their villages of origin.

Compared with immigrants from Hunan and other provinces in the interior of China, Han peasants from Mojiang and other poor places within Yunnan very rarely had experiences of being migrants in larger cities in the east and southeast of China. Most of them had not considered this a possibility since it was far to travel, they had no relatives or other contacts there, they were poorly educated (sometimes without any schooling at all) and they feared that they would have nothing to offer (or to gain) in a far-away highly modernised metropolis. Some had tried out the possibilities in Kunming (the provincial capital of Yunnan), but border areas that were developing tourism within the borders of Yunnan were a more likely choice for Han (and other) peasants from the poorest areas in the vicinity. Hunanese and other peasants from provinces in the interior of China, by contrast, clearly saw more options and possibilities in other areas if their attempts failed in the minority area. Many told me that 'if business is good we stay, if not we leave.'

The people settled in state farms were generally among those Han immigrants from the period of the PRC who felt most 'at home' in the minority area, and they rarely had any plans to return to their *laojia*. Some referred to their *laojia* in Hunan as their 'previous *laojia*' (*yiqian de laojia*), suggesting that after resettlement in Panna they had established a new *laojia* that would be the real home place for their descendants. The people within the state farms had lived there for a long time, they had left their villages when land was collective, and they had therefore also not been given any contracted land in their villages of origin when land was distributed in 1981–2. They had re-settled permanently and few had any intentions of leaving:

> 'Most people from the state farms really like to be here. So although we are allowed to return to our previous *laojia* with some financial support when we retire, about 90 per cent of us decide to stay. We have a good life here. We have much better houses than before.

We are a small society (*xiao shehui*). We have everything: schools, hospitals, living quarters. What would we have if we went back?' (Previously worker in state farm, now lower official)

Like recent Han peasant immigrants, people employed in state farms and Han cadres working in local administration outside the state farms emphasised again and again the importance of children's whereabouts and their working opportunities for their own decisions on where to settle. Their children were born or had grown up within the minority area and the vast majority of them would also find work within that area. Some people expressed the feeling that they were caught in a dilemma between wanting to return to their *laojia* when getting old, and wishing (and needing) to stay where children and grandchildren would most likely remain:

'We still don't know [if we will return to Hunan]. Many people want to go back when they get old. You know, 'a tree may grow a thousand *zhang* high, but its leaves fall back to the roots'. The system of household registration of course has changed this way of thinking. More and more people want to settle where their children are. Most people whose children have a registration here will stay. If you have your closest family here, even if you would like to go back, you don't do it. You don't leave your children.' (State farm employee who had later started a shop in Panna with his wife and their four children who were now adults)

The highest retired cadres and Party officials in Panna were offered the chance of returning, for instance to Kunming, to live in houses supported by the government. Some had used this possibility while others explained—in the same way as numerous other cadres and workers in state farms and in local administration—that since their children were settled and worked in Panna they would rather stay. Being old, one needed children and grandchildren around, and after death they would take care of the graves in the proper way. Places of ancestors were important and constituted a *laojia* with which connections were often still rather strong, but for most cadres and workers in state farms and the local administration and the Party, considerations of their own and their children's future were much more important when making actual decisions on where to settle after retirement.

In this respect there were, at the same time, some differences between Han state employees working in Panna and in Xiahe. These
were connected with the fact that in addition to the importance
attached to children's place of living, economic development (and
thereby access to markets, education, and communication) was highly
significant for the ways in which state employees viewed their homes
and expressed their wishes for future settlement or return. In Panna
most of the interviewed state employees praised the environment,
climate and social atmosphere in Panna. Relations with local minorities were generally regarded as unproblematic with only minor conflicts, and the weather was perceived as beneficial for older people's
health and for plentiful production. However, the most important
positive factor for many was the level of economic development
since the mid-1980s—especially after the tourist industry started to
boom and the massive influx of mainly Han tourists resulted in the
building of numerous hotels, restaurants and leisure parks, and secured an abundance of goods available on markets and in shops. The
hardship that most of the people who had arrived in the 1950s and
60s recalled was, according to themselves, repaid by the fact that they
were now living in an area where at least the prefectural and county
capitals were probably at least as developed as their own places of
origin. And, importantly, they felt that it was first of all their own
work and their own efforts that had laid the ground for this new
modernisation. They had served their country, they felt, in rough
times and now they were justly harvesting the fruits of their efforts:

> 'Among the workers from Hunan about one fifth went back quite
> early [in the late 1950s and early 1960s] after less than a year. They
> found the work here much too hard. Some had no families, some
> had come by themselves and they just found it too hard. Then
> when they saw how Panna developed during the 1970s and 1980s
> they came back and said they regretted and wanted to work here
> again. I told them, "sorry, we don't want you anymore". There
> was no state farm who would take them back!' (Party secretary in
> state farm)

The Maoist period with the establishment of local governments
and Party organisations, and with the large-scale immigration of Han
to the new state farms in the area, continuously strengthened the
influence of Chinese language, education and customs, and laid the

ground for an unprecedented integration of Panna into the Chinese state. The modernisation period after the reforms of Deng Xiaoping since 1978 was regarded by many interviewees as having added economic development and provided a much more pleasant life for those Han who were already resettled in the area. Development to them implied more than mere economic gains. It was also a prerequisite for having a well-developed educational system based on the national standards and therefore beneficial to the Han immigrants' descendants. Most of the interviewed state employees—in spite of some regret at having lost what they saw as Panna's more pristine, simple, sympathetic and natural pre-modern past—celebrated the recent developments which they saw as based upon their own ground-breaking work in the minority area during the Maoist period.

The importance attached to levels of economic development in decisions on settlement or return was shared by Han state employees in various positions, from teachers to high level cadres in Tibetan Xiahe. In Xiahe, however, state employees were generally more critical about the economic situation as compared to state employees in Panna. They were much less optimistic about the future of their children staying in the area, and they were not optimistic about the prospects for achieving substantial development of the economy and culture in the direction that they thought was the most desirable. Xiahe had developed its tourist industry since the late 1980s, but it remained on a much smaller scale than in Sipsong Panna. Tourists would mainly come for one or two days only to see Labrang monastery and visit one of the tourist destinations on the grasslands. Being situated at an altitude over 2,000 metres with cold and windy weather, Xiahe was seen as hazardous for the health of elderly people and children especially. More goods had become available to the inhabitants in the late 1990s than ever before, but there was still no comparison with the larger cities or more popular tourist destinations such as Panna. As a Tibetan area with a very important monastery, attracting Buddhist monks from all over China and abroad, the area was also under relatively strict political control. A history of prolonged conflicts between the Communist government and Tibetans, as well as between Han and Muslim Hui in neighbouring Linxia, also made Han immigrants more aware of the potential for local ethno-political conflicts.

Nevertheless, in the state employees' accounts it was first of all the factors of children's future, economic development and climate that were used to describe or suggest where their home was, where they wanted to spend their lives, and where they wanted to be buried. For the retired cadres at the highest levels in Xiahe and Gannan prefecture special treatment allowed them to resettle in the provincial capital of Lanzhou or in some cases in their places of origin. Most would only accept this offer if their children also found working and living opportunities in Lanzhou. One doctor born in 1940, for instance, was educated in Lanzhou and assigned to Gannan together with ten others from his class after graduation from medical college in 1964. All were assigned to different hospitals and medical centres. According to him, the Tibetan Gannan was, at that time, considered to be one of the toughest (*xinku*) areas in Gansu province. The majority of Han doctors went back to Lanzhou as soon as they were able to, but some stayed mainly because they married other Han who were already living within Gannan. The interviewed doctor stayed in Xiahe with his wife, but since his children finally had found work in Lanzhou—and thereby also got a household registration there—he and his wife were both planning to leave the area permanently and resettle in Lanzhou after retirement. Most others did not consider this as an option because their children were bound by their work and registration to the Tibetan area. With a new road between Lanzhou and Xiahe it was only four hours' drive to the provincial capital, but many Han cadres nevertheless found it impossible to return even if they would like to:

> 'When we came in the fifties our life was really hard. Much harder than we were used to. We certainly hoped that we would be able to go back. Even now I would like to move to Lanzhou. But how could we do that? All our [six adult] children are here, they all have work and they would never find work in Lanzhou. I could get some money to establish a home in Lanzhou but that would not nearly be enough. My health is very poor and the main reason is the high altitude. Most Han who retire want go back to their *laojia* precisely for that reason. But we have nobody to look after us in Lanzhou.' (Retired teacher)

Compared to interviewees in Panna, few state employed Han were enthusiastic about staying in Xiahe, but many were pragmatic and saw it as the only realistic option. Most acknowledged that the educational level was relatively low in Xiahe and used this to explain why their children often had no other option than staying, with the consequence that they themselves also stayed:

'Before I always wanted to go back to Ningxia. When finally it was possible for me I did not leave anyway because of my children. Children who have been to school here are not good enough to continue into schools in the more developed places. The better ones can continue in school here and then get work here. That is what happened to my children and that is why my home remains here.' (Retired cadre, now running one of the many private pharmacies)

'Most children of the retired Han cadres are still here. They were born here and they got work here. Only the very best find work in the big cities. The ordinary ones (*yiban de*) and the less clever ones stay here.' (Retired cadre and soldier in PLA)

In particular the early soldiers, cadres and others working for the Communist cause in the 1950s in the Tibetan area talked about how their relationship to 'home' had changed, first through migration and then again after retirement became a reality they had to face within a reasonable time. Many had been used to returning yearly, or as often as possible, to their *laojia* to burn incense and sweep the graves of ancestors. As one explained, this was 'of course superstition, but after all Chairman Mao said that it did no harm to commemorate and honour your parents.' However, some recalled that at the time when they were actively working for the CCP it did not even cross their minds that they would ever be able to make the decision themselves to return home. They did what they were told—at least that was what they recalled—in accordance with the demands and needs of the Party. Only when they got older and the situation had changed did they start to reconsider their position as Han living in a Tibetan area. Then many realised that they had the opportunity of deciding themselves whether to stay or return, and some started to feel that they had been betrayed by their leaders, having now few realistic options other than to stay as retired cadres in an area far less developed than the cities of China, and with much fewer opportunities for children's promotion:

'The government told me that I could get a piece of land for free to build my own house near my *laojia*, but apart from that I would have to take care of myself. Nobody would give me special consideration as a retired soldier having fought for the Communist revolution. So why should I go back? How could I go back?' (Retired cadre)

As shown in this chapter, immigrants' narratives of home did not involve any romantic idealisation of movement as such. While one could argue that the recent peasant immigrants in particular were 'at home' in their movement, because they were used to moving between, and adapting to, different socio-cultural environments, they would probably themselves have been amazed by such a suggestion. For recent peasant immigrants, 'home' was not equivalent to 'movement', because home was perceived as something connected first of all with ancestors as well as descendants. Movement was regarded as unavoidable, as a necessary but insecure way of life that was not idealised, but presented pragmatically as a strategy to accumulate capital and do what was necessary for the family. Obviously, one can have many homes, but only a minority of recent peasant migrants expressed anything that suggested that they conceived home in terms of multiple spaces or places. In their narratives of home most of the recent immigrants made a clear distinction between a fixed place which they regarded as their 'home' and the multiple places they regarded as temporary places of settlement. In particular those who had settled down with all their children in the minority area eventually came to regard the new place of living as their 'home'. The place of their ancestors that they or their parents had left was then still their *laojia*, but they would explain that their 'new old home' (*xin de laojia*) was in the minority area. Some would even call it 'the *laojia* of their children' as opposed to their own *laojia*. The new home was regarded as permanent, not in the sense that they or their children would necessarily stay there all the time or for ever, but in the sense that they *expected* to be buried there, and that children would take care of their graves there. They assumed that this would be the place for descendants to relate to as their *laojia*.

The most important factors in people's decisions on whether to return, migrate to somewhere else, or stay permanently in the minority area were the prospects for children, possibilities for accumulating capital, the level of economic development in the area, and the opportunities (or lack of them) for making a satisfactory income back home. When social practices of home in the new place of immigration fulfilled certain expectations, narratives of home also changed and allowed for new concepts of where and what home was. People found new homes when they were able to make them fit into strategic plans of accumulating capital and ensuring a future for their children within their new area of settlement. When this was not conceivable, migrants were oriented towards moving to other places and then eventually returning to the place of origin—'home'—where they still had land, schooling for children and grandparents to take care of. This suggested—in some contradiction to common assumptions about Chinese culture—that descendants, as much as ancestors, were central in Han notions of 'home' and place of belonging.

5

RATIONALISING RESETTLEMENT
CONTESTED NOTIONS OF HAN 'MIGRANTS'

'….identity is always mobile and processual, partly self-construction, partly categorization by others, partly a condition, a status, a label, a weapon, a shield, a fund of memories, et cetera. It is a creolised aggregate composed through bricolage.' (Malkki 1992, p. 37)

Han settlers in minority areas have different reasons for having resettled and they also recalled and accounted for their own migration experiences in different ways, emphasising different aspects. But interviewees had in common that they were always able to reproduce or (re)construct reasons for migration. Adults' migration to an ethnic minority area was rarely seen simply as an outcome of a way of life where migration or movement had coincidentally led them to the border region. Migration was always accounted for as a matter of importance—an event—which had included various considerations of pros and cons that had then resulted in a conscious decision. At least this was how migrants mostly represented their experience of migration. It is very likely that many of them had actually been much less conscious of the reasons behind their resettlement than they recalled in interviews years later. However, conscious choices and decisions were often accounted for as highly relevant factors providing legitimation not only for resettlement but also for the right to claim certain rights within the minority area in the current time. Often social differentiations between Han immigrants were constructed on the basis of different reasons for migration. Some could claim to have taken part in the state's explicit modernisation programme, and because of this they saw their own role and position in the minority area as of a different nature from the role and position of those of the settlers who had come on their own initiative with the development of a market oriented economy. Within the large group of people who had migrated to the various minority areas, social status was connected not merely to occupation and level of education, but just as much to possibilities for claiming certain reasons rather than others for immigration in the first place.

Consequently settlers also employed different concepts to distinguish between what were considered different categories of Han settlers. Notions of 'migrants', 'supporters of the borderlands', 'floating population' and 'new local nationality' were far from neutral, but implied social attitudes and distinctions which were important in interactions between immigrants. Certain categories were used to legitimise immigration and thereby also demands for local rights vis-à-vis the ethnic minorities and other groups of Han immigrants. These popularly employed concepts also sometimes implied other meanings than similar concepts conveyed by Chinese scholars and bureaucrats in writings about Han settlements in minority areas, and other types of internal migration.

Debating immigration of Han

Reading through Chinese newspaper and journal articles, reports and books from the 1950s and up to the mid-1990s concerning the impact of Han Chinese migration to border areas, one gets a picture of a massive discourse generally praising the initiative of the CCP since the 1950s to organise large-scale migrations especially to Xinjiang, the southwest, Mongolia and Tibet. In combination with TV and radio programmes celebrating the contribution of Han immigrants in minority areas, the dominant political discourse in China on Han migration to border regions has had a strong impact on migrants' own possibilities for legitimising immigration vis-à-vis the local ethnic minorities. It made resettlement easier for many Han of the pre-reform period of the PRC especially, since it provided them with publicly sanctified support and sympathy for the hardships many felt they were going through.

A number of interviewees resented that the earlier official support for their resettlement, in their opinion, had been replaced in the 1980s by lack of interest in their contributions. They had entered an era in which economic development and private initiative were so much more important than revolutionary spirit and sacrifice. However, since the end of the 1990s, and not least in connection with the launching of the state project to 'open up the western regions' (*Xibu da kaifa*), scholars and bureaucrats have once more argued for the need for new rounds of organised migration of Han into border and minority areas. Often Xinjiang has been the focus of attention, but the arguments include other border regions as well. As a result of the last twenty years of increased individual migration to minority areas, the new discourse on the need for more Han migration to minority areas tends to make a clearer distinction between organised and unorganised migration, and between qualified and unqualified immigrant workers. It is no longer merely 'the Han' who are encouraged to migrate to minority areas. It is emphasised that what the minority areas need are first of all *certain* groups of Han people (though it could also be people belonging to other ethnic groups), namely those who have skills and abilities that the minority areas seemingly lack. The focus on *rencai*—skilled personnel—is stronger than it was in the earlier discourse on Han migrations which tended to emphasise sacrifice, idealism and patriotism of the Han in general.

People in the 1950s and 60s who either themselves considered signing up to go to a minority area to work, or who were sent as soldiers or cadres, or who were part of one of the campaigns to send youth to the countryside, were all exposed to the Party's propaganda about the heroic sacrifice that was needed from them: a sacrifice which they were told was for the benefit of the minority areas and the entire country. People interviewed in the 1990s recalled that they knew little about the areas before they arrived, but that they were normally well accustomed to the Communist rhetoric that surrounded the organisation of their resettlement. Many of the young intellectuals, especially, had also read novels describing heroic deeds and struggles of young city folk going to the rough border regions. One of the most popular novels from the Maoist period among settlers in Panna was the 400-page novel *Song of Dawn at the Borders* telling the story of young people signing up to go to subtropical border areas in Yunnan to participate in the Socialist mission among ethnic minorities.[1] The novel's opening exemplifies the style

[1] Huang Tianming 1965.

of many novels and articles read by youth going to the border areas. It focuses on the heroic spirit of people participating in civilisation campaigns, taming nature in unexplored, wild and mysterious border regions:

> The trumpet of battle has sounded! Young people are just about to leave the beautiful City of Spring, embark on their journey and hurry to the subtropical border region of the Motherland. There, the land is dark green by nature. It is a mysterious piece of land almost cut off from traces of human presence. It is a large emerald buried in the vast mountains of Yunnan.... The young people are just about to face the sunlight of the subtropics where they will break through brambles and thorns, launching a fierce struggle against nature. They are determined to make use of this emerald and make it shine with unique lustre in the Motherland's era of Socialism. (Huang Tianming 1965, p. 1)

Today the novel almost reads as an ironic description of naive young people who swallowed raw any propaganda about minority areas and Han immigrants. My young Chinese fieldwork assistants, and a few young local Han who also read part of the novel, laughed at it and found it amazing that their parents would have been so infatuated by its rhetoric that it could have contributed to their decision to resettle in Panna. However, older interviewees who had read the novel when they were young recalled that it had indeed moved them immensely to read about youngsters of their own age who struggled to manage the hardships in a minority area and thereby serve ethnic minority brothers, the country and their great leader.[2] Most of the young intellectuals anyway went back to the cities as soon as it became possible during the late 1970s. However, those I talked to who had remained in the area up to the 1990s mostly felt that their contribution at that time, though in their view not always appropriately appreciated by the locals, had been worthwhile because it had laid the basis for the current modernisation.

While several former young intellectuals told me that they would probably find the novel *Song of Dawn at the Borders* dull or maybe

---

[2] That many of the intellectual youth in Panna in reality suffered from diseases and psychological problems was recently documented by Judith Shapiro (Shapiro 2001).

slightly amusing now, most insisted that when they were young they had been moved and encouraged by the novel's characters to make a similar sacrifice themselves and resettle in what was regarded as a very tough border area with low living standards and serious risk of tropical diseases. The novel contains intrigues, disagreements and debates among young people about whether or not their work in the border area (clearing the forests to make room for rubber plantations) was a waste of their intellectual talents. However, the most politically correct characters in the novel always get the final word, and thereby the novel supported the 1960s' official discourse describing in virtually 100 per cent positive terms the contributions and heroic deeds of the Han who had either voluntarily resettled or been in practice forced to take part in the Party's campaigns. In one debate among youngsters concerning the purpose of their resettlement, one of the conclusive remarks emphasises the importance of the immigrant Han and their achievements and goals, for the good of the local area, the local minorities, and the nation as a whole:

> Comrades! If we say that we can create miracles here in the border region we have to throw out our chests and eliminate all obstacles. We simply have to use our two hands to thoroughly get rid of all useless things in the Peacock Plain. Hereafter, according to our scheduled plan we will paint a beautiful and splendid picture from scratch! This is, just like the [Socialist] construction in other areas of our Motherland, a course that shakes heaven and earth. Of course I have to say that to rely alone on the efforts of those of us here will not be sufficient. Young people from the interior will maybe still come in group after group to assist us. But in any case, in order to raise their confidence in the renewed flourishing of the Peacock Plain, we first of all need to get a firm foothold here, closely unite with all the nationalities in the border regions, use ironclad evidence, and take action. (Huang Tianming 1965, p. 120)

Yunnan and Gansu provincial newspapers from the 1950s, 60s and 70s often contained brief statements or articles about the number of new settlers in the border areas and about new projects to exploit natural resources through the assistance, and under the guidance, of Han immigrants in minority areas. Journals sometimes included longer articles describing the results of the resettlement of Han in terms of changing the economy and the political system among minorities, or praising the contributions to the local area as well as the entire country. Strong support for immigrants was also expressed in articles written by local Party and government representatives who were themselves members of minorities. These articles were important for the Party to show that their programmes of Han immigration were supported locally by so-called 'progressive' members of the ethnic minorities. Such articles were also sometimes referred to by Han interviewees in the 1990s (especially cadres) who wanted to explain that their immigration was not only a great contribution from an 'objective point of view' focusing on the general interest of the state, but also from the local, subjective view of people of the ethnic minorities themselves.

One such article was written in 1957 (published in 1958) by a Mongolian government official, Ma Litu, and it indirectly acknowledged that although it was not possible to publicise critical views on Han immigration at the time, there was nevertheless considerable local criticism of the CCP's strengthened activities to promote migration into Inner Mongolia. Ma's article went against the critical arguments which, according to him, held that immigration of Han people into Mongolia was comparable to 'imperial colonialism' (Ma Litu 1958, p. 39). Ma, to the contrary, argued that in order to exploit the rich natural resources of Inner Mongolia, especially Han Chinese labour with good qualifications had to be encouraged to migrate there. He further insisted that state organised and planned migration to areas where there was a lot of land but few people was generally of help, not merely to the entire country but to specific minority areas such as Inner Mongolia. Through this kind of immigration Inner Mongolia, according to Ma, got direct help to establish and increase industrial and agricultural production and thereby develop economically and culturally:

> My general opinion is this: it is a necessary tendency that the Inner Mongolia Autonomous Region will hereafter see an annual increase in the number of Han workers and Han cadres, and this is to the mutual benefit of all the nationalities united in the great family of our Motherland and to our common development. It is necessary for the Socialist construction of the Motherland, for the

establishment of the Autonomous Region and for the flourishing development of the Mongolian nationality. It has a lot of advantages and does no harm. Therefore, in terms of the principal nationality of the Autonomous Region it is unavoidable that the proportion of Mongolians compared to Han will fall, but I am afraid that assimilation is in fact 'a case of the man of Qi worrying lest the sky fall' [i.e. things may not be as bad as they seem]. (Ma Litu 1958, p. 42, see also p. 41)

In spite of Ma's one-sided praise of large-scale immigration into Inner Mongolia there are clear indications in his article that he first of all preferred state planned immigration of people with technical skills. Unorganised, spontaneous migration was viewed with more scepticism. In this regard there are also clear connections between the official discourse of the Maoist period on Han immigration and the renewed discourse today on Chinese immigration to border regions in connection with, for instance, the project to develop the western regions. A range of publications and reports from the late 1980s argued the need for new *organised* migration, after a period of more than ten years where unorganised, individual migration had been the dominant trend. In the early reform period, as well as in the 1950s, it was common for articles about Han migration to minority areas to focus on what was regarded as the backwardness of minority areas. 'Backwardness', cultural and economic, is also today perceived as a historical phenomenon that may partly be changed through the immigration of Han who can assist the minorities in their development. It is argued that the minority areas are extremely rich in natural resources, but do not have the capacity to exploit them to the benefit of the country and therefore themselves. Since the establishment of the PRC this problem could, according to many authors, only be solved through organised mass immigration of Han people with more advanced technical skills:

> The border areas where the ethnic minorities live are strategically very important for the policy, economic development and building of national defence in our country. But for historical and social reasons the development of the economy and culture in minority areas has been slow. They especially need trained personnel within technology, education, and economic administration. After

Liberation, while the Party and the government organised the ethnic minority areas to become self-reliant and to struggle, they also organised in accordance with their plan migrants going to the ethnic minority border areas. They provided vigorous support in terms of, for instance, manpower, material resources and financial resources. (Peng Xun 1992, p. 243)

It is quite common for authors writing about minorities, or about Han migrations to minority areas, to blame the minorities for lacking openness towards new things and having a self-sufficient attitude. In this regard, some find that the immigration of millions of Han to the minority areas has promoted a type of exchange between Han and minorities that has helped the minorities to gradually improve themselves and open up to change (e.g. Tian Fang and Zhang Dongliang 1989, p. 73). Therefore, according to Tian Fang and Zhang Dongliang, the minority areas in particular have to work hard to attract more *rencai*, that is people with education, talents and skills, and they believe that minorities themselves will also benefit from migrating to Han Chinese areas where they are exposed to modernisation and advanced forms of production and trade (ibid., e.g. p. 74). Tian and Zhang's book emphasises that immigration is first of all positive for development in the case of incoming Han being better educated than the locals, and when their 'quality' as professionals is high (*suzhi gao*). They support an argument I often heard from local cadres in the mid- and late 1990s, namely that larger numbers of immigrants with advanced knowledge will have a more direct and lasting influence on the direction of development in the minority areas. Continued or renewed large-scale immigration of Han is legitimised not merely as a way to solve unemployment problems in Han areas, but also to promote a certain direction of development—a development that is regarded as the only possible way for non-Han to achieve the same level and stage of modernisation as the rest of the country, become more integrated into the national (and eventual global) economy, and adapt to what is regarded as the modernised culture of the Han.

Furthermore, it is frequently argued that the degree to which the incoming Han can influence the minorities is directly proportionate to their number. In order to have a lasting and, in the view of the authors, definitely positive influence the Han immigrants have to constitute a community, or at least an obvious *group* of people. If not they will instead adapt to the culture of the minority area and become assimilated with the minorities. The minorities themselves, according to Tian and Zhang, are going to change anyway, owing to the general process of modernisation and the direct impact of media, books and newspapers, but large-scale immigration of Han will help speed up this process (ibid. p. 90).

The distinction between 'organised' and 'unorganised' immigration of Han is an important one for most Chinese authors writing on the topic of Han immigration, not least those writing from the local levels of administration. Immigration of Han in general is praised for its 'civilising effects', but local officials concerned about Han immigration in minority areas have also started to take part in the ongoing debate about obligations, rights, advantages and disadvantages of the so-called 'floating population'. Writing about migration to minority areas, Tian and Zhang simply define the difference between the 'floating' (*liudong*) and 'migrating' (*qianyi*) populations as that between those who are continuously moving around, or at least not planning to stay permanently in one place, and those moving with the purpose of settling down permanently (ibid. p. 71). My research showed that this distinction is difficult to make since even those who plan to stay sometimes end up moving again, and those not planning to stay may end up staying long-term anyway. Non-registration is regarded as a common signifier for *liudong*, but this is also problematic since many migrants on the move have to take a temporary registration to be able to perform the work they are employed to do, while other migrants who in practice settle permanently do not register. In any case, the discursive distinction between *liudong* and *qianyi* is a powerful one in China today, because it has implications for the ways migrants are perceived and described in official discourse, and for the ways in which they are treated on the labour market and by local inhabitants. *Liudong* has become a negatively loaded label that often suggests a low level of education, poverty, and unskilled, unorganised and uncontrollable people, but it also suggests cheap labour that may relatively easily be dismissed by the employers.

Even though people defined as belonging to the floating population are probably more accepted by local authorities in minority areas than in the larger cities, and maybe also less exposed to discriminatory views on the part of the locals, they nevertheless encounter some of the same negative attitudes in the minority areas. First of all they are directly or indirectly described as 'a problem' in local reports and publications about immigration. It is not only the economic development of private markets and the encouragement of private initiative and establishment of enterprises in minority areas that have attracted large numbers of individual settlers who would be defined as belonging to the floating population. Many private entrepreneurs have also actively recruited them because they are cheap labour and often less demanding (according to the entrepreneurs) than other workers. They are therefore an important group of people in terms of making possible the kind of economic development that the government wants to achieve in ethnic minority areas. At the same time they are often regarded as a problem by the authorities, first of all because they are difficult to control in terms of number of children, attendance at school and tax payment, and because they sometimes create problems with regard to housing facilities and the local environment.[3]

The fact that critique is mostly directed towards this specific group of immigrants is not necessarily due to their special status as unregistered or temporary migrants. It can also be explained by the fact that it is politically acceptable to criticise the impact of precisely this group, while it remains much more politically suspect to criticise the influence of the immigrants who have been organised by the state and whose resettlement has been almost unanimously praised in official discourse. Critical voices against unregistered migrants may also be connected to the fact that many Han belonging to the group of state organised immigrants or their descendants find their own working positions threatened by the increasing number of individual immigrants, fearing the increased competition on the private market.

---

[3] See for instance Feng Jianjiang 1993 for a critical attitude to unorganised immigration in the northwest by peasants who have no education and are regarded as more or less useless while posing great pressure on housing, food, etc.

One unpublished local report from 1990, critical of the impact of Han immigrants in Panna, explained that whereas 60 per cent of Jinghong county was covered by forest in 1953, the forestry area was in 1990 down to 40 per cent. It believed that a further increase of the population in Jinghong would have a damaging effect on the natural environment and consequently on the economic development of Sipsong Panna. The report therefore suggested that the population growth should be held in check, partly through a more tight control of births among ethnic minorities but also through direct restrictions on immigration. It recognises what it calls 'the great contributions' of the large numbers of immigrants, but finds that there are major problems especially with continued immigration of unskilled peasants. Problems mentioned include an insufficient amount of grain in the county; immigrants tending to take jobs from the locals; more than 65 per cent of the female immigrants coming to marry, with the consequence of an even greater population increase; and too many immigrants having a low level of education and few other qualifications (Office in Charge of the Fourth Census of Jinghong County 1990, p. 10).

According to the same report, the estimated number of people belonging to the floating population in Jinghong was 32,446 in 1990—an increase of 267 per cent compared to the estimated figure in 1982 (and by the late 1990s this number had definitely increased much more). The report estimates that more than 85 per cent of the floating population had stayed in Jinghong for more than a year in 1990, but had their permanent household registration in other places; 63 per cent had already been in Panna for more than five years. Two-thirds of the floating population had their origin in rural areas. The report emphasises that approximately half of these came from rural areas in Zhejiang and Jiangsu which were more economically developed that Panna; interestingly, the report argues that precisely for this reason these immigrants tended to have a more positive impact on the ethnic minorities and the development of Panna (ibid. p. 128). Nevertheless, the report continues, some had gone bankrupt and lost their investments, some were engaged in the drug trade, some had become prostitutes and others had become customers of prostitutes. Therefore it suggests a much stricter control over people belonging to the floating population, and insists that only immigrants with local household registration should be allowed to stay and work in the area (ibid. p. 131). Such suggestions were otherwise rarely heard among local (especially Han) officials.

In terms of immigrant Han potentially outnumbering local minorities in some areas, or having in practice control of the emergent market economy, this is rarely regarded as problematic by authors because the influence of immigrant Han, whether organised or unorganised, is generally seen as beneficial for promoting what is regarded as a necessary modernisation of education, language, customs and beliefs. Other authors have been more explicit in arguing that owing to the specific historic development of a common Chinese nation—the *Zhonghua minzu*, created through blood relationship of multiple ethnic groups in Chinese history—no ethnic groups within the PRC should be entitled to special territorial rights. On the basis of such an argument, rather than the argument of specific Han contributions, the scholar Long Xijiang has defended the free movement of Han into all ethnic minority areas of China, including Tibet:

> The Chinese nation is unified, based on common religious culture and blood relationship. But it also contains diversity, particularities, and richness. It is just as Dr Ji Xinge has pointed out: although China's *minzu* do not share one common language, they have a common history and culture. And, it is necessary to add, they have common blood ties. In the Chinese nation, the Han is the ocean and the fraternal ethnic groups are the ocean's brooks and river waters. For all, it is a situation where you are in me and I am in you. [...] Consequently, *the ethnic minorities have the natural right to reside, work, live and labour in the central areas of China, and the Han have the same rights in the border areas of China. China is the common territory of the Chinese people and not divided according to ethnic groups.* (Long Xijiang 2001, my italics)

Long's view goes against the government's policies and none of my interviewees expressed similar views. The general assumption manifested in the dominant Chinese discourse on minority areas remains that Han immigration is by and large benefiting the officially recognized minority areas as well as the ethnic minority people. These should still have certain rights in accordance with the law on regional autonomy.

The significance of being 'immigrant' or 'supporter of the borderlands'

In recent Chinese books and articles it is common for immigrants in minority areas to be called *yimin*, 'immigrants' or 'migrants'. The term *yimin* usually, but not always, suggests that migration has been compulsory, or organised by the state. However, interviewed Han settlers who had themselves taken part in one of the Communist state's modernisation projects and been resettled because of that were practically all opposed to the suggestion that the term *yimin* could be used in a sense that included them. When I started my fieldwork I frequently used the term *yimin* when referring generally to Han immigrants in the areas. However, I stopped this practice after being corrected in virtually every conversation with people who had taken part in the state planned immigrations between the 1950s and late 1970s. Numerous interviewees would have agreed with this cadre who criticised my use of the term:

> 'You have misunderstood! We are not *yimin* [immigrants] because we came to *zhibian* [support the borderlands]. We did not come on our own initiative but were sent by the government. Our aim was not to make money for ourselves but to serve our country. We are definitely not *yimin*.'

From those people's perspective the most important general distinction between different groups of Han settlers in the minority areas was that between those who were immigrants, *yimin*, and those others who had come to 'support the borderlands', *zhibian*. Ignoring this difference, they felt, placed them within a category that was often looked down upon locally (quite often by themselves, as well as by many of the people belonging to ethnic minorities). Many of those defining themselves as 'supporters of the borderlands' considered that, unlike themselves, the *yimin* had no legitimate way to make claims for local power and influence, because they had no special relationship with the government, state and Party. The distinction between *yimin* and *zhibian* superseded to a certain extent, and in some situations, differentiations based on class, and it was for instance also emphasised by many ordinary workers in state farms. Although some cadres in state farms insisted that all workers who were not directly sent by the government or should be described as *yimin*, most cadres agreed that no workers within state farms should be called *yimin*. They regarded them as peasants who had aspired to become workers in state farms, and they represented them as people generally less educated, and on a lower level of a social hierarchy based on perceived class affiliation, than themselves. But they did not regard them as 'immigrants' in the sense of *yimin*, because they had after all taken part in the state's political project to support the borderlands and had therefore contributed much more to the development and integration of the minority areas than 'true' immigrants, the *yimin*, could ever do. The only common denominator for all immigrants that seemed to be accepted by almost all interviewees as neutral was the concept of 'people who had come from the outside' (*waimian lai de*). In daily conversations, this term was frequently used to include all Han immigrants, but also other people staying for longer periods of time in the area and frequently returning, such as myself for instance. When responding to requests for an interview I was frequently met with the answer, 'Of course, we are both from outside'.

Most of the interviewed Han who had come as cadres or qualified personnel in the 1950s, 60s and 70s emphasised that although many had themselves signed up to go, they had in fact had no other choice. This was a factor which they also felt provided them with a special position in the minority area today, as opposed to the individual and voluntary recent immigrants. They themselves had felt a strong pressure to become 'voluntary' participants in the CCP's projects in the border areas during the Maoist era. Even in situations when people were not directly assigned to go to a minority area, the psychological pressure had been immense according to the stories of most interviewees, because staying or leaving could well determine whether or not one had a job, was accepted as a good Communist, and was likely to advance within a workplace later. This was of course the case not merely for people sent to ethnic minority areas, but also for intellectuals and others sent from the cities to the rural areas during various campaigns. However, those who were interviewed in connection with my research project had mostly remained in the minority area, and they strongly emphasised that not only their own lives, but the lives of their children and grandchildren, would have taken a very different direction had they not been sent to the ethnic minority area without ever having a realistic opportunity for returning.

Obviously, it is impossible to know exactly what the people signing up to go to minority areas, or being assigned to certain positions there, actually thought and felt at the time when this happened. But clearly the collective psychological pressure on intellectuals, Party members and people with various qualifications had made a strong impression on many of the settlers. Often people became very emotional when talking about this, and although the atmosphere of the interviews cannot be given due representation here, the following quotations hopefully suggest some of the feelings involved:

> 'At that time we never thought about how hard it actually was [to have moved to a border region] and what kind of work and life we might otherwise have had. We knew we did not have a choice. That's why we did not think about it. We just knew that where the government sent you, you would go, or else you had no job.' (Han doctor who was sent to Xiahe after graduation from medical school)

> 'I was sent to Xiahe as a cadre in 1964. Of course the spirit of the time was that you should preferably go to the toughest areas. But at the same time we had no choice. What would you do if you did not go? Everything was run by the state. If you did not take the job you were assigned to you had no food. You went wherever you were sent, and at the same time you felt that you should be happy for the chance to go to one of the toughest minority areas.' (Graduate from medical college who had lived more than thirty years in Xiahe)

In people's accounts of their lives, resettlement was emphasised as a major event. This event took place under political conditions that remained important for the ways in which settlers years later, and in a different political climate of economic reform and a higher degree of political liberalisation, legitimised their positions within the minority areas and sometimes tried to extend their power and influence locally. The special circumstances surrounding their original resettlement were also often important for their current perception of the government and the Party and the political changes since the time of their own resettlement. In particular, the cadres and intellectuals who described themselves as *zhibian* could roughly be divided into two groups on the basis of their expressed views on the political changes since the 1978: first, there were those who felt that their contribution in another political context and atmosphere had paid off through a better material life today and the satisfaction of seeing the 'wilderness' now transformed into a modern society. Secondly, many felt (often at the same time) a certain degree of betrayal by the Party which they thought had forgotten about their original contributions in the minority areas and had abandoned its lofty aims of helping the poor against the rich, and supporting the minorities through the assistance of the Han immigrants. One cadre, like many others, explained his resettlement in a way that suggested that the political pressure at the time was so intertwined with personal feelings of responsibility and the urge to sign up that the two levels of motivation were impossible to distinguish from each other. Therefore, the disappointment of the changing path of the Party was almost felt as a personal betrayal.

Recalling migration....and feeling disappointed thirty-seven years later (extracts from interviews with a retired Han high level official in Tibetan Xiahe)

Mr Wang: 'After China was liberated and the Northwest region was established, the central government wanted a number of cadres from advanced areas to go to these more backward places and carry out the policy of the Party. That was why I was sent here. I also wanted to come myself. I was working in administration at a high level [in Beijing] and at that time the most important thing was to do what the Party thought best. We all had a very strong sense of responsibility. The responsibility towards the Party and the country came before anything else. It was not like today. Now everybody wants to decide themselves where they live and where they work. It was certainly not like that before. If the Party wanted to send us somewhere, if the leaders thought we were of better use somewhere else, then we would of course go there. We wanted that ourselves. [....] This [the Northwest] was really a backward place when you look at the economy and political leadership at the time. Therefore the Party needed people from the more advanced places to help, to support the remote areas. [....] But I was only in Xiahe for a month in 1956. Then I made a mistake. I had come from Beijing so I always spoke out and also told my opinions to the local Party secretary. That was a mistake. I was transferred to Luqu county where I had to drive a tractor in a state-farm. I was even criticised for being right-wing. I had to stay for five years in Luqu which was a peasant area, even more backward than Xiahe and much poorer than the present day rural areas here.'

MHH: 'Did you have contacts with the other Han outside the state farm in Luqu?'

Mr Wang: 'We had no contact with them at all. They were peasants. We worked for the government. We had our work to do and that was also political work. We were sent here as part of a government organisation. They were like all other peasants here. Of course they wore somewhat different clothes and they spoke Chinese. But we had no contact with them. They had fled Hui uprisings and settled as peasants. [....]. We were first of all government administrators and our kind of work was basically the same everywhere. It did not require any special knowledge of a local area or of the language. We knew what our work was and we were very motivated to work for the Party. [....] So you see, I am really of Chairman Mao's generation. Not of Deng Xiaoping's. I believe that everybody should be equally rich. We have to take care that the poorest peasants benefit from development. I do not believe that somebody should get very rich and others not rich at all. Now, all governments do good and bad things. Take for instance the Guomindang. I helped to fight against Chiang Kai-shek. That was really necessary at the time because people were suffering and they did not want his kind of government. But Guomindang has changed now. Now Taiwan is richer than the Mainland. The peasants in Taiwan are richer than here. If people think a government is good, then it is good. If they think it is no longer good, they should get a new one because then it *is* in fact not a good government. The people decide these things. But there are lots of things I cannot talk about. We [old cadres] like to talk about our experiences. We have experienced a lot. We have seen many changes and have our opinions. But some things we cannot talk about. That is just the way it is. We will only talk about the things we find possible to talk about.'

Especially among the earliest participants in the Party's projects in the minority areas, many shared the views of this cadre although few expressed themselves in equally clear terms. They felt that they had taken part in a very important political movement, but that the acknowledgement of their unique contributions had been somewhat reversed with the modernisation policies of the 1980s and 90s. At the same time, there was a notable difference between interviewees belonging to the earliest group of immigrants in Panna and in Xiahe. Those in Xiahe in particular tended to be more disappointed with the way things had turned out, while many of those in Panna felt that modernisation during the reform period had brought a much better life to them also. The Han living in Xiahe felt that modernisation had been too slow, that the impact of Chinese education, tourism and trade had brought fewer changes than in many other areas, and that nothing could change the fact that this was a Tibetan region on a high altitude with grasslands and nomad production— something that was seen as a predominantly negative factor which could not easily be changed even by the current modernisation processes. It was often pointed out that the food in the Tibetan region was impossible to get used to, and that the high altitude was in any case damaging to older people's health.

The discrepancies in standard of living between areas such as Xiahe and the Chinese metropoles on the east coast in particular was something that Han interviewees who had been sent by the government to the area often referred to, and expressed ambivalent feelings about. Through TV especially, people living in some of the poorest areas of the country were exposed to numerous Chinese (and foreign) soap operas and journalists, reports, which in their different ways demonstrated to them the immense inequalities in economic development that had deepened since the 1980s. And Han immigrants from earlier periods of the PRC, who lived in areas that had gone through a relatively slow pace of economic development and were still considered among some of the poorest in the country, were often unsatisfied with this, feeling that they had been sacrificed for a cause without receiving the proper reward.

On the other hand, in Panna many cadres had not wanted to return to the city after retirement. One important reason (as discussed above) was their children, but another was the fact that Panna was seen as having developed in a very positive direction that made the lives of the Han immigrants and their descendants not merely more bearable, but in some respects even better than in many other areas, including the cities, some said. Importantly, this was emphasised by many of the interviewed cadres within and outside state farms to be a direct result not only of the CCP's policies after 1978, but of their own personal contributions in the 1950s, 60s and 70s. Without this, they argued, the minority areas would not have developed to the current stage of modernisation. This again was the basis for their strong emphasis on the distinction between the earlier *zhibian* and the later *yimin*. They, the *zhibian*, generally felt certain that in spite of the problems the state projects had eventually produced (especially for the environment), their own work during the earlier times of the PRC had created the very foundation on which the current modernisation was based. This was a factor that strengthened their urge to make the distinction between the category of *zhibian* on the one hand and, on the other, 'the rest' of the Han in the area who, they thought, had mainly benefited from the foundations laid by themselves. Many earlier state organised settlers, especially those with cadre status or working for the Party, stressed that they had come to the minority area at a time when people were engaged in politics and had high ideological goals, while the later immigrants, the *yimin*, had come at a time when personal gains and individual needs were the only motivation that could drive Han settlers to the border regions.

However, in spite of this common focus on the distinction between the state organised and the individual migrants, the majority of interviewed cadres supported the increased influx of peasant immigrants. While they were careful to make sure that they themselves were not included in a broad categorisation of Han settlers denominated as '*yimin*', they still expressed themselves in ways that were in accordance with the official discourse, positive towards the impact of more Han immigrants in developing minority areas:

'Now people come from everywhere to work or do business here. This is good for Panna because it helps develop this place. We need to modernise this place even more, and they help with that.' (Retired local Party leader)

'Most people from outside come from poor rural areas. With an income of 3–400 yuan a month here they can solve their basic problems of food, clothing and housing. The influence of those people on the culture here is not so big because they mostly do all kinds of small business to make money for themselves. Those who really have a big and lasting influence mainly come from the big cities like Shanghai and Guangzhou and open hotels, tourist parks, etc.' (Party secretary in state farm, born 1940)

In the minority areas even Han peasants who in some contexts were criticised for their low educational level and poor moral qualities were put forward as being at least more advanced, more educated than the local ethnic minorities, and they were therefore seen as bringing 'modernisation' to the minority areas.

The term 'modern' (*xiandai*) was often used when state organised immigrants in administrative or political positions tried to explain how some people, in this case mostly the Han, possessed 'modern skills', 'modern techniques' or 'modern knowledge' as opposed to what were regarded as 'pre-modern' or 'traditional' (*chuantong*) forms of production, trade, behaviour and political systems. When I asked questions about the impact of recent Han immigration, interviewees with a longer education working in the state sector, or having been sent to work for the Party and government, would often use words and concepts involving variations on the term 'modern' to explain a certain positive path of development, or to provide a positive description of certain groups of people. 'Modern', to most, implied better living standards, Chinese education as opposed to local religious training, and developed trade that ensured an abundance of different goods and housing facilities and public buildings of a standard approaching what was seen as the standard in the large Chinese cities and symbolising prosperity and global outlook, possibly with a touch of local tradition. And often 'modernisation' (*xiandaihua*) was used to legitimise large-scale immigration of Han.

Cadres and other state employees tended to regard Han immigration on the whole as a positive and significant factor without which 'modernisation' of the minorities and the minority areas would perhaps have happened, but at a much slower speed. It was therefore also important, especially for state employees, to maintain a clear-cut distinction between those—themselves—who came as participants in the state's projects to modernise the minority areas and those who came on an individual basis, not as *part* of the state's later policies to modernise but to *exploit* the results of them.

In comparison, peasants who had signed up to become workers in state farms in the 1950s and 60s were much less inclined to emphasise this difference between *zhibian* and *yimin* when talking about their own migration experiences and histories. They also rarely used the terms 'modernisation' or 'modern' to explain their own and the new immigrants' impact in the minority areas. Although they normally defined themselves as people who had taken part in the movement to 'support the borderlands' they did not explain their migration in terms of high political ideals and aspirations, but much more as a necessity in times of poverty and lack of other alternatives. One female worker who arrived with one of the first groups of recruited workers to a state farm in 1956 told her story of immigration in this way:

'They came to our village to ask if anybody wanted to sign up to go to Panna to plant rubber. Six or seven from my village signed up, but only two of us were accepted. In 1949 when Liberation came, I was 15 years old and I dreamed of becoming a worker. I did not want to be a peasant in the mountains like my family. My mother had died and life was very hard. She had made some money for the family by going out doing all kinds of work but when she died we were very poor peasants. I always wanted to get away. I was 22 when I got the chance to go to Panna and I was never in doubt. I never regretted, and I never wanted to return. My grandmother and brother cried when I left and everybody said that Panna was a terrible, frightening place, that there was a lot of dangerous diseases and that it was not a place for human beings.[....] When people told me that Panna was a dangerous place I always thought that if other people could live there, so could I. I found it really hard to work here, but still better than it would have been at home.' (Han female worker recruited for Panna in 1956)

Many other workers and retired workers told similar stories of how poverty and sometimes even starvation in the aftermath of the Great Leap Forward had caused them to sign up for going to one of the minority border areas as soon as they got the chance. Life in the minority area was also very hard, and they often had to leave their families for good, but at least they had their working points in the state farms and thereby a guaranteed minimum income.

Maybe their own experiences as migrants participating in the state's project to change the minority areas, while at the same time trying to create a better life for themselves and their families by escaping poverty in their villages, explained why the workers often expressed a much higher degree of understanding and sympathy towards the recent immigrants than the cadres in the group of people 'supporting the borderlands'. State farm workers often pointed out that the recent immigrants had first of all come to make an increased income for themselves and their families. But so had they themselves, and they would often take account of this when telling their migration stories and trying to make sense of why they left and what impact migration had had on their own lives. This feeling of having a certain amount in common with the recent individual immigrants did not prevent them from also calling attention to their own specific role as people who had come at a time when the area was much less developed, much rougher, and much harder to adapt to than now. So they often stressed also that they had after all contributed to development in ways unthinkable for those recent immigrants, the *yimin*. This argument could be used to legitimate their permanent resettlement and, for instance, their children's access to a better schooling system within the state farm. Many state farm workers (like other people defining themselves as belonging to the group of people 'supporting the borderlands') considered that with their particular background it was only reasonable for them and their children to be given better opportunities than recent immigrants for employment, both in the state sector and in the private sector when establishing enterprises and small-scale businesses.

How did the recent individual immigrants themselves respond to these views, and did they regard themselves at all as *yimin* in the sense of constituting a specific group distinct from other groups of immigrant Han? The recent immigrants' stories of migration were, like those of other immigrants, formulated in terms that stressed movement to the minority area as an event. In life stories where questions were not framed to focus specifically on the period of migration, many nevertheless highlighted decisions and experiences connected with resettlement. Even for those who had already lived and worked as immigrants in other areas of China, moving to an ethnic minority area on the borders of the country was seen as a different kind of experience, and the decision to move was made on a different basis. Moving to one of the large cities in the east or southeast was often represented as an action where one followed in the footsteps of the majority of other peasants seeking work in areas with large concentrations of industry and potential working opportunities. Moving to a border region inhabited by ethnic minorities was, on the other hand, seen as a larger step with more open ends and less certainty about the final outcome.

Still, reasons given for moving to the minority area were largely consistent with state organised settlers' perceptions of the *yimin*: the vast majority of the recent immigrants told me that they were motivated first of all by the prospects of making a living for themselves and their families. Their use of language differed profoundly from that of many of the state organised migrants (excluding the workers) in that they rarely referred to political ideals or ideology when accounting for their own experiences, their reasons for migration and their aspirations and rights in the area. Many felt that they were contributing to the development of trade, service and agriculture in the minority area, but this was hardly ever presented as an argument for them to constitute a special group of people with a specific political purpose in the area, and therefore also with specific obligations and rights for themselves and their descendants. They did not have anything against being called *yimin*. They would sometimes refer to themselves and also all other Han immigrants as *yimin*, although they knew that they had come at different times, as a result of different policies and in different political contexts. *Yimin* to them was not a derogatory term and it did not necessarily imply that people had been forced to move because of government policies. It simply suggested that people had immigrated in a not too distant past, and that they did not belong to one of the so-called 'local ethnic groups' (*dangdi minzu*). At the same time, few felt comfortable about suggestions that they could be included in the term 'floating population', because they were highly aware of the explicit negative connotations this term carried in the official discourse. Having settled down as an *yimin* was clearly more morally acceptable to most than 'floating' from one area to another.

Towards a new 'local ethnic group' (bendi minzu)?

Most Han in the two areas of Xiahe and Panna shared notions of being 'from the outside', of having moved from somewhere else into an area which was mainly inhabited by Tibetans, Tai, Akha or other ethnic minorities. Xiahe was only one of several counties in the prefecture of Gannan, and in many of the other counties Han people as well as Hui had lived for decades among the Tibetans, often in mixed villages inhabited by all three groups. The county of Xiahe would nevertheless be described by locals belonging to all the three ethnic groups as a 'Tibetan area'. All were aware that before the PRC the area had been dominated by the Tibetans living there and to a large extent ruled through Labrang monastery. The area was historically Tibetan and the oldest Han and Hui who lived in the rural areas of Xiahe, and who could still remember the times when they or their families resettled in Xiahe, had a clear notion of themselves as being 'from the outside'. However, their own children and grandchildren were born and had grown up within the area, living and working together with the Tibetans in small villages where Han had no special political or economic status or position vis-à-vis the Tibetans or Hui. They had rarely retained their connections with their ancestors' place of origin and burial, and their 'home' was clearly in their villages in Xiahe. They had no sense of having maintained a home in another place, nor any sense of belonging connected to movement in itself, but they were aware of being part of a Han family that had resettled and therefore had ancestors in another place. They were Han from the Tibetan Xiahe, but they nevertheless regarded the area as a Tibetan one, and saw its history and culture as being to a very large extent formed by the Tibetans inhabiting it.

It was the Tibetans of Xiahe who could be called *tribal* in the loose sense used by James Clifford in his well-known article about diaspora identities: '[tribal] loosely designate[s] peoples who claim natural or *first-nation* sovereignty. They occupy the autochthonous end of a spectrum of indigenous attachments: peoples who deeply "belong" in a place by dint of continuous occupancy over an extended period' (Clifford 1994, p. 310). The Han immigrants and their descendants seemed also to recognise the Tibetans as those with the strongest attachment to the place because of their much longer history in the area. However, in the process of time that had caused profound changes of political power, and with the new generations of Han growing up in the minority areas, general concepts of who and which ethnic groups had which kind of belonging to the place were also changing.

As noted by Clifford, 'precisely how long it takes to *become* indigenous is always a political question' (Clifford 1994, p. 310). In both Xiahe and Panna it was especially in the course of a large number of second-generation Han growing up and establishing their own families in the area that new concepts of who were 'local' or 'native' (*bendi*) and who were 'from the outside' (*waimian lai de*) developed. The Han second-generation has become a large group in Panna (mainly because of the state farms) and it was among them—rather than among the smaller group of second-generation Han in Xiahe— that I encountered the most vocal and engaged expressions concerning the issue of who could claim status as locals or natives. The Han people who were locally called 'the second generation' (*di er dai*) in Panna were mainly sons and daughters of Han who were recruited by the government or the state farms. As discussed in earlier chapters, their parents had transmitted to them feelings of affiliation with their ancestors' or parents' place of origin. They had learned to speak the language of their parents' place of origin as their mother tongue, they had celebrated the same festivals as their parents and the other Han in the community, they had worshipped the same ancestors and they had heard stories from the myths and memories of the 'old home'. They had learned to share a community consciousness based on solidarity among people identifying with an ancestral home, and their parents had not regarded them as 'local' or 'native' people of Sipsong Panna. At the same time, they were the first Han in Panna to feel a strong contradiction between this community feeling and the fact that they were born in, very likely to stay in, and officially registered as inhabitants in the Tai Autonomous Prefecture of Sipsong Panna.

When asked about their identity as 'locals', Han people belonging to the second generation in both Xiahe and Panna would normally reply that they regarded themselves as locals, *bendi*, because they were born in the area. This did not refer to their status as members of the Han *minzu*. It was not necessarily their *minzu* as such that was *bendi*, but themselves as individuals because they were born in the area or had lived there since they were so young that they had no memories of living somewhere else. At the same time, in the case of people belonging to the second generation of Han in Panna, there was more political weight to their identification as a new 'local' ethnic group than there would have been if various individuals were simply maintaining that they were local because they were born, or had grown up, in a certain geographical space. In informal talks and interviews, the second generation of Han in Panna would, to a much larger extent than the second or third generation of Han peasants in Xiahe, themselves take the initiative to introduce the topic of who were to be defined as 'locals', and which status the Han had and should have as an ethnic group settled in a minority area. They talked of themselves as the second generation of Han who were born in Panna, whose parents had come for an important political purpose directly supported by the state, and they saw themselves as descendants of people who had sacrificed a lot for the sake of the country and the non-Han. Therefore they also felt that they were entitled locally to the same preferential policies as other 'local ethnic groups'. However, their arguments for this did not include the recent Han immigrants since they had come for profoundly different reasons. Their sense of who the 'Han' as a 'local ethnic group' actually were therefore did not simply correlate with the official definition of the 'Han' as a 'nationality' or *minzu* category. It was not, at least for the time being, the 'Han' *as such* who were regarded as a 'local nationality', but the specific group of second generation Han who were brought up in state farms or as children of other state organised immigrants.

The state organised settlers and their children had of course enjoyed the support of the political system as Han settlers in a minority area, but in the new era of economic reform the Han belonging to the second generation were faced with different political and social realities that made it relevant for at least some of them to negotiate the identification of 'the Han' as a new 'local nationality'. For their parents it was not so important to be identified as 'Panna people' (*Banna ren*), because although they mostly ended up staying in the area for their entire lives, they preserved memories of their 'homeland' and had maintained an attachment to their place of origin and their ancestors' homes that was not replaced, but rather supplemented, by a new kind of attachment to Panna. Migration had been an event for them that marked a new period in their lives. However, although most of them stayed for the rest of their lives in their new 'home' they did not regard themselves as locals, but as people who had moved into the area for a specific purpose. They represented themselves as pioneers in a 'backward' region among 'backward' people, and for a long time they had assumed that when their mission was accomplished they might return home. They had no objections to using the term 'local nationalities' or 'local ethnic groups' as referring only to the ethnic non-Han groups who claimed historical heritage to the area and who were accepted as having a deeper sense of belonging based on their historical occupancy of the land.

Unlike them, the second generation was born into, and grew up as part of, a large and influential Han immigrant community which had already assured a dominant role in the area. Through the Party and the national direction of policies, Han people had come to dominate much of the political life and direct the development of the economy from a largely agriculturally based one to an increasingly modernised market-oriented one, while the 'local minorities' largely remained occupied in small-scale agriculture or small-scale trade. The second generation grew up with the conviction that the clearly demarcated community of Han had remade a backward wilderness of poverty and humiliating living conditions into a prosperous, modern, civilised area. This, they believed, was to the indisputable benefit of everyone. At the same time the second generation had 'lost' a homeland in the sense that many found it increasingly difficult and unattractive to identify with their parents' place of origin—places which their ancestors had come from but which they themselves had rarely or never visited. On the other hand, they had not been completely provided with a new homeland, because even though the upper strata of the Han to a large extent controlled the policy and the economy in Panna the area remained a Tai Autonomous Prefecture and the Han were in some contexts still faced with resentment (often expressed very subtly) on the part of some members of the Tai and other ethnic minorities. As discussed earlier, the Tai and other recognised minorities had certain advantages in education and in employment in government offices, and the last point in particular bothered some of the people belonging to the second generation. They suggested that considering the contributions to the area by their parents, themselves, and even the 'Han *minzu*' as a whole, they, as the only Han born in the area, should not be prevented from gaining the same kind of access to political power as 'other local nationalities':

> 'The Han here are more clever than the minorities. They learn faster. But the problem is that the Han here do not have a high

status [*mei you diwei*]. This is a Tai Autonomous Prefecture so the Tai and Aini enjoy special treatment because they are minorities. When a unit needs to employ cadres the Tai and Aini have an advantage and it is also easier for them to get an education. Is this fair when we were also born here?' (Second-generation Han woman, running a private business)

On the other hand, as discussed above, there were also quite a few among the second generation who did not resent the fact that they as Han were disqualified for some positions in administration and government. One man who had, according to himself, reached the highest possible post within the local administration, but had ambitions to go further up in the political system he saw no other way than to try to be transferred to the provincial capital. He would have stayed, he explained, if it was possible to further his career in the local political system as a Han, but at the same time he accepted the need to provide the local ethnic minorities with special rights to occupy higher posts in the government.

Many interviewees belonging to the second generation in Panna believed that owing to the recent influx of Han in search of jobs and business opportunities the local Tai, especially, had come to resent Han in general. Many Tai did indeed express a critical view of the Han, especially those Han immigrants who were most visible on the streets and most often came into direct contact with local Tai in connection with trade, housing, etc. Some Tai criticised them privately for controlling too much of the local trade, for being 'dirty', for 'living poorly', or they looked down upon them for doing service jobs which they themselves would not do. Others pointed out that the ever increasing number of Han immigrants made competition on the markets so fierce that local Tai people and other minorities were losing out. Han belonging to the second generation wanted to distance themselves from this particular image of the Han as a group. Therefore their views about themselves as 'local Han' were often manifested in opposition to precisely these new immigrant Han. Some of the strongest criticism and derogatory views about the recent Han immigrants were expressed not by Tai or other minorities but by some (though far from all) of the Han belonging to the second generation in Panna.

With the development of tourism in Panna many new shops, restaurants and other small-scale businesses were run by newly arrived

Han. Previously that had not been a major problem for the second generation of Han in the state farms because until 1993 they were mostly guaranteed jobs (though on a contract basis) in the state farms. After the state farms had to cancel this system it became much more difficult for the second generation to find jobs, and they had to compete with new immigrants to get into the same market. Many of the people belonging to the second generation felt that as 'local Han' they had by definition more legitimate rights to take advantage of the opportunities offered by the new economic development, to buy cheap agricultural products from the non-Han peasants, and to get access to the best located trading stalls. They used their 'local identity' to create a distinction between themselves and the new immigrants when trying to attract customers among the local minorities, when dealing with authorities about matters related to business, and when seeking opportunities in the tourist industry where it was an advantage vis-à-vis the tourists to be 'local'.[4]

An important asset in the second generation's attempts to be accepted as 'local Han' was the reproduction of their parents' concepts of *their* own motives for coming. The state organised immigrants of the Maoist era were able to use a political argument to explain why they migrated—sacrifice for the motherland, support for the backward, revolutionary spirit—as a resource while establishing themselves and legitimising their being in a border region historically inhabited by non-Han. Their children, the second generation of Han, had taken over this way of legitimising resettlement in their own claims for positions, access to markets, and rights to certain jobs in opposition not first of all to the local ethnic minorities, who were rarely regarded as competitors on the market, but rather to the recent immigrant Han. Regardless of what the original reasons were for peasants, soldiers and cadres leaving Hunan for Panna in the 1950s, 60s and 70s, the younger generation tended to highlight an image of their parents' generation's outstanding contributions to the long term economic and cultural development of Panna as an argument for their own current and future status as 'local Han', as a new 'local *minzu*'.

To be worthy as a citizen with the same rights as the non-Han in Panna, you had preferably both to be born or raised there and to be

---

[4] By the late 1990s there were several hundred small travel agencies in city of Jinghong alone, many of them run by Han from the second generation.

able to argue that you or your ancestors originally came there for an ideological purpose larger and more admirable than merely a personal need for money. Parents' motives for coming were as important as your own. If your parents could argue that like many other Han they had settled down a long time ago for reasons other than selfish ones you, as their child, should be considered part of a new 'local *minzu*'. Although no special legal rights would be granted a new 'local ethnic group', the common identification as such by more and more descendants of earlier Han immigrants would probably facilitate arguments for greater inclusion of Han in leading official positions and other administrative posts which some of the younger Han today feel that they have a legitimate right to. Interviews with cadres and other state employees belonging to the first generation of Han immigrants suggested that they often shared an understanding of the second generation's specific problems in the areas, being born and raised there and having their future there while, on the other hand, not being completely accepted as 'locals'. Some admitted that the second generation in some cases would be treated better than the recent individual immigrants by officials when applying for permits to start businesses or rent shops in attractive areas, and that other state organised Han immigrants would rather assist them than others in various matters of business and employment.

Labelling and categorising is rarely an innocent activity, and while I had expected that the Chinese term for immigrants, *yimin*, would be accepted as a relatively neutral term covering people who had for one reason or another moved into the minority areas, this turned out to be wrong. Even though many recent Chinese publications about Han settlers in minority areas use the term in a broad sense to include also immigrants who have voluntarily moved, the term had important political implications for some Han who therefore rejected my use of the term as including themselves. The Chinese term for immigrants, *yimin*, was actively employed by state organised immigrants to categorise only one specific group of Han in the minority areas, namely the recent immigrants who had *not* taken part in a state organised project, but had decided to come mostly for economic reasons. And among the Tai in Jinghong in Sipsong Panna, too, it was common to hear the term *yimin* used to describe the recent individual immigrants only.

When early state organised immigrants were debating the political and economic contributions *in general* of Han people in minority areas, they often emphasised that they saw 'the Han' as an 'advanced *minzu*'. In this respect many of them would echo the dominant official discourse on Han settlement in minority areas under the PRC. However, in other contexts where interactions among different Han immigrants were the topic, and where concrete local conditions were in focus, most of the state organised Han immigrants I talked to would emphasise the perceived differences between themselves as people who had come to 'support the borderlands' and those who had 'just' come as *yimin*, as 'real' immigrants without direct state support. It therefore had important political implications to call the state organised immigrants *yimin*, and especially among the second generation, many of whom had started to argue for their own status as a 'new local *minzu*', it was unthinkable that the Chinese term *yimin* should be accepted as including themselves. Thus the use of different categorisations and ways of labelling was always contextual, and the Han who had themselves moved into the minority areas perceived 'Han in the minority area' both as a group corresponding to the dominant official discourse on the Han's role in minority areas, and as a group of people first of all characterised by differences in class and status.

6

HAN IMMIGRANTS' IMAGES
OF ETHNIC MINORITIES

Many people working, studying or doing research in ethnic minority areas of China have been struck by the strong prejudice towards minorities expressed by Han in those areas. Even more people have experienced how a massive discourse in China on the ethnic minorities as an exotic and less developed 'Other' nationally permeates media and publications concerning ethnic groups. This might too easily be translated into a generalised conception of how 'the Han' as a group view the non-Han. However, few have actually studied how people identifying as members of the Han majority, and living within an ethnic minority area, perceive the ethnic minorities and the areas they have moved into. Obviously racist comments about 'less intelligent' and 'incapable' minorities cannot simply be taken to represent 'Han views' or 'Han images' of 'minorities' in China. My research on this topic has attempted to discover if and how different views were expressed by different immigrants belonging to the Han majority, and how expressed views on minorities were related to social practices and to the dominant discourse in China on ethnic minorities and the majority. As shown in this chapter, common perceptions of ethnic minorities were to some extent expressed by Han immigrants regardless of social status and gender, and these often corresponded to the dominant images of minorities as manifested in public discourse. Common stereotypes attributed to the local ethnic minorities characteristics such as special talents for singing and dancing, concern with aesthetics, laziness, fear of 'eating bitterness', plainness and hospitality. Also lack of hygiene, low level of intelligence and lack of initiative were common themes when Han immigrants talked generally about differences between minorities and the majority.

At the same time, there were data pointing towards significant differences in Han immigrants' ways of expressing their views and concepts of the ethnic minorities they lived among. While I found no striking differences across gender, factors such as social position, education and reason for migrating to the minority area had a strong impact on how Han immigrants expressed their views of the local minorities. Cadres and people with a longer education were normally those who expressed themselves in the strongest paternalistic terms, and who most vividly constructed images of minorities as child-like, innocent people who had benefited enormously and indisputably from Han immigrants' self-sacrificing help and assistance. Many recent economic immigrants (most of them with a peasant background and a shorter education) did not talk about local non-Han at all. Or else, owing to their direct social contacts with members of ethnic minorities, many expressed more personalised views on individuals rather than representing non-Han peoples as a group.

This chapter attempts to represent and analyse both the diversity of expressed images of minorities and their common features. This hopefully produces a more nuanced picture of how members of the Han majority regard ethnic minorities in China. Long term encounters between Han and non-Han living within the same minority areas have helped to form and transform Han immigrants' views on minorities, and at the same time the minority images promoted through the dominant public discourse clearly continue to inform especially those Han immigrants with an educational level beyond primary school.

The chapter includes sections on how in interviews Han immigrants represented their first impressions of the minority area, how some of them perceived minorities as 'problems', how others remained silent on the issue of ethnic minorities, and how a certain Han nostalgia for the past in the minority area was formulated. Since both research areas were popular tourist destinations, Han tourists' images of the areas they visited and the minorities they encountered also provide a relevant entrance to further understanding of Han views on minorities expressed by individuals, and not merely through public discourse. Han tourists were in close contact with Han immigrants through their visits to restaurants and encounters with guides, staff in hotels and tourist offices, and they were often heard discussing their impressions of the area with local Han immigrants. Most tourists had consciously chosen a minority area as their destination and had certain expectations as to what they would find in the area. These tourist images, as expressed in interviews and in conversations among tourists and with local Han, were therefore part of a broader picture of 'Han images of minorities' circulating within the minority areas.

An increasing number of studies have analysed and discussed the public Chinese representations of ethnic minorities as female, as childlike exotic 'Others', natural and naive, less developed, and sometimes even dirty, dangerous and uncivilised. Most Han who have never been to an ethnic minority area within their own country have formed their own images of these regions and the peoples living there through the media, their education, or visits to parks or other locations exhibiting 'live minority culture'. For most Chinese themselves belonging to the Han majority, ethnic minorities are peoples living within the PRC with whom they rarely come into contact. Even among Han in Kunming, the capital of Yunnan Province hosting a large variety of China's ethnic minorities, Susan D. Blum's study found that Han people regarded minorities as 'intriguing embellishments on an otherwise uniform human world', and not as people who were 'intersecting much with the world of the Han' (Blum 2001, p. 97).

The media representations of minorities had influenced Han popular views on ethnicity so that they often focused on certain characteristics or traits believed to be possessed by minority groups and minority groups were differentiated on basis of these traits. According to Blum's study, the Han interviewees in Kunming regarded the Tai as a prototypical model of the ethnic 'Other' because they were seen as possessing all the characteristics attributed to minorities in general: they had beautiful costumes and colourful festivals, could sing and dance, and had their own distinctive customs. The Tibetans, Wa and Hui, on the other hand, were regarded with what Blum calls 'distaste' because they were seen as backward, separatists, slightly scary people resisting Han assimilation. Naxi and Yi were regarded as backward, but colourful and harmless peoples. And finally, the Bai were known as a familiar ethnic 'Other', having long embraced assimilation with the Han while maintaining a certain degree of identification as an ethnic group distinct from them (Blum 2001, pp. 102–73).

The Han in Kunming, described in Blum's study, are living in a province nationally known for its many ethnic groups. More than most other Han in China they are exposed to a variety of journals, TV shows, tourist publications and other activities that all, in their different ways, represent dominant views of ethnic minorities as exotic 'Others'. And as shown in Blum's study, many of the interviewed Han in Kunming were able to reproduce images of the ethnic minorities that were largely consistent with the images created and communicated through this discourse. Many Han in Shanghai, Beijing or other large cities would probably share the same general views on the ethnic minorities, having also been exposed over a long period of time to similar images of non-Han within China. In a survey of images of ethnic minorities among Han students at a university in Tianjin, Rowena Fong and Paul R. Spickard found that students ranked selected groups in the following way: (1) 'Admirable': Han, overseas Chinese, Uighurs[1] and Koreans; (2) 'Positive primitive': Dai[2], Yi, Manchu and Mongolians; (3) 'Barbarian': Tibetans (Fong and Spickard 1994). While the smaller ethnic minorities from Yunnan, like the Bai and Naxi, were probably not well known among Han students in Tianjin, their general images of the Tibetans and Tai, for instance, fit into Blum's descriptions of Han views in Kunming as well as into a dominant picture of these groups in China.

The Han in the two studies mentioned above only had sporadic direct contacts with minorities, if they had any contacts at all. Their images of ethnic minorities were therefore almost entirely constructed on basis of their encounter with official discourse and popular media descriptions. In this respect the Han living within ethnic minority areas differ considerably because they inevitably encounter people belonging to ethnic minorities through local policies, in connection with work, in trading relations or in social contexts. They

---

[1] It was interesting that the Muslim Uighurs of Xinjiang received the highest positive ranking among the non-Han. Possible explanations could be that the students in Tianjin had heard much less about the Uighurs in the media than about the other groups. The answers would probably have been different if the survey had been carried out by the early 2000s after years of reported incidents of Uighur separatism in Xinjiang.

[2] Referring to the Dai *minzu* (*Daizu*) of which the Tai in Sipsong Panna are part.

therefore also have a different basis, in addition to the discourse they have encountered in school and through the media, on which to form their opinions and perceptions of ethnic minorities and thereby also of themselves as Han.

According to Barry Sautman 'it is well known, though not officially acknowledged, that the vast majority of Han Chinese regard only their own ethnic group, whether living in the PRC or elsewhere, as Chinese (*Zhongguo ren*) and hence descendants of the Yellow Emperor' (Sautman 1997, p. 83). I do not know what the 'vast majority' of Han think about this issue, but my fieldwork suggested that in fact Han living among non-Han in minority areas today do regard the Tai and Tibetans, for instance, as Chinese in the sense of '*Zhongguo ren*', simply because they are regarded as citizens in the state of China, *Zhongguo*. But they definitely do not regard them as Han, nor therefore as descendants of the Yellow Emperor. Whereas the notion of *Zhongguo ren* was generally accepted by Han interviewees as including all the ethnic minorities as citizens of the People's Republic, the notion of a common 'Chinese nation'—the *Zhonghua minzu* so heavily promoted through the patriotic education in schools—seemed to have reached only intellectuals and cadres who were themselves specifically concerned with promoting nationalism and national identity.[3] For most people interviewed in connection with my study of Han settlers in minority areas, the concept of a *Zhonghua minzu* was highly abstract, it conveyed little meaning, and it was very rarely used spontaneously.

The past revisited: first impressions of minority areas

One of the topics that engaged many Han immigrants in interviews and more informal conversations was their own migration stories and memories of first encounters with the minority area. Through such personal stories concepts and notions of what constituted Han and non-Han, and what characterised ethnic minorities, were often vividly expressed. Many immigrants from before the 1980s recalled having reacted with surprise and even disbelief when first encountering the minority area to which they had moved. They had found

[3] See Xie Benshu 1994 and Liu Weihua *et al.* 1995 as examples of instruction books for teachers and others engaged in patriotic education.

the conditions appalling and many recalled feeling pity and compassion for the minorities because of this. First impressions in the context of this study were of course 'first impressions' as recalled and retold years later. They were distilled through years of experiences in the areas, and marked or even formed by the continuous official discourse on ethnic minorities and ethnic relations. To the immigrants of the 1950s and 60s ethnic minority areas were almost by definition 'backward' compared to Han areas. Therefore studying those 'first impressions' was first of all important for understanding how Han immigrants conceived the minorities decades or years *after* their first encounters with the minority areas, how they represented them and thereby reflected upon their own role as immigrants and as Han.

It was always the earlier immigrants from the time before the economic reforms of the 1980s who expressed their own first impressions most strongly and most vividly. They had experienced profound changes in the fields of economic activity, production, education and culture since the Maoist era, and they often emphasised that their first encounters with minorities and minority areas took place in a different time from now. Notions of changing times and social evolution were strongly represented in the group belonging to the state organised migrants, especially those with longer education and positions as cadres. Their concepts of social evolution had largely been shaped prior to immigration through the discourse they had encountered at school, in the media and through Party training, but social evolution gained a new and more personal meaning when they actually arrived in the minority area. Most found 'proofs' that the official accounts of unequal levels of economic and social development of different ethnic groups were correct. And many made use of this officially objective and non-discriminatory claim to Han superiority vis-à-vis most of the non-Han to explain their own shock at seeing the conditions in the minority area. On the basis of Morgan's and Engels' theories of social evolution it was officially confirmed by the Communist Party—and therefore not an expression of politically incorrect 'great Han chauvinism'—that minority areas were 'backward'. Thus personal experiences and feelings of encountering cultures and living styles that were profoundly different from what one knew before could easily and without political risk be formulated in terms of encounters with a backward and less civilised world.

Among interviewed immigrants from before 1980 some of the more impersonal outbursts about how social evolution constituted an indisputable theoretical way of understanding the world manifested themselves almost in the form of lectures:

'Every dynasty, every new epoch is a step forward. It is inevitable that a country always develops forward. It is a natural law and China is no exception. Through all the dynasties China has developed forward until the PRC. And that still goes on. That has to do with history. It is inevitable that we always move forward, not backwards. That is an objective way of putting it. From a more subjective point of view, of course only very capable peoples will develop very fast, less capable peoples develop more slowly.' (Interview with retired Party official)

Declarations like this could easily be read as simple and unreflective statements of the order of the world. However, in this example the body language of the interviewee revealed uncertainty of the statement as if he was trying to convince himself, as much as me, about the truth of his claim. The interviewee moved about on his chair while talking, shaking his knee as a sign of nervousness or discomfort. He hesitated before the statement and his tone was almost asking, either suggesting doubt about the truth in the statement or expressing apprehension that I might not agree with his view. I do not hereby claim that manifestations of opinion concerning social evolution, or the backwardness of minorities, were generally not really meant by the people who expressed these views, but they need to be understood in the contexts in which they are made and in connection with Han immigrants' personal experiences.

The retired Party official who gave the statement above was in many aspects very critical of the policies of the Party, and his 'lecture' on social evolution was delivered in the middle of a much longer talk about his own experience of migration. He was not endorsing the policies of the Party, but almost reciting a lecture that he himself had clearly listened to numerous times. He used it to somehow make sense of what he himself had experienced as a profound difference in culture and economic conditions between the Han city he came from and the Tai area he had arrived in. Like many other Han immigrants of the Maoist period he had, prior to his migration, only been prepared for an encounter with a 'backward' area that needed help from Communist revolutionaries such as himself. His way of making sense of migration, and of understanding the social differences he experienced, was through the officially promoted discourse on social evolution and the historically 'objective' backwardness of the minority areas as compared to the Han regions. Seen through this discourse, his own personal sacrifice of migrating made sense. It was even celebrated in a political atmosphere where it was precisely personal sacrifice and revolutionary spirit that characterised a good citizen and Communist. Other Han immigrants from the Maoist period could, in similar ways, employ the official discourse on minorities and minority areas which they had been exposed to during many years of education, training and political meetings to make sense of their own personal experiences as immigrants in an area which they found difficult to understand and adapt to.

Many interviewed Han who had migrated to minority areas before the 1980s mixed expressions of their own personal feelings of shock when arriving in the minority areas with such objectified statements about the laws of social evolution. Very often concepts of social evolution were used as ready-made explanations of why the experienced differences were so pronounced. While most immigrants of the 1950s and 60s were from rural areas, some of the cadres, teachers and educated people came from cities, or had at least spent some time in a city before their immigration. They recalled feeling the highest degree of discomfort when realising what conditions they had to live under in the area they arrived in. In Xiahe, Han immigrants arrived in a Tibetan area in the mountains, and most of those interviewed focused on how they had been shocked by difficulties of communication, poor and strange clothing, religious practices and strong beliefs, weird eating habits and what they saw as a general backwardness of the Tibetan population:

> 'It was hard to come here. There was nothing here. Even the villages in Hebei were more developed than this place. Life in Beijing [where the interviewee had worked for the Party for some years] was quite pleasant. We ate well, had good clothes. The government took care of everything for us. When I came here, my first thought was, "ayah, our country still has this kind of place!" The Tibetans only wore big sheep skin as coats. They had no trousers under them. Only the big coats. There were no real houses.

This really was a backward place, and the Party needed people from the more advanced places to go to the more backward places to help.' (Retired cadre who came to Xiahe in the early 1960s)

Interviews with immigrants in Tibetan Xiahe provided data which in some ways resembled those from a study made by the Chinese sociologist Ma Rong of Han immigrants' views on Tibet (TAR) prior to, and immediately after, their immigration. Ma Rong carried out interviews partly to find out why fewer Han had, it was presumed, been willing to migrate to Tibet than to Xinjiang. His interviewees regarded Tibet as an unfavourable place mainly for the following reasons, which also largely corresponded to replies from especially government organised immigrants in Xiahe in my own study:

(1) The geographical conditions of the Tibetan high plateau caused physical reactions that Han were afraid of. They feared that their children's health would deteriorate, and that their hearts and other organs would suffer.
(2) Owing to undeveloped lines of communication between China and Tibet, life in the TAR was described as being dull (*kuzao*).
(3) The level of cultural and technological development in Tibet was regarded as being much more backward than in other provinces. For this reason young Han, especially, blamed Tibet for not providing them with proper working conditions and opportunities. After returning home they would for instance discover that they had come to lag behind other people they used to study with.
(4) Many worried about their children's education if they were to be brought up in Tibet. (Ma Rong 1996, p. 78)

In my own interviews with earlier state organised Han immigrants, comparisons between the minority areas and the Han areas migrants had come from were often focused on degrees of development. Sometimes interviewees tried to place the minority area on a time scale defining their development at a certain point in history as compared to Han areas. By defining, for instance, Tibetan Xiahe in terms of a linear history, the present of Xiahe became equivalent to the past of the area the interviewee knew best. Difference was thereby made more understandable, and the changes that immigrants were sent to achieve seemed more realistic and practicable because they would simply accelerate a familiar development that would inevitably take place according to the presumably objective laws of history. This was exemplified by the following conversation that took place between a retired Han cadre, Mr Zhang, who had lived in Xiahe since 1956, his Hui friend Mr Wang, who came as an intellectual in the early 1960s, and myself (MHH). One of the issues that engaged the two men was the topic of how many years Xiahe was 'behind' the rest of China, and it was not uncommon to hear, among Han immigrants, such different estimates that attempted to place the minority area on a linear history in direct comparison with the Chinese interior (*neidi*). The following extract from the conversation is also one of many examples of how immigrants sent by the government perceived development and social evolution in the minority area and put this in the context of their own personal experiences and memories:

> Mr Zhang: 'After graduation [from an agricultural university] we were assigned to a job (*fenpei*). I wanted to go to a really rough area....To show that I was a good Communist [both laugh]. I could go to Jinan [in Shandong Province], but I said no. Some of us were sent to Tibet [laughs]...ayah, that was really considered one of the toughest places. Then I was asked to join the army and go to Xiahe. I had no idea where that was and what kind of area it was. They just told me that it was in the south of Gansu, and that it was an area where different nationalities lived [*minzu zaju*]. That was all I knew, so I said yes. I expected it to be a rather backward place. That was also what I wanted. But, really, I had no idea of just how backward it actually was! When I got here, I could not believe that there were still places in China like this.'
> Mr Wang: 'Yes, this place was probably twenty years behind the interior (*neidi*).'
> Mr Zhang: 'TWENTY! What are you saying? No, no, no, it was several thousand years behind. Really, I assure you, at that time I had already learned a lot about China's history, about all the different dynasties, about feudal society and that kind of things. So I had expected that maybe Gannan was still a feudal society. But really, this was a slave society in 1956. I saw the way the lamas punished other lamas who had done something wrong. I saw one who had to sit in a hole in the ground like in a prison. Really, this was a slave society. Incredibly backward! When I just came I also

saw a head hanging in a tree. But that was the head of someone who had fought against the CCP....a counter revolutionary. In the beginning I did not really dare to go to the monastery [of Labrang], but some of the others told me to go and have a look, so I went....I did not like it there. All the others wore guns when they went there, but I had not taken mine.'

Mr Wang [directed towards MHH]: 'Maybe *now* Xiahe is twenty years behind!?'

Mr Zhang: 'The problem with the Tibetans here is really that the quality of their brains is not very high (*naozi suzhi tai di*). They also do not have a proper education. But they are the most honest of all the nationalities here. In this respect they are much better than the Han and the Hui. If you are good to the Tibetans, they are very good to you. They do everything to help you. Of course if you have once scolded them or treated them badly, then... [show his fist, and both laugh]. But the problem is really that they believe too strongly in Buddhism. It is not good. It influences all their actions. Take the herdsmen, for instance, they are the richest people in Xiahe, but how do they spend their money? They basically give it all away to the monastery. Ayah, you see, this really prevents development here. How can they develop when they give away their income to the lamas?'

Mr Wang: 'Yes, that is true. They just give away everything instead of investing it and helping develop this place. This place is now about twenty years behind the interior, but it will slowly change. Before the number of sheep and yaks in front of their tent would show how rich they were. Now they often sell their animals and keep some money in their pockets instead.'

Mr Zhang: 'They believe too strongly. Just see how they kowtow all the way from the door of their house to Lhasa! Yes, many of them really do this. They kowtow maybe 20,000 times to get to Lhasa. Ayah, this is not good....'

One of the major differences in the experiences of Han immigrants in Tibetan Xiahe and in Sipsong Panna was the fact that Han immigrants in Xiahe came to an area with a predominantly nomadic Tibetan population, while Panna was dominated by the agricultural Tai living in the plains. The Han in Xiahe settled in the towns and some in the villages among Tibetans, but the grasslands remained entirely Tibetan. Immigrants like Mr Zhang and Mr Wang from the conversation above were acquainted with basic Marxist theories of the evolution of societies before their arrival in Xiahe. They were able to strengthen their feelings of belonging to a 'more advanced' ethnic group because they had been taught that people organised by the government to move to minority areas came not merely with a more developed political system, language, script and broadly 'culture', but also with advanced technology, for instance agricultural tools. Nomadic production, society and style of living were incomprehensible to most Han and many expressed surprise that the nomads were not readily willing to take over and adapt to what they themselves had learned was a 'more advanced' settled agricultural life.

The conviction that a settled agricultural society was a more advanced one, and certainly an easier controlled one, dominated the views of those earliest Communist Han immigrants whose mission had first of all been to establish a new political system and firmly integrate the Tibetan areas into the PRC. They had experienced how forced nomad settlement and agricultural production in the grasslands had disastrous consequences in the aftermath of the Great Leap Forward, but many of them continued to regard the nomadic life of Tibetans as a problematic issue because it created a conflict between a necessity to adapt production to geographical conditions on the one hand, and a necessity to enforce political control on the other. While there was a clear tendency among some of the earlier Han immigrants organised by the Communist Party to look down upon the nomads as even more backward and culturally incomprehensible people than the peasant Tibetans, descriptions of them also often contained a certain admiration of and attraction to what was seen as a dangerous, wild and therefore exotic way of life. But what made earlier Han immigrants slightly insecure in the Tibetan area, and made it less comfortable for them to live there compared to Sipsong Panna, was partly the fact that the Tibetan nomads' persistence in their own way of life and their religious practices made it difficult for the Han sent by the Party to maintain their belief in the superiority of the settled agricultural life and the Han as a 'more advanced ethnic group' which others would eventually (and gratefully) learn from and adapt to.

Han immigrants in Panna were also generally more satisfied with their current living conditions than immigrants in Tibetan Xiahe.

More than anything, this was due to the speed of economic development. But also the climate, and simply the large number of Han in the area, were determinants of a more positive evaluation of Panna compared to Xiahe. However, with regard to the representations of first impressions of the minority areas at the time of immigration, and the first encounters with the local non-Han, there were a number of similarities between the perceptions expressed by immigrants in Xiahe and in Panna. In both areas immigrants with an education beyond primary school, or with political training in the Party, tended to integrate politicised statements relating to official minority policy into their personal accounts. They would, for instance, emphasise how their own initial shock on seeing the bad conditions in the area had led them to feel pity and compassion for the minorities. Their distress, they told, had then motivated them to help the minorities to achieve the same level of political consciousness and cultural development as the Han. Their views were in this respect closely connected to the official discourse on social evolution and on the Han as the 'older brother' destined to help and assist the more child-like minorities. Paternalistic feelings towards the ethnic minorities were politically correct and, at the same time, they could help young immigrants to make sense of their resettlement and give meaning to their daily work and sometimes loss of close family relations.

For most of these interviewees, feelings of responsibility to help what were seen as the more backward and innocent ethnic minorities were regarded as positive and as the basis for correct attitudes towards minorities. And those who most clearly expressed what could be described as parental feelings towards the minorities were often also those who used the most positive expressions when describing them. They represented minorities as children and therefore as people not really accountable for their own actions. The minorities were, many said, at the same time naive and extremely polite and friendly if only treated properly by the Han. This was an especially blatant attitude among state organised Han immigrants in Panna and was related to the fact that the Tai were seen as a mild and friendly nationality, not aggressive towards the Han and largely accepting the policies of the Communist Party. They were settled people and they fitted well into the dominant theory of social evolution that allowed the Han to feel superior in terms of technological and cultural development.

The early Communists had taken part in a mission that was partly directed at helping the ethnic minorities, and in this process they had personally encountered a number of people belonging to those minorities. With some of these they had developed more equal social relationships, and their paternalistic feelings were therefore sometimes also combined with personal experiences of friendship and equality with at least a few individuals belonging to non-Han local ethnic groups. The story recounted below of one female Communist soldier in Panna, Liu Hua,[4] suggests how initial feelings of loneliness and estrangement in a minority area were partly resolved through a process in which she developed. It also showed how these motherly feelings were sometimes superseded by experiences of companionship and mutual friendship with individual members of the same ethnic minority. Liu Hua was particularly engaged in work to improve the situation of the Tai women and in her work she made use of her political training which in spite of her young age allowed her to feel like an older sister, or mother, towards the local women. At the same time, she herself was struggling with the dilemma of being a women in a male dominated Party that was presenting itself as the ultimate solution for eradicating inequality between ethnic groups, as well as between men and women. Belief in social evolution and the mission of the Party to some extent helped ease these personal troubles. It became a resource that allowed young state organised immigrants, like Liu Hua, to situate the minorities and their incomprehensible lifestyle in a distant past occurring in the present. And it enabled them to claim that the Party and they themselves were merely helping the minorities follow the only possible road forward—the road towards an ideal political system as formulated by the Party. This trust and conviction gave meaning to their own lives and helped compensating for personal feelings of loss.

Being Han, woman and Communist soldier in an ethnic minority area: experiences of a female fighter.[5]   Liu Hua was born in 1930, came to Panna

---

[4] Pseudonym.

[5] This is an edited version of several long conversations with a retired female Communist soldier and cadre. Although it has been reduced to a very short version of the original interviews, it attempts to provide the main viewpoints and memories as expressed by the interviewee.

as a guerrilla solder and member of the Communist Party in 1950, married another Han Communist soldier and stayed in the area. When interviewed in 1997 she had retired and had no intention of leaving Panna. This is a fraction of her story of immigration:

'The CCP sent me to Panna, but I also wanted myself to go. I wanted to go to a border area to help the Party. But my parents did not want to let me go. They were afraid that I would die because they had heard that Panna was a place with a lot of diseases. I insisted on leaving, and later on when I got my first child they came here to visit me.

'We were sent here to establish the new government and spread knowledge of the Party's policy. When I first came I truly regretted it. How I wished to return! I thought this place was really backward and poor. We only had rice to eat, only water to drink, and we could not even talk to the common people. The Tai looked down upon us female soldiers because we had to sleep together with the male soldiers. They felt pity for us and asked if it was not really tough for us being so few women with so many men. They did not understand that we had very good relations with the men, and that all women slept in the middle with the men to the sides so that they could protect us. Some of the Tai women I got to know offered to find me a handsome man in their village. Somebody I could be together with instead of the male soldiers. I could choose one myself because they found me very pretty.'

After a few months Liu Hua became the head of a local administrative area. Shortly after she got the chance to return home, but did not want to any more:

'I told them that I had actually come to do some work, to establish the power of the new government. Since that work was not yet finished, I did not want to return. In the beginning I found it hard to get used to the fact that many Tai and other minorities were afraid of the Han. When the children saw us they shouted, "the Han have come!", and they ran to hide in their houses. The parents warned their kids that if they were naughty, they would give them to the Han people. No wonder they were afraid of us. So even after a year or so I was really in conflict with myself. I did not feel secure working here. I did not feel well, and part of me wanted to go back. But then again, I knew we had to educate local minority cadres to continue our work. We had to learn the minority language although we had no chance to really study it. We had to live according to the rule of the 'three alike' (*san tong*): eat together, live together and work together with the common people. Slowly we learned to speak Tai, and the Tai got used to us. They felt pity for us because they thought that we had no parents and that we had come to look for spouses. But they also called us *Han guan*, the Han who had come to take care of them. This showed that their minds (*sixang*) had changed. They had started to understand that we were there to help them. In the beginning they found that since we were Han and they were Tai, those were two entirely different things. Slowly they started to understand our point of view—that we were all nationalities united in the Chinese nation [*Zhonghua minzu*].

'People in Panna were for a long time still afraid of the traditional local Tai leaders. Once the local headman[6] told me in the Tai language that if the Han women would actually run this place the result would be a lack of food. I did not really understand what he meant by this, so I asked the head of our county [another Tai]. He said the headman was simply criticising me and the fact that the Han were here. So he went to scold the headman. He was really angry. He told him to stop saying these kind of things to the people who had come to help them. Then the headman suggested that I become his third wife. That really made me furious. He wanted to make a lot of money together with me because I was Han. But I told him calmly about the new laws of the Communist Party, about the new marriage law and that nobody was allowed to violate it. Just imagine how young I was, and what I had to cope with!'

When Liu Hua was twenty-six years land reforms were started in Panna and from that time on she became increasingly engaged in work related to minority women:

'Living in the villages of the Tai, I developed a very close relationship with some of the women. They let me sleep in their own

---

[6] Here the interviewee used the word *tusi* for a local Tai leader who was related to the Tai court in Jinghong from before 1949. He was in fact not a *tusi* in the common sense of having been granted this title by the Qing courts. I therefore translate the term as 'headman'.

sleeping rooms which they normally would not let outsiders do. They accepted me completely, and still today I am very well received in those villages. Therefore I wanted to stay in Panna. It is not due to the policies any more but because of the changes here. We had never imagined that this place would change so much. After I got children I still wanted to work. I took my children to the villages and I was very happy at that time. I felt I was doing the right thing, that I was really helping. I also found friends among the Tai women. We [the people working for the Party] wanted to change the low position of the women. The position of Han women was not as low as the position of the Tai women. When they had their menstruation they could not do anything because their blood was considered dirty and no man could get into contact with it. They only wore skirts, so the blood ran down their legs and they had to go to the river to wash. They could only sit on chairs covered with ashes. We taught them to use cloth and pants so that they could sit on ordinary chairs. Therefore they came to regard me as an older sister or a mother. Some told me that because I had taught them this, I was like a mother to them and they would do as I said (*ting wo de hua*). Because of this problem with menstruation and chairs it was also difficult to make the Tai women participate in political meetings. And anyway they did not dare to speak up. I was also a woman and I spoke up, but they said that I could do this because I was a Han. Therefore we found it necessary to teach the minorities how to propagate the policy of the Party. The best thing was to teach themselves how to propagate it. But most women were afraid of this. They would hold my hand or sit behind me. I supported them, told them that they should not only talk about their own thoughts but speak in accordance with the policy of the Party.'

'Many of the Tai now do not want us to leave. They say, "You are the same as us". If you are good to them, they are good to you. We told them that the meaning of socialism is "a two-storey house for everybody, electricity for everybody and a telephone for everybody". When we came here people did not have shoes. They had not even seen shoes, and they were so happy when we let them try ours. At that time the Tai made their clothes themselves. Now they have beautiful clothes, even better than ours. The common people cannot forget that all this came because of the policy of the CCP.'

Liu Hua's memories of her life as a young Communist, having to learn to live in a minority area with the purpose of establishing a new political system, contained a strong flavour of idealism and trust in the course of the Party's policy towards minorities. Long conversations with many of the early immigrants showed that feelings of personal loss and insecurity had been strong as well, but that the collective revolutionary mood of participants in the Party's mission, combined with the leadership's insistence upon the need for self sacrifice, became a kind of resource that some could use to overcome these feelings. Still, those who stayed in the area, even after they were allowed to return, were not necessarily those who had adapted best to the area or developed the strongest feelings of attachment to it. As discussed above it was mostly a matter of coincidence and family organisation that determined whether the earliest immigrants would stay or leave.

Many of the earliest immigrants in Panna expressed—after experiencing a culture shock at the time of their first encounter with the minority area—a feeling of satisfaction at having helped to change the areas o thoroughly that one could live a relatively pleasant and uncomplicated life there as a Han. This implied that the area had developed good Chinese state schools for the children, nursing homes for elderly cadres, means of communication that were predominantly based on the Chinese language, a market offering the kind of food and other goods preferred by Han, and a political system entirely consistent with the rest of China. It also implied a good climate. In all these respects, Xiahe came out less favourably than Panna. While the first encounters of early Han Communist immigrants with the Tibetans and the Tibetan area of Xiahe were also described as very distressful, immigrants in Xiahe were less confident that they had managed to transform the area as much as they had expected to. Xiahe was still rather poor, Tibetans were still loyal to the Dalai Lama and to Buddhism, tourism had not brought in a large settled Han community, education was not well developed, and it was difficult for them to see how this would ever change.

The image of the helping Han and the problematic minorities

Impressions of the minority areas—both recalled first impressions and current concepts of the areas—were closely related to Han immigrants' ways of describing the ethnic minorities they lived among. In my research among Han living in minority areas I had no problems collecting material that documented many Han immigrants' derogatory views on minorities. Some Han immigrants were more than willing to talk about their perceptions of local non-Han, and quite a few introduced the subject spontaneously. However, the main problem was to understand what was actually meant by their statements, and to what extent expressions were derived from the immigrants' long-term encounter with the official discourse on ethnic groups in China. What consequences, if any, did these expressed views have for the actual relationships between Han immigrants and minorities, and to what extent could strong racially discriminatory expressions be taken as representative of local 'Han images of ethnic minorities'? In fact a number of Han immigrants did not talk at all about their concepts of local ethnic minorities, or only did so only in neutral or predominantly positive terms. This silence on the topic of minorities, or the lack of discriminatory or negative descriptions, was obviously much less noticeable than extreme statements which also tend to get the most attention in foreigners' reports about Han images of minorities. But in order to understand more about majority-minority relations and especially Han images of ethnic minorities, it is relevant to focus on what prompted the pronounced differences in various Han immigrants' ways of expressing their views on Han versus non-Han.

Strongly promoted ideas of social evolution, and scales of development that place the vast majority of non-Han on the lowest levels, could easily be transformed by Han immigrants into popularised notions of the minorities as simple, less intelligent and, by and large, backward people. They could be used as ready-made explanations of social and economic inequality which at times implied a racial distinction between 'capable' and 'incapable' ethnic groups, between 'developed' and 'backward' peoples, between 'civilised' and 'less civilised' people, between ethnic groups 'open to outside influence' and those that were 'closed and inward looking'. These were distinctions commonly made in interviews, and used spontaneously in conversations by Han immigrants themselves belonging to different social groups. They are also constructed distinctions which may be found in numerous popular and scholarly publications on minorities since the 1950s, and they have been used more or less directly in the education system to teach about historical development and ethnic composition of the PRC.[7] It will be clear from the examples below of Han immigrants' descriptions and characterisations of local ethnic minorities that a number of concepts and labels were repeated by many people belonging to different social categories of Han. Nevertheless, interviews with Han immigrants who had themselves lived within a minority area for a period of time showed diversity in attitudes towards and concepts of minorities. There was no such thing as *the* Han view on ethnic minorities from the perspective of Han themselves living within ethnic minority areas, but there was among a large number of Han a range of largely similar expressions that were frequently repeated. Though they should not be understood as expressions of one common attitude towards minorities, they may be regarded as manifestations of some common notions and perceptions shared among many Han immigrants.

State farms' images of Han and non-Han. One of the local arenas where Han immigrants employed by the Party and state were found to produce, in published form, strong images of local minorities as contrasted with Han immigrants was the state farms. Through their publications of state farm histories, biographies of state farm employees and stories of state farm model workers, state farms and Land Reclamation Bureaus in minority areas have contributed actively to the construction of a common identification among state farm employees as 'Han supporters of the borderlands'.[8] Thereby, they have

---

[7] Other distinctions, such as those between 'raw' and 'cooked' barbarians known from Chinese historical discourse about people living on the geographical periphery of the Empire, have been eradicated from official Communist discourse. These distinctions were also never used by Han interviewees in the minority areas. One of the latest examples that I came across in my research in Panna and Xiahe of descriptions based on these distinctions was the local gazetteer of Xiahe from the 1930s. This gazetteer divided the Tibetans (*fan*) living in Xiahe into three groups: the 'half-Tibetans' who had assimilated with the local Han peasants; the 'cooked Tibetans' who were simultaneously farmers and herdsmen and understood Chinese; and finally the 'raw Tibetans' who were the herdsmen that had not adapted to Chinese culture at all (Zhang Qiyun 1978 [1934], pp. 40–43).

[8] See for instance, Sipsong Panna Branch of Land Reclamation Department 1992a, Sipsong Panna Land Reclamation Department 1990, Sipsong Panna Branch of

also produced certain images of the ethnic minorities, partly as a counter image to the immigrant Han, partly as the objects of the culturally transformative power that is attributed to the state farms and their predominantly Han employees. Since the 1980s, with the countrywide promotion of the writing of local histories and gazetteers, state farms in Panna have engaged in the production of booklets that introduce their official state farm history and describe selected personalities connected to the farms. These booklets are often for internal state farm use only, or for offering to higher officials visiting state farms. It was therefore not always easy for me to get access to these publications, and more than once I was asked by leaders to immediately return books that a lower level cadre had offered me, trusting that it could cause no harm for me to read such stylised and politically correct versions of state farm histories.

There was a widespread uncertainty among state farm cadres of how these books were to be used, and it was often a matter of coincidence whether people within state farms had read them. It was an integral part of state farms' political and propaganda work to produce such booklets, but they were not necessarily widely distributed or read. In spite of the uncertainty about how books were to be distributed, interviewed cadres (but sometimes also workers) in state farms sometimes recommended me to read them to get the 'true' picture of what state farms were and what it meant to have come to Panna working as a Han 'supporting the borderlands'. In particular, people working in schools and various sectors of administration in state farms used the images produced in state farm publications as reference when they presented themselves as part of a selected group of Han settlers distinct from the individual Han immigrants and the Han working in *difang*, the state sectors outside the state farms. The publications helped to create and strengthen feelings of belonging to a special community—a community consisting of people with different levels of access to power and with different types of work, but still ideally united in a community feeling of having resettled for a special purpose and sharing a special mission.

Land Reclamation Department 1991, Jinghong State Farm 1992, and the collection of newspaper articles about state farms in Panna, Sipsong Panna Branch of Land Reclamation Department 1992b.

State farms often had 10–15 per cent non-Han employees but representations of the local non-Han in the publications leave no doubt that state farms were established and developed by a predominantly Han population, settled since the 1950s. Minority people in state farms are presented profoundly differently from the Han, mainly as examples of how the civilising mission of the state farms through employment of local non-Han after 1979 transformed these 'backward' mountain people into modern workers with an understanding of scientific rubber producing methods and eventually a modern commodity market. There are also often sections in state farm publications about state farms' special units and employees working specifically with minority issues, carrying out so-called 'minority work' (*minzu gongzuo*). These units were established to improve relationships between the Han population in the state farms and the local ethnic minorities living in their vicinity. The main objective of the published sections on the issues relating to local ethnic minorities is not in itself to create a certain image of ethnic minorities. It is rather to formulate a history of state farms and their employees which can ensure that people within state farms understand the very purpose and mission of those farms, as well as their own role and identification as Han settlers taking part in this mission. Minorities represent a significant counter image to the immigrant Han, and descriptions of them serve to exemplify how the mission of state farms was broader than merely to produce rubber for the country. Thus, a powerful image of 'Han settlers in state farms' is established through the creation of stories of minorities which highlight a presumed transformative power of state farms over local culture and psychology.

Examples from local state farm contexts also show how officially sanctioned perceptions of ethnic minorities can conveniently be employed and used, for instance by leaders in state enterprises in their attempts to improve production and output. The following example from a state farm in Panna in the late 1970s exemplifies how a rhetoric of assistance to minorities through assimilation with Han was instrumental in arguing for the positive outcome of recruitment of minority workers—a recruitment that was in fact first of all initiated for pragmatic rather than idealistic reasons.

After the end of the Cultural Revolution state farms in Panna were instructed to introduce measures that could help improve the strained relationship between state farms and the local population. Since 1978 state farms had to train cadres to work specifically with 'minority issues', and administrative sections dealing with minorities (*minzu ke*) were established. One of the measures introduced by state farms was to recruit workers belonging to local ethnic minorities. This was presented as a political move to improve relations, but it was at the same time a pragmatic way of solving the problem of a sudden decrease in staff on state farms. By 1979 the intellectual youths from the time of the Cultural Revolution had all been allowed to return to their cities of origin, and this resulted in a dramatic, sudden fall in the number of employees in state farms. In Mengpeng state farm alone, the number of 8,000 employees was suddenly reduced to 1,900 (Sipsong Panna Land Reclamation Department 1990, p. 45). Suddenly there was nobody to guard the gates, schools had to cancel their lessons, hospitals stopped treating people, and nobody could drive the cars. At the same time new directives had already instructed state farms to pay special attention to the strained relationship with ethnic minorities that had resulted from the Cultural Revolution. This provided a good opportunity for the Mengpeng state farm to solve its employment problem, while at the same time taking the initiative to improve ethnic relations through the recruitment of minority workers. Seven villages inhabited by Akha people (*Hanizu*) were invited to take up work in the state farm because they had shown 'love for the Party, Socialism and the state farm' (ibid. p. 23).

By 1990 there was a 17.6 per cent proportion of minority workers among the Mengpeng state farm employees (ibid. p. 24). A publication from the Land Reclamation Department subtitled *Panna Friendship* strongly emphasised that more than ten years of influence from the Han community in the state farm had positively changed the cultural habits of the recruited minority people—Akha, who were considered to be even more backward than Tai. The broad civilising mission of the state farms was manifested in the book's description of how the state farms' recruitment of these 'backward' people resulted in positive cultural and also psychological changes for them. Descriptions of these changes clearly suggest how the author and the political leaders of the state farm looked upon the Akha as a people, and which areas of a perceived Han culture they found especially important for them to reproduce:

(1) For hundred of years the Hani had eaten, lived and been poor in the mountains. They were satisfied with a full stomach and they found it disgraceful to go out and sell their surplus products. They did not have the slightest idea of market, prices, commodities or profits. Today, however, the Hani workers understand the market even better than the Han workers. They are more active in ancillary businesses than the Han workers. They become wealthy faster and their houses are more modern.

(2) When the Hani workers came they could not speak Chinese. This created not only language problems but problems with regard to the way of thinking. After several years of hard work the Hani can now speak Chinese and write some simple characters, and some can even write a letter in Chinese.

(3) Old habits have been replaced with modern consciousness. Before the Hani did not use toilets or fertilisers. They did not eat with chopsticks and did not wear shoes.

(4) It has become common that Han and Hani marry and the Hani's old custom of valuing boys higher than girls has been abandoned.

(5) The Hani have come to feel that the state farm is their home. They all say, 'My family is in the state farm, the state farm is my family. The Han will maybe go back to their places of origin, but we will live here for generations to come.'

(6) The second generation of Hani in the state farm is growing. There are now [in 1990] about 800 Hani children and young people who all speak Chinese and go to school. (ibid. pp. 54–6)

Such generalised descriptions of the state farms' presumed power to positively transform minorities are supported by other publications containing success stories of individual minority employees. Of the numerous stories of how state farms and their employees have contributed to the development of Panna, and have in fact been the main engine for modernisation and change, none are more forceful than those claiming to speak through the voice of local minorities. By letting members of local Tai or Akha communities speak on behalf of the local minorities as such, emphasising how the Han in the state farms have helped them and their fellow villagers, a picture is given of state farm employees as sacrificing beneficiaries without them having to claim this role themselves. One of the more interesting stories of this kind is about a Tai monk who was employed by the Jinghong state farm and eventually became its most important connection to the local minorities. The story is presented in the form of a short autobiography of the former monk, He Tan. In fact the account is written not by He Tan himself but by a Han author speaking with the voice of He Tan. It is unclear if the story is based on quotations from interviews or if it is partly fictional, but in the context of the book in which it is published this is less important. The main point is that the story provides one of the stronger examples of how a positive identity of being 'Han settlers in state farms' is established and supported through a constructed account by a member of the Tai minority.[9]

Through the constructed voice of the former monk himself the story tells how He Tan (from Jinggu near Sipsong Panna) together with thirty-one other monks and eight novices, to the great despair of their villagers, resumed secular life in 1958 because of the policies of the Great Leap Forward. After having worked in both a salt and a sugar factory, He Tan contacted the Jinghong State Farm, moved to Panna and started working in the rubber plantation together with twenty friends he brought along. However, life turned out to be not so pleasant in the state farm. Through the description of how tough a Tai monk found life in the state farm—hard work, simple food, less affection among people—an indirect picture of the suffering Han in state farms is also drawn. When even a member of a 'backward' and 'poor' minority found it harder to work in a state farm than to live in his own village, how hard would it then not have been for a Han immigrant from a faraway Han village now living in an unfamiliar region without his family? He Tan himself is on the verge of leaving, but what would he tell his villagers if he returned? Would he have any 'face' (*lian*) if he, as a former monk, could not 'eat bitterness' (*chi ku*)? Through the voice of He Tan the author asks these questions using expressions such as 'face' and 'eating bitterness', typical Chinese expressions which indicate how He Tan had already adapted to Han customs and language. He Tan finally decides to stay and his work in the rubber plantation improves. Then, owing to He Tan's understanding of Tai villagers and his own conscious choice of con-

---

[9] The story about He Tan is found in Jinghong State Farm 1992, pp. 408–22.

tinuing his affiliation with the state farm, the leadership realises that it can use He Tan as a bridge to improve strained relations between villagers and state farm. Therefore, in 1965 He Tan is assigned to work specifically on minority issues.

In the story He Tan is depicted as a model example of an ethnic minority person in every way: a Tai monk who voluntarily resumes secular life, takes up work in a state farm, denounces both 'great Han chauvinism' and 'local nationalism' (*difangzhuyi*), and uses his cultural competence—developed through his combined minority status and long-term adaptation to life in the state farm—to convince the local minorities of the self-sacrificing spirit and contributions of the Han working in the state farms.

As a former highly-educated monk, He Tan enjoys a high degree of authority among Tai villagers. Therefore he becomes a powerful spokesman for the state farm in one of its frequent conflicts with the neighbouring Tai villagers. According to the text, villagers in 1984 started activities to drive out the 'people from Hunan', referring generally to Han employees in the state farm branch. At the same time, the township had financial problems and He Tan suggested that the township government should use its income from a rubber plantation that the state farm had helped it to start up to build a rubber factory to generate collective income. Villagers at that time, however, had put up posters demanding that Hunan people return home, that land inherited from the Tai ancestors should be given back to the Tai people, that the state farm should be closed down and rubber plantations distributed to the Tai (Jinghong State Farm 1992, p. 419). At a public meeting villagers asked He Tan to explain to them why they should agree to build a rubber factory, saying that they would listen to his words rather than their own leaders'. He Tan then delivered a speech emphasising how the Han in the state farms in particular had helped and assisted the Tai in their recent development, and how the Tai should be grateful for this:

> 'They were listening to me, so I said: "Did the Hunan people and the Han come to Sipsong Panna because they themselves wanted this? No, it was the Communist Party's Chairman Mao who told them to come, to open up the borders and construct the border areas. And we Tai people, and the masses of all ethnic groups, also beat drums and gongs to welcome them. Think about this, every-

body: if it was not for the Han would there be electricity and a road to the village? Would we have wrist watches and cars? Could there be television to watch and refrigerators? Some people become jealous when they see how many rubber plantations the state farm has. They use it as a pretext to say that if the Han would just leave, they themselves would become rich. These people do not think. What skills do they have? They do not understand science or techniques, they do not know how to administrate. Is it enough just to want to get rich? Who came to build roads? Who came to set up electricity? Now there are many kinds of enterprises, would they know how to operate all these strange machines? No, they would not. They do not understand anything. They are just greedy. In their hands, would this wealth not simply be destroyed..."' (Jinghong State Farm 1992, p. 419)

After some discussion following He Tan's speech, the villagers start shouting, 'He Tan, don't go, lead us to build...' (Jinghong State Farm 1992, p. 420). The paternalistic and parental tone in He Tan's speech, combined with the overwhelming positive response of Tai villagers, serves to convince the reader of how grateful minorities in fact are for the contributions of the Han. They just need the right person to come along and make the facts understandable for them. Minorities, in this image, are not vicious or hostile by nature but possess a child-like innocence which makes them incapable of immediately perceiving complicated facts. Therefore, according to the image presented in this and many other local texts, only more knowledgeable persons with a correct understanding of state farms and insight into the psyche of the minorities are capable of turning minority villagers' ignorance into acceptance of and even support for Han immigrants. Through the reconstruction of He Tan's speech, He Tan himself is exposed as an ethnic minority member who is so bright and forward looking that he understands that 'we' (the Tai) would be backward and undeveloped if not for the help of 'them' (the Han). And the majority of villagers are in the end characterised as being basically good, but simply too naive to make their own decisions and therefore thoroughly in need of proper leaders who understand them and their situation better than themselves. He Tan's speech also emphasises another aspect important in many other published stories about Han settlers in state farms and brought up in interviews as well: the fact that immigrants of the Maoist period were organised by the government and did not merely come on their own initiative. This is often repeated and it brings into focus the difference between the earlier government organised immigrants and their offspring on the one hand, and the more recent individual immigrants on the other. At the same time it emphasises sacrifice and unselfishness on the part of the Han working in state farms. Through these publications state farm employees are reminded that they should regard themselves first of all as people taking part in a government and Party mission, and that criticism of large-scale Han immigration can only be partly legitimated when it is directed against the recent economic immigrants—those who, alas, have no other mission than to increase their own standard of living.

The culturally transformative power of state farms is emphasised in another story which also indirectly constructs a strong image of the 'advanced' Han. In *Stars of the Rubber Plantation* (one of numerous publications praising model workers and cadres within the state farms) an outstanding Akha rubber plantation worker, A Er, is praised (Sipsong Panna Branch of Land Reclamation Department 1992a, pp. 184–8). Already the title of one chapter, 'This was How the Eagle Flew off', next to a photo of A Er brings associations of primitive wild mountain life rising to new and better standards. The metaphor of a flying mountain bird is used several times in the chapter to emphasise how A Er is seen as a lonely, outstanding individual, willing and able to set off from his mountain life, raising himself towards the sky and reaching new goals in the state farm in spite of his background as a simple Akha hunter:

> You flew away from the village in the high mountains. Together with numerous known and unknown sisters and brothers did you, with your different face, different language but similar youthful vigour, fill the hole that the young intellectuals had left behind and help to ensure that the state farm regained its exuberant vitality. (ibid. p. 184)

The book portrays 31 outstanding state farm workers, most of them female. A Er is one of three Hani workers of the book, and he is the only man to have come directly from a mountain village to the state farm. The chapter about A Er is also the only one with a second person narrator who speaks directly to the main character, A Er, in the form of 'you'. This strengthens the chapter's patronising tone because A Er's deeds are recounted by the narrator directly to A Er himself in order to praise him almost like a child. In the beginning of his career in the state farm, A Er was asked to administer a rubber forest. This, it is explained, did not require many technical skills but first of all a sense of responsibility which A Er possessed. A few years later he was instructed to tap rubber. This did not go equally well and the narrator explains in a paternalistic tone: 'When you [A Er] were given the knife used to tap the rubber it was obvious that it would not obey you like the hunting rifle used to do.' Retraining was needed, A Er had failed, and the narrator again explains to the reader, through the monologue directed to A Er himself, how A Er came to realise that his own cultural background as a Hani (Akha) accounted for this failure:

> Was it that you were stupid? Or was there another reason? After having turned this over and over in your mind, you came to the conclusion that it was the latter. You were born and had grown up in the mountains, and hunting naturally became your first interest. The village fostered in you the freedom not to care about heaven or cultivate the land, and taught you careless and undisciplined habits. Living for a long time in a backward atmosphere also made you incapable of knowing what science was. In the state farm you became a worker, but you had not cut off the connection with your past, especially when it came to hunting in the mountains. You even dreamed about it at night. (ibid. p. 185)

Then, the chapter goes on, thanks to help and warm concern from his team leaders A Er decided not to give up, but rather to work hard in order to learn scientific ways of tapping rubber. A Er had understood the correct way of handling his problem. The author indirectly suggests that in this process a positive transformation of A Er's personality had taken place. He quotes A Er explaining his motives to go on working in a way that would be understandable to most Han: 'Please tell the leaders not to worry. I could not let the Aini people loose face (*diu lian*) again.' By letting A Er use the concept of 'face' to explain his personal motives to make a bigger effort to adapt to state farm life, the author creates an image of a largely assimilated Akha who is loyal to the state farm and its leaders, but also finds it

important to show that the Akha can live up to the performance demanded by the state farms. They may come from a backward life
but they do not need to be stuck there. A Er even uses the local Han
name for the Akha, namely Aini.

In the image of the story, A Er really becomes 'the eagle' who has
'taken off' from the mountains to seek a better life, and who has
come to understand not merely the 'science' of rubber tapping but
the Han's ways of life. A Er therefore manages, in the spirit of the
chapter, to contribute positively with his previous experiences from
hunting to these new and more modern surroundings. Tapping rubber early in the morning before dawn, A Er gets the idea to use the
headlamp which he used to take for hunting. This habit spreads to a
number of other workers with the result that rubber production in
A Er's team increases. A Er is entitled an excellent worker four times,
and in 1990 he becomes a national model worker as well as a Party
member. The transformation is complete and the book has produced a simple and conceivable image of the childlike, helpless minority 'saved' through the right kind of assistance combined with
personal effort.

Lack of national consciousness and inability to change. The view of ethnic minorities as characterised by a general incapability to adapt to
broader structural changes of society was in different contexts something brought up by Han immigrants working in all sectors of society. There were especially two topics which were often brought
forward by interviewees in both Xiahe and Sipsong Panna to exemplify this: minorities' presumed lack of national consciousness, and
their inability to adapt to the modernised market economy. In connection with the first—a lack of national consciousness—this was a
characteristic which government, Party and state farm leaders had
found especially blatant in the earlier periods of the PRC. This was
also a viewpoint that had spread to lower level cadres, teachers and
administrators within and outside state farms. Although it mainly
pointed towards the minorities in the earlier periods of the PRC it
remained a topic of debate because it was seen as a characteristic that
could still potentially pose great problems.

One of the major sources of local conflicts between local villagers
and state farms after their establishment in Panna related to land and

forests. The government, as well as the state farms, had to convince local peasants and hunters that state farm employees were entitled to cut down the forest and to establish rubber plantations, and that only the agricultural land of villages could not be confiscated. To convince people of this proved to be a great challenge, and a number of immigrants organised by the government recalled their surprise at what they regarded as a lack of national consciousness on behalf of the minorities. This was expressed in different ways by numerous interviewees and the following are just a few examples from Panna of how people would talk about their earlier experiences of the minorities' lack of identification with national policies, their own role in changing this, and their concepts of how a feeble consciousness of the nation and national property was still manifest among Tai and Akha in the late 1990s:

'We started to plant rubber in larger and larger areas, and some rubber trees were very close to the Akha villages. At first the Akha were annoyed by this and got really angry. But then we calmly talked to them, explained to them that this was the land of the country and that our job was to plant rubber. They gradually came to understand our reasoning. It was not like in Hainan where the people fought against the state farms. The Aini could not really hunt any more, but we gave them a road, electricity and access to water. Recently we even installed cable TV for them and they only had to pay for the materials. They could use the road to the other villages and buy their meat instead of hunting animals. Our way of thinking was that the land belongs to the country, but we still have to take care of the ethnic relations. Today they come to give us things. Of course there are still some backward elements who try to steal rubber. Then we have to teach them that this is not allowed.' (Lower-level administrator in state farm branch)

'When we came here, the Tai did not know much about the country. They did not understand that they were part of China. They were for instance used to letting their cattle walk within a rather large area, but suddenly they saw their land getting smaller and smaller. Therefore they complained to the local government that the Han had come to steal their land. They did not realise that this land belonged to the country. This was the main problem before, and maybe it still is. The Tai saw that the rubber plantations made money on rubber, and they tried to take it. We had to teach them that it belonged to the country and that they could not take it.' (Retired state farm worker)

'Some Tai really hate the Han because of the disputes about land, but others realise that this development has been good for them. Many are angry because they believe that the Han came to steal the land on which they had lived for so long. They do not know that the land belongs to the country. They have no idea about what the country is. They just know that there is Panna, Jinghong and Kunming.' (Lower-level cadre in government whose mother was Tai, his father Han and his wife Jinuo)

In Tibetan Xiahe similar experiences were expressed very strongly by earlier immigrant Han, and it was often brought up by people working in local administrative offices. The feeble national consciousness of ethnic minorities was seen as a special challenge of these immigrants whose role was to spread the message of national unity of the PRC to minority people, presumed to be living in ignorance of their own minor role in a much larger game.

There were many examples of how minority people were seen as inherently incapable of adapting to structural changes of society, and interviewees often emphasised what they saw as their inability to adapt to and make use of the opportunities provided by a new market-oriented economy. Among interviewees in both Xiahe and Sipsong Panna it was not uncommon to explain a perceived incapability to understand the demands of the new market economy in biological terms, insisting for instance that minorities 'did not have the brains' (e.g. *naozi bu tai hao* or *naozi suzhi tai di*) for doing the kind of work that immigrant Han took up in construction, trade and the service sector. Sometimes it was explained as a result of slow cultural development that had so far made it difficult for minorities to enter the modern world and adapt to its demands. And often, especially in the case of the Tai and Tibetans, it was explained as a result of religious beliefs that were so strong that people would spent money on 'unproductive religious activities' rather than make 'rational' productive investments. In all cases, the fact that an increasing number of Han immigrants were visible in the markets and known to run many of the new enterprises, shops, tourist offices and restaurants was attributed to deficiencies of the minorities and their cultures: deficiencies which according to interviewees could mostly be overcome by long-term contact with the Han, continued influence of a modernised economy, and a higher degree of acceptance of 'modern things from outside'.

While the Tai were strongly criticised by many Han immigrants for believing too much in Buddhism and not being clever enough to adapt to the market economy, they were nevertheless described as an ethnic group with inherited cultural characteristics that tended to be considered more positive than those attributed to Tibetans. The cultural distance between Tibetans and Han, especially the nomadic Tibetans as argued above, was perceived as much deeper than that between Han and Tai, and political conflicts in Tibetan areas were regarded as potentially more likely by many Han immigrants. The Tai were more often described as calm, easy to get along with, and friendly and open towards other people. Some described them as mild, warm and hospitable. The Tai's settled agriculturally based life was conceivable to the Han immigrants and considered less threatening and uncontrollable than the life of the nomadic Tibetans. But sometimes descriptions of Tai in predominantly positive terms were first of all due to the interviewee's comparison of the Tai with other minorities living within Panna which were perceived as even more backward and less civilised than the Tai:

'There is such a difference between the Han and the minorities. Compared to other minorities the Tai minority is one of the most intelligent and clever ones. The Tai belong to one of the most advanced (*xianjin*) minorities. They have a script, they have Buddhism, but they are still a very closed-off ethnic group and the Han are much more developed and open than the Tai. Of course the difference between the Tai and the Jinuo, for instance, is huge. The Jinuo have a primitive society...although today the Jinuo are ashamed of their long houses and have eliminated them. They are also embarrassed of their Jinuo costume. Concerning education, almost all Jinuo children now go to school, but you cannot say that their society has jumped over some stages of development. They were forced to change when the Communists came, but in fact their society is still at the stage of a primitive society. It would be unscientific (*bu kexue*) to claim that they have jumped over some stages of development.' (Successful private Han entrepreneur and cadre)

Other interviewees expressed very direct negative stereotypes of minorities in general, and of the minorities living in the mountains of Panna especially. Like this woman who focused her description on the aspects of minorities that she found most repulsive:

'When we arrived, the Han were very different from the other *minzu*. Nothing was the same. Language, way of living, customs... Now many young people have adapted to the Han. They wear the same clothes. Before the minorities here did not bother about their clothes. If their shirt fell down they were not even shy. They did not mind if you saw them without their clothes! Now that has changed. They are shy about the body the same way we are. But of course there are still differences. The mountains are poor, Jinghong is rich. The reason is that the Lahu in the mountains have a primitive society (*yuanshi shehui*). The Lahu cannot work. They are lazy and if they get money they go drinking. They are dirty and so are their villages!' (Woman belonging to the second generation of Han)

Since there have been few open conflicts between Tai and Han in Panna, most Han regarded Panna as a safe and relatively comfortable place where they could live and work in a pleasant climate and atmosphere without risking being openly criticised, attacked or discriminated against. This was sometimes brought up as a difference between the situations of Han living in Panna and those in Tibet and especially Xinjiang. A few interviewees had been to Xinjiang or had friends, family or colleagues who had been there, and they had the clear impression that with many Uighurs' sceptical attitude towards the Han and the Communist leadership Xinjiang was a far less safe and pleasant place to be a Han. Thus the negative images and stereotypes that local Han expressed when discussing local non-Han in Panna were often supplemented with positive evaluations that praised the minorities in Panna for being also friendly, non-aggressive, hospitable and generally not making it difficult for Han to settle there.

In Xiahe there was a tendency for more Han immigrants to express discomfort about the Han's relationship with both the Hui and especially the nomadic Tibetans. Some described the Hui as people belonging to a 'closed' minority that because of religion was potentially hostile towards the Han and would not engage in close social relationships either with Han or with Tibetans. Tibetan farmers and Tibetans living in Xiahe town were often seen as docile, not capable of adapting to modernisation, but after all friendly. This did not differ significantly from Han cadres' views on Han peasants often living in villages with Hui and Tibetans. Although many cadres described the Buddhist beliefs of the Tibetans as being 'too strong' and therefore incompatible with modernisation, Buddhism was also a religion that was regarded as peaceful, civilised and acceptable for both the government and most Han cadres. As one Han cadre explained, 'It is good for the Tibetans and for the development of tourism here that they believe in Buddhism, as long as they do not believe too much!' This view was shared by many interviewed Han cadres and teachers especially.

The new familiarity with minority areas

Stereotypes and derogatory expressions are easy to take notice of and register as part of a dominant discourse. People who remain silent on the topic of ethnic difference, who ignore the topic, or who are clearly not interested in it at all tend to be less noticeable when enough vocal and articulate people are willing to promote their own stereotypical views on ethnic minorities. My experience when doing research among Han immigrants in Panna and Xiahe was that quite a few Han interviewees did not talk at all about the local ethnic minorities as groups representing difference, or as an ethnic 'Other'. Not everybody was interested in the topic of ethnic groups, relations and policies, and quite a few clearly regarded these issues as completely irrelevant for their own lives, even though they were living within an officially designated minority area. These were especially recent economic immigrants as well as the Han farmers in Xiahe living in ethnically mixed villages. While some of the recent economic migrants joined in the common discourse maintaining that minorities in general were incapable of living up to the Han's swift adaptation to a modernising economy and culture, others seemed largely unaffected by the propagation of social evolution and the media's exoticisation of ethnic minorities. While some used biology to express the view that minorities were not only historically backward but had some kind of inherited deficiency making them less intelligent, others made no such distinctions at all, even when being directly asked for their impression of the local minority areas and the minorities living there.

Among a number of Han belonging to the recent economic migrants it was more common to express stereotypes about Han from other parts of China (other provinces or other counties within the same province) than to comment on the ethnic minorities. This was most obvious in cases when Han immigrants from different regions often came into contact with each other and competed on the same market for the same jobs or costumers. In conversations about their migration experiences and their impressions of the area they were currently living in, they would talk about differences among people working in different sectors of society, discrepancies in people's income and their unequal levels of power. More concretely, they would refer to how people had highly unequal possibilities when it came to influencing decisions on, for instance, who got access to which kind of jobs, who got which kind of customers, who got permission to open new shops or restaurants, etc. They would almost always compare their own economic life in their places of origin with other places they had migrated to, including the minority area, and sometimes they would emphasise differences between men and women in terms of which kind of job one could expect, how much money it would provide and how good or bad the job was compared to opportunities in other places. Often discussions on these issues centred around what were in essence differences of class, and often they included strong criticism of cadres' power (regardless of whether they were Han or non-Han) and 'ordinary people's' (*laobaixing*) dependence on cadres' often arbitrary decisions.

But these discussions and conversations did not necessarily include any references at all to 'Han' or 'ethnic minorities' as groups, and it was clearly possible for some Han immigrants to account for their experiences of migration to a minority area without paying special attention to possible differences in cultural practices, physical appearance, language or religion. Some had apparently no concept of a perceived backwardness of minorities, and did not first of all regard them as 'minorities' but rather as other people living, working and seeking to improve their life situation in the same area as themselves. Those who indirectly expressed such attitudes through silence on the topic were often those *not* working in sectors where they came into daily contact with Chinese and foreign tourists;[10] they were for instance working as farmers or in construction rather than in transport, hotels or restaurants. When I sometimes tried to direct the attention of these interviewees towards the issue of ethnic minorities by asking questions, for instance, about what, if any, differences they found between themselves and the Tai, some would say that they did not know any Tai and therefore did not know what the possible differences were; others would point out a few examples of difference like language or religion but describe these in neutral terms. Others on the other hand would rephrase notions of 'backwardness', 'less intelligence' or, more frequently, the Tai's lack of capability to work in a modern market economy.

What then were the reasons for the pronounced differences between some immigrants' willingness to talk at length about their perceptions of the minorities as contrasted with the Han, and others' seeming disinterest in the topic and lack of comments on the local minorities within the area where they were living? Silence on a topic such as ethnic difference could of course mean that the people remaining silent were simply unwilling to reveal their own thoughts. This sometimes turned out to be the case, especially in Xiahe where some interviewees who had remained silent on the topic of Tibetans turned out to have rather negative attitudes towards them—though these views were only revealed coincidentally in later conversations with me, or with other people while I was present. However, this was the exception rather than the rule. More important were differences in exposure to the official discourse on minorities, as well as the time of immigration. Especially for many of the recent economic immigrants, possible ethnic and cultural differences were by and large irrelevant for their own experiences and current lives within the minority area. Unlike the Han immigrants of the Maoist period they had arrived in a minority region where the towns (in which most of them were working and living) were dominated by buildings in the

---

[10] Taxi-drivers for instance, in contrast, were often very willing to talk about their concepts of the local ethnic minorities. They were used to both foreigners and Chinese tourists being interested in this topic, and they were used to driving to the various local tourist destinations talking with other Han living permanently in the area. Moreover, quite a few of them were second generation Han with parents working in the state sector.

same style as in other Chinese towns, where a familiar Chinese political system had already been established for a long time, where schools were largely similar to Chinese schools in other parts of the country, and where the dominant language in the business sector was Chinese. The larger towns, especially Jinghong and the other two county capitals in Panna where most of them settled, were inhabited by large numbers of Han. The minorities were not seen to dominate the city area, and most of them were living either in the villages on the outskirts of the city areas or in work units within the city.

Furthermore, most recent immigrants were of peasant background and had limited education. Although they were all aware of having moved to a 'minority autonomous area', often they had not thought about what this designation implied, and they had no opinions about minorities' eventual rights to self-determination. These issues were too far removed from their own lives to make sense or constitute a topic of interest, and partly for this reason they were also seen by many cadres as 'Han peasants with a relatively low level of civilisation' (*suzhi di*). But the main reason why many recent immigrants were not concerned with minorities as such and did not talk about them in conversations about their own migration experiences was probably first of all that perceived cultural differences were less relevant for them than they had been for those Han immigrants who arrived forty years earlier in an area then largely dominated by local non-Han. They had been pioneers who had to set up a new political system, displace local authorities with new ones, change the ecology and ensure that the border areas would be thoroughly changed and integrated into the PRC. Even those peasant immigrants from that era who had been less conscious of their participation in a lofty political mission had encountered areas that were in many ways profoundly different from what they had come from. They had encountered people who talked, lived and behaved differently from themselves— people who were not necessarily eager to accept the newcomers and their projects to transform the area and themselves, and exploit the available natural resources. For the recent economic immigrants, in contrast, life in the minority area was perhaps somewhat exotic, but not necessarily very different from life in another Chinese developing town or city at a county or prefecture level. Therefore, they did not express anything comparable to the feeling of shock that many

earlier immigrants so vividly recalled having sensed on their first arrival in the minority area.

While some recent immigrants remained silent on the topic of minorities versus majority, others were largely positive or neutral in their
indirect or direct references to ethnic minorities. In these cases they
also tended to express their positive attitudes towards ethnic minorities
in different ways from cadres and people with a longer education. In
general positive aspects of minority images were often strengthened
through interviewees' own experiences of friendship or acquaintance with individuals belonging to ethnic minorities. Through such
experiences the image of minorities as impersonal groups with collective and static characteristics was fragmented and supplemented
with more personalised and individualised views. People working in
the state sector who, for instance, expressed largely critical views on
how 'minorities were not capable of adapting to the market economy' would sometimes at the same time have colleagues and friends
belonging to the same ethnic minorities. These minority friends
normally shared the same kind of work, lived in the same unit, spoke
fluent Chinese and sent their children to the same schools as Han
colleagues. Derogatory views and stereotypes about 'minorities' as
such would not necessarily influence personal social relationships. It
was—in a way well known from studies of ethnic stereotyping in
other parts of the world—perfectly possible for interviewees to have
close personal contacts with individual minority people, and at the
same time express stereotyped views of the 'cultural characteristics' of
the minority group as such. Similarly, intellectuals and cadres belonging to an ethnic minority sometimes expressed equivalent negative
views themselves on the perceived cultural characteristics of their own
ethnic group, especially the peasant or non-educated members of it.

People from among the individual immigrants (often with no or
only a few years of education) more often based their descriptions of
minorities only on personal experiences of encounters with individuals, not at all on general images of minorities as impersonal
groups or an ethnic Other. In Panna some of the immigrants renting
rooms below Tai houses would make references to their landlords
when talking about ethnic minorities by explaining, for instance,
how they were well received by them and accepted as workers in
Panna. They did not have a close social relationship with the land-

lord and his family, but on the basis of their personal experiences with renting rooms they would sometimes explain that 'the Tai' were 'friendly' towards immigrants. The most common positive reference by recent individual immigrants to the local minorities was based upon comparisons with their previous experiences as migrants in larger Chinese cities. Many had negative experiences of living and working in one or more Chinese metropoles, and in comparisons with how they were treated by the locals there the ethnic minorities came out favourably. Only few interviewees with a background as 'floating population' in a large south-eastern city of China would characterise the ethnic minorities in their new place of living as 'backward' or as possessing any specific cultural deficiencies as compared to themselves. They had moved to an area which was familiar because of the strong influence of the large number of Han settlers, the similarity with other Chinese towns and smaller cities, and the lack of dominance by the ethnic minorities living and working in the towns. One female restaurant owner from Sichuan explained her satisfaction with the atmosphere of Panna in a way which was common among those recent immigrants who ran successful small-scale businesses:

'It is maybe impolite to say so, but the quality of schools here is not so good. That is why my daughter is still back home. But it is hardly the fault of the Tai here. Panna is really a nice place. People are polite and hospitable. In the beginning it was difficult to run a restaurant because of the language problem. And I did not know what the Tai liked to eat. Now it is good to do business here, and I get along well with my customers and neighbours.'

Another Han woman from Zhejiang Province had started a very small restaurant selling cheap dumplings together with her husband four years earlier. They had both been peasants, but the government had claimed their fields because of the expansion of an industrial area. The couple was not interested in the jobs in a factory they had been offered instead, and had migrated. They now both worked in their restaurant from four in the morning till ten in the evening (not uncommon among individual immigrants) and were happy with their income which amounted to about 3,000 yuan a month. The woman only had the following comments relating to ethnic minorities during a total of several hours of interviews in addition to a number of more informal conversations:

'Why we decided to come to Panna? Doesn't everybody say that Panna is a nice place? I do not know anything about the history or culture, or in fact anything at all, about Panna. I have no relatives who have been here. But I had heard that it was a nice place, the weather is good, and I hoped people would like our dumplings. I thought, maybe they do not have so many dumpling restaurants in a minority area. We are only here to make business. People here are friendly, the minorities are polite to us, they do not look down upon us. What else is there to say? I like to be here and business is good.'

Panna was seen as 'a nice place', the local minorities there were not posing any specific problems for the immigrants, who were also received better by the authorities than in many other areas. Peasant immigrants were also rarely concerned intellectually with the issue of ethnic relations in China, the notion of social evolution, or the ideology of nationalism, and they rarely echoed the official discourse on minorities when referring to their local experiences in the minority area.

Ironically in view of their more frequent positive views on ethnic minorities and fewer paternalistic and derogatory descriptions of them, the economic immigrants themselves were often described in negative terms by local people belonging to ethnic minorities. In both Xiahe and Panna many locals in the county towns described them as dirty, uncivilised, uneducated and socially disturbing. When negative views on the Han as a group were spontaneously expressed they were frequently directed towards precisely these immigrants. The reasons was that they belonged to a low social group of unskilled workers, sometimes taking up jobs that locals regarded as unattractive and even degrading. The Han who were most despised within the larger towns were for instance those selling second-hand clothes or collecting garbage, prostitutes and women in massage parlours and other businesses directed towards male Han tourists, drivers of tricycles and sometimes those with very small stalls doing, for instance, shoe and bike repairs on the street. With the influx of Han immigrants searching for work and income, many local minority

people felt increased pressure on a changing market, and they directed their frustration towards these newcomers rather than towards
the Han working as government cadres, in the Party, as teachers, or
in the rather isolated communities of state farms.

As mentioned earlier, Han from the second generation were often
aware of local minorities' critical attitude towards the recent spontaneous immigrant Han, and some were therefore very keen to establish distance between themselves as second generation Han or 'local
Han' and those recent immigrant Han. The recent economic immigrants were accepted by the government and Party for contributing
to the improvement of trade and service, and most Han welcomed
the increased offer of goods and services ensured by these immigrants. But in the cities especially, there was at the same time no
doubt that both state organised Han immigrants and many people
belonging to ethnic minorities (including cadres and educated people) regarded the recent individual immigrants with different degrees of contempt, and sometimes as the lowest social group within
the county capitals.

Longing and regretting: Han nostalgia and tourist images

Some images of ethnic minorities and minority areas provided by
Han immigrants highlighted ambivalent feelings of having lost forever a more pristine time, mixed with hopes and longing for further
modernisation. Han immigrants who had migrated to the minority
areas in the early period of the PRC would frequently express despair over slow economic and cultural development, while at the
same time complaining about the loss of an innocent, more human
pre-modern era. The past they imaged (as with so many other people living in the modern world) was a time when people were more
friendly, nature more beautiful, and human relations more intimate.

This Janus-faced nature of modernisation sometimes made it difficult for Han immigrants to explain their own complex feelings
about the area they were currently living in. Practically all earlier immigrants agreed that the minority areas had improved significantly
since their own immigration, and largely because of their own, and
other Han immigrants', contributions. The economy was better off,
nature had been tamed and diseases eradicated, living standards had
been raised, secular education had become more available, and the

political system had improved the administration and degree of political control. In this process, however, something was lost. This feeling of loss manifested itself in a nostalgia for the past and the characteristics attributed to it. Han immigrants from the Mao period would express this in different ways, emphasising different aspects of the loss they believed had been the inevitable price of modernisation. But mostly it was nature, human relations and the honesty and hospitality of ethnic minorities in the past that were emphasised. One Han shopkeeper who had lived in Xiahe since he was a child explained:

'Before people here were very honest, but they did not have a high level of education (*wenhua shuiping bu gao*). Therefore they were easily cheated by others. Now people have become more wise. They understand things that were incomprehensible to them before. Therefore they are not easily cheated. But they are also not so honest any more.'

One interviewee who had retired from an important position in the Party was one of the few Han immigrants I met who was directly critical of the impact of the government's organised migrations of Han to Panna. He clearly found that Han culture was 'more advanced' than that of the minorities, but in his view the problem was that the government had allowed this 'advanced culture' to more or less eradicate 'minority cultures'. The interviewee expressed a feeling of a dilemma related to the complexity of promoting modernisation, which necessarily implied more immigration, while at the same time insisting that minorities 'keep their characteristics'. His way of describing this also suggested a feeling of a paternalistic obligation of the Han to take care of and direct the development of the ethnic minorities, including taking care to protect their culture:

'Heaven and earth have been turned around in Panna. There are so many people coming from outside now. They come to sell all kinds of things. All the tricycles are biked by people from the outside, the houses, roads, furniture…everything is made and sold by people from outside. The local minorities rarely do that. They have an easy life in their villages. They can live without doing much. Their attitude towards work has not changed. They do not want to do physical work for others. They look down upon people who do that kind of work. But the influence of the advanced Han culture has been too strong. We have not taken enough care to protect the minorities' own cultures, their own characteristics. Take for instance Manjinglan which used to be a Tai village. Now it is taken over completely by business people from outside. It is important to protect their culture and we have to work to achieve that. The advanced culture should be combined with the minorities' own cultures. Before the Cultural Revolution we had a policy supposed to benefit the minorities. But at the same time we were expected to transmit Han culture.' (Retired Party employee in his 60s)

Feelings of loss connected to the gains of modernisation were expressed most strongly among (a minority of) early immigrant Han and some intellectuals, but they very rarely combined this with a critical attitude towards Han immigration in general. However, generally it was not immigrants but Han tourists visiting the minority areas who expressed the strongest disappointment about a seemingly vanished pre-modern paradise in an undeveloped though modernised minority area. Both Xiahe and Panna were popular tourist destinations and Han tourists' images of the minorities they encountered during their visits provided a relevant entrance to a further understanding of Han views on minorities, expressed by individuals and not merely through public discourse. Tourists were often in close contact with Han immigrants through their restaurant visits and contacts with guides, hotels and tourist offices, and I often overheard tourists discussing their impressions with local Han immigrants. Their impressions of and expressions of views about the ethnic minorities they encountered during their visits were important for many of the Han immigrants who were dependent on the tourist industry for their living, as well as for the many who regarded tourism as the most important industry for both Panna and Xiahe. At the same time tourists' views and perceptions were also clearly shaped by the stories they were told in some of their encounters with Han immigrants living in the areas.

In the process of modernisation that allowed an unprecedented number of Chinese people to seek pleasure, adventure and distraction from daily life in tourist destinations all over the country, some minority areas became very popular sites during the 1980s and 90s. Many tourists hoped that the minority areas they had chosen as their destination would have preserved remnants of times, cultures and human relations that they thought were lost forever in the more modernised and homogenised areas of China. Their expectation was supported and partly created by media images of ethnic minorities and the areas they live in. Interviewed tourists could roughly be divided into two groups: those who came first of all to seek pleasure in what they had heard was a 'hot' area with lots of opportunities for having fun, eating well and relaxing, and those who first of all sought a pristine culture and nature in what they expected to be a culturally different and exotic minority area. At the same time they all wanted to have a pleasurable stay, preferably in a good hotel. The first group was mainly represented in Panna while the second was found in both areas. Tourists going to Xiahe knew beforehand that they were going to a Tibetan area at a high altitude where the tourist industry was not yet highly developed, the number of hotels limited, evening entertainment sparse and the climate rough. They came to experience Tibetan Buddhism in a 'natural surrounding' through a visit to the famous Labrang monastery, and to make a trip to the grasslands visiting one of the tourist tents serving traditional Tibetan food and drinks.[11]

Practically all Han living in the town of Xiahe welcomed the tourists and hoped for more in the future. They saw this as the only hope for modernisation and economic development of Xiahe, and they often emphasised that tourism had an immense, and wholly positive, impact on the area and the minorities:

> 'Tourism influences everything here: the way people live, the way they think, their economy, the clothes they wear. Everything! Before the Tibetans were afraid of new things. They were closed-off (*fengbi*), they did not understand people from the inland of China. Now they are used to them, and much more open. They are even used to seeing foreigners now.' (Local Han administrator who came in 1952)

In both Panna and Xiahe, cadres and local leaders saw tourism as one of the only solutions to dwindling resources and the limited number

---

[11] Foreign tourists generally hoped to 'experience genuine Tibetan culture', and according to local authorities the number of foreign 'backpackers' and tourists in smaller organised groups tended to increase when access to Lhasa and other places in the TAR was restricted.

of other industries. As shown in Tim Oakes' comprehensive study of tourism in Guizhou, many local village leaders in Guizhou shared the belief that only tourism could help their villages escape poverty and overcome their dependence on scarce natural resources. To reach this end they were therefore willing to commodify and market their culture (Oakes 1998).[12] In Panna and Xiahe Han immigrants generally considered the tourist industry so important that negative tourist views on the area became a cause of concern both for cadres and individual immigrants:

> 'We have some tourists coming here now because of Labrang monastery. But that is really the only reason they come. People from Guangzhou and Shanghai laugh at us when they come here. 'Is that all!', they say. They do not think that there is anything special here.' (Same interviewee as above)

As in other places of China tourists tended to travel in larger organised groups with a guide and a tight organisation of the programme. But an increasing number of especially younger tourists were also coming on their own initiative, independently of the formal tourist groups. With the high expectations of finding at the same time 'authentic Tibetan culture', 'primitive life' and good hotels, Chinese food and leisure activities, many were disappointed. My fieldwork periods in Xiahe were outside the main tourist seasons in June, July and August when the weather was warmer, but locals told me that even during the high peak season the vast majority of Chinese tourists came only for one day. Interviewed tourists confirmed locals' accounts of tourists' impressions of Xiahe: most found that the monastery was beautiful but that it was too hard to stay for more than one day because of the difficulties of adapting to climate, altitude and food. There was also, as several said, 'nothing to do for fun' (*mei you hao wanr de*) in the evenings, and therefore many Han working in tourist related businesses were complaining that the government did not do enough to adapt to the needs of Han tourists. Some were frustrated because they themselves had been attracted to the place precisely because of the prospects for doing business related to a developing tourist industry.

Interviewed tourists made the same complaints and added that the place was dirty and badly kept and that a one-day visit was more

---

[12] See also Schein 2000 about tourism and Guizhou.

than enough to see everything. Nevertheless, tourists found their images of a 'pristine culture' partly confirmed through their visit to Labrang and the visual presence of monks and Tibetans coming to visit it. But at the same time they made clear that their negative expectations of encountering a 'backward', 'dirty' and 'primitive' place were fulfilled as well. Many were able to situate their experience within the dominant discourse on social evolution and modernisation, and thus both the positive and negative impressions made sense through the filter of the images of minorities and minority areas they had already formed before their arrival.

'Beautiful Sipsong Panna' has for a long time been pictured in literature, TV series, films, art, exhibitions and 'nationality parks' as an exotic, sub-tropical paradise with beautiful Tai women, stunning nature, picturesque monks and an atmosphere of friendship and hospitality. As discussed earlier, the tourist industry in Panna boomed during the 1990s, and even though it slowed down after more people got the opportunity to travel to Southeast Asia especially, there were by year 2000 still more than one million tourists visiting Panna every year. Owing to the massive exposure of Panna as a tourist destination expectations of tourists in Panna tended to be higher than those of tourists in Xiahe. Most came for three to four days, taking part in organised tours, conferences and meetings or travelling in smaller groups hiring guides through one of the numerous private local tourist agencies (many of them started by Han of the second generation). Most tourists made at least one visit to an organised 'minority village' where a fee was paid to enter an 'ordinary' village featuring minorities in 'traditional' clothes, selling various minority items. Visits to at least one of the monasteries, the minority park, the botanical garden and a 'Tai restaurant' (normally owned by a Han immigrant) with minority dancing were also 'musts' for most tourists. Then there were plenty of massage parlours, as well as organised trips across the border into Burma.[13]

---

[13] Many organised tours to Panna included a visit to one of the very popular drag dance shows in Burma. These were also organised for a short period of time on the Chinese side of the border, but were quickly banned by the government. According to people in Panna, the performers were boys who had been treated to develop female bodies, and some of them could be hired as prostitutes as well. Between 1995 and 1999 the stories surrounding these shows and their performers were plentiful. There were posters of the performers in many places, and

In Panna as in Xiahe tourists expressed a certain disappointment about their encounter with the minority area and the minorities. They were surprised that their destination, Jinghong, was in fact a busy city and that only organised bus tours and guides would take them to see 'nature' and 'minority villages'. At the same time they felt that they experienced the expected 'backwardness' of minority areas when driving in buses on narrow mountain roads through non-Han villages. The dilemma of wanting a certain kind of familiar modernisation and, at the same time, experiencing disappointment at the fact that the very same modernisation had seemingly ruined an attractive image of minorities characterised many tourists' views of minorities and minority areas. This was for instance expressed by a woman who had travelled from the city of Guiyang in Guizhou to Panna for a short holiday with her husband and parents:

> Woman: 'I think Panna is very backward. Don't you also find that the minorities here are very backward? Here they are more backward than in Guizhou. Our place is of course much more developed.'
> MHH: 'What did you do today?'
> Woman: 'We went into a Tai restaurant. But really, we were simply not able to eat the food. It was Tai food [makes a face expressing disgust]. It is anyway not so interesting to see the dancing [of people dressed in minority clothes in the restaurants]. [in a tone of regret]: Ayah, this modernisation is going to eradicate all the characteristics of the minorities. There will be nothing left. In a few years they will be like us.'

The paradox of tourists complaining that an area is overrun and ruined by (other) tourists (a well known phenomenon all over the world) was widespread also among Han visitors in Panna. Interviewed male tourists were sometimes even complaining that the famous sex industry and night life in Panna were overrated and that there was 'nothing fun' about evenings in Panna. Others emphasised that precisely the night life and massage parlours in Panna were among the main attractions of the place. While complaining quite a lot, most tourists were grateful for the abundance of Chinese restaurants, the

---

tourists (men as well as women) talked with excitement of their visit to these shows in particular. On the topic of prostitution in Panna see Hyde 2001.

widespread use of the Chinese language, and organised bus tours and activities that were only possible precisely because of the numerous tourists.

Since tourists in Panna expected to encounter Tai women colourfully dressed in the characteristic Tai dress and performing songs and dances, hotels and restaurants run by Han immigrants struggled to recruit enough minority girls from villages to work in the tourist business, dressed up as 'proper minorities' and providing the right image of a minority area (a common alternative was to hire and train young Han to perform as minority people). While many entrepreneurs complained that minority girls were often not willing to work in their businesses (they were too 'lazy' or 'too satisfied with the little they had in their villages') a number of girls belonging to local ethnic minorities did find work in the towns, serving or guiding tourists, and often performing singing and dancing as part of the job as well. Mostly they would carry out the jobs they were asked to do, politely attempting to answer any questions from tourists about their ethnic group and the area, and those I interviewed were generally grateful for having a job at all although wages were low and working hours long. However, sometimes the pressure in the form of questions relating to the imagined backwardness of minorities and their exciting and exotic customs became too much for those working daily with tourists.

One such instance occurred in the popular 'minority park' in Jinghong where tourists visit 'traditional' minority houses getting a short introduction to the customs of Panna's minorities. I was walking with a group of Han tourists, visiting the various houses, listening to tourists' comments and questions. In the Blang house two Blang girls of nineteen were responsible for presenting the 'traditional customs' of the Blang when about fifteen Han tourists and myself came into the house.[14] Immediately one of the Han women

---

[14] Like most young women recruited for work in the tourist industry these two Blang women had a junior secondary education. People from the park had come to their village looking for minority girls capable of speaking and reading Chinese. Before starting as guides, when they were fifteen years old, they had both had a brief introduction to the Blang's 'traditional customs' and how they were supposed to introduce them. Their wages were 500 yuan a month and they worked seven days a week, guiding in the Blang house during daytime and performing minority dances and songs for tourists in the evenings.

in the group loudly commented to another one that this girl was really pretty, but that her costume was of course not as nice as the Tai costume. The Blang guide went on talking about the 'eighteen strange things of Yunnan' ('an old woman can climb up a tree faster than a monkey', 'monks may engage in love affairs' etc.) and the tourists started asking questions. One man in his forties explained that he himself came from the north of China, but he had once met a man from Sipsong Panna who told him that he had been to a Hani village, and that this had proven to him that China still had 'backward minorities'. Now the man wanted to know whether or not the Blang were more backward or more developed than the Akha. The Blang guide was clearly embarrassed and avoided the question. Other questions were asked and the group started to talk about food. One woman asked how the Blang cooked their food. Again the question was avoided by the guide. This, however, was a question that engaged many in the group and several insisted that she should explain how the Blang made food. Finally, the young woman, clearly annoyed, answered in a quick and very tense voice: 'We happen to cook just like everybody else! We make a fire, take a pot, put some water in it, add some rice and boil it! And then we eat it like everybody else!' This response, and the rather unusual way in which it was delivered, put a quick end to the visit of this group. They did not laugh. They quietly left the Blang house, looking for other houses with more exciting information about the exotic customs of minorities.

For a short while the image of the docile, friendly and hospitable minority women in interesting and original costumes was scratched by this young Blang woman's outburst of annoyance with what she regarded as completely stupid and ignorant questions, insisting upon essential cultural difference rather than common human experience. Tourists' images of minorities, as they were recounted to me, were hardly changed through the visit itself. It was my impression that most tourists prior to their visit already had clear notions of what they expected from minorities and minority areas, how they thought 'minorities' as such looked, and how they acted. Although the areas rarely lived up to their more romantic images most of them had quite a good time and also felt that they had been provided with a first hand insight into the 'backwardness' of these areas. Pre-formed images were confirmed.

With the strong public discourse on the ethnic minorities as 'younger brothers' to the Han, as peoples who were on a lower stage of social evolution by the time of the Communist takeover, as exotic remnants of times gone by and peoples in need of special assistance from more advanced members of society, it is not surprising that largely similar views were expressed by many Han living in minority areas. In particular those taking part in the Communist government's and Party's project to establish firm control over the border areas, partly through organised immigrations of Han people, had to a large extent shaped their images and opinions about the minority area before actually going there. In addition the education system and the media's frequent programmes containing references to minority areas and ethnic minorities played a significant role in shaping images and concepts of how minorities were, who they were, and how they differed from a perceived Han majority—a majority whose image was largely created in the same process.

Most Han in China have never personally encountered people belonging to ethnic minorities, and their perceptions of them are first of all shaped by the dominant public discourses on ethnic groups and relations in China. However, owing to their migration the Han of this study were inevitably confronted with their own status as Han as compared with those who were 'ethnic minorities'. Their concepts and images of ethnic groups in China, as they expressed them in interviews and other forms of conversation, had not merely been shaped by the ongoing and dominant national discourse on ethnic relations. They had also been shaped through direct encounters with people who in many contexts identified themselves as different from the Han, sharing different histories, languages and customs and also being officially recognised as distinct non-Han ethnic groups.

The discourse on ethnic relations expressed in the media, through education, and locally, not least in state farm publications, supported a dominant national image of the Han immigrants living in minority areas as constituting a special group of people, sacrificing themselves to help build up 'backward' regions and thereby the motherland. A largely similar image was provided mainly by those immigrants who had an education beyond junior secondary school and possessed positions as cadres and state employees, as well as by others who migrated in the Maoist period when the areas were poorer, when Chinese schools and the Communist political system were not well developed, and when the general influence and sheer number of Han in the areas were much smaller than today. Among these Han immigrants a common pride in being Han was manifest.

It was by no means difficult to collect examples of strong prejudice and racially discriminatory views on minorities expressed by Han people living and working in minority areas. But there were also quite a large number of Han who remained silent on the topic of ethnic difference, or who only had positive (and not necessarily paternalistic) comments. Putting important individual differences aside for a while, it was first of all the social status and position of immigrants that seemed to determine how images of minorities and Han were represented. Roughly one could say that high position and education tended to go together with paternalistic judgements focusing on minorities' presumed lack of 'development'. Modernisation (*xiandaihua*) was seen as an ultimate goal for change, created and passed on to the minorities by the Han immigrants.

In comparison it was striking to see how, in particular, Han immigrants who had come as individual migrants after the 1980s were often uninterested in the topic of ethnic relations and minority-majority differences. They had not experienced anything like the cultural shock that other migrants referred to when arriving in the minority areas, mainly because the larger towns they mostly settled in during the 1990s had already been transformed by the long-term presence of a large community of Han settlers. They made no claims to a special idealistic mission as Han in a minority area, and the fact that they had come with the specific and explicit purpose of improving their and their families' economic situation helped to explain their lack of interest in ethnic minorities as such. They often judged the minorities on the basis on their own personal encounters with landlords, neighbours and shopkeepers, while expressing satisfaction with the fact that there were jobs locally which they, rather than the local minorities, were successful in.

It would be possible and plausible to argue that Han in minority areas tend to identify themselves as part of a national dominant ethnic majority vis-à-vis the ethnic minorities which they in a national perspective see as numerically, economically and culturally almost insignificant. But in the daily encounters between minorities and immigrant Han, this abstract understanding of a 'Han majority' has little relevance for most. Class distinctions among Han immigrants and among members of ethnic minorities were profound, and the Han's ways of describing the local people they lived among were clearly formed by education, position, and the concrete situations in which they interacted with other Han and local non-Han.

AFTERWORD

During one of my conference presentations of research on Han migrations to minority areas a discussant pointed out that I had said a lot about how Han immigrants perceive their own situation as immigrants, how they recall their histories of migration and regard their own role in the minority area; but what happened *in reality,* the discussant asked, and was immigration a good or a bad thing for the areas involved? I could not answer these questions. The response depends on the people who answer, and these kinds of contradicting answers are precisely what I have been interested in during this research.

There is no doubt that since the large-scale immigrations took off after the mid-1950s minority areas have experienced immense political, economic and cultural changes, many of which have been instigated by Han immigrants who took up new and influential positions in government, Party, education, production and trade. Although many Han immigrants regarded the minority areas they came to as sealed off, backward and isolated, Gannan and Sipsong Panna had already for a very long time been areas on the cultural borders of China and Tibet, and China and Southeast Asia, with all the mutual contacts and influence this implied. Many current minority areas, for instance Inner Mongolia and areas in the southwest, have also had a long history from before the PRC of receiving Han immigrants and colonisers. The reasons why the Communist period's immigration of Han has been so remarkable are first of all the scale of migrations, their often tight organisation, and their continuing direct influence today on policy, the economy and culture in regions which were historically dominated by non-Han.

While colonialism has often been regarded as a phenomenon of the past, characterised by domination over indigenes by European men, this book has presented Han settlements in ethnic minority areas within China as part of an ongoing Chinese internal colonisation project. This could also be described as a modernist project in the sense that the Communist leadership envisioned a modernity that would transform the ethnic minority areas, considered to be at a lower evolutionary stage of development, through the input of more advanced technology, improved means of production, secular mass education, the dissemination of ideas of participation in politics guided by the CCP, and new notions of citizenship in the Communist state. Seen from the point of view of the government and Communist Party, this project has largely been successful. The population within most ethnic minority areas in China has accepted the areas' integration into the Chinese state and only a minority of people in some areas (notably Tibet and Xinjiang) engage in direct struggles for independence. The areas have been firmly integrated into the economy and policies of the Chinese state, and the civilising aspect of the government's modernist project has led to the establishment of a dominant Chinese education system, accepted by most as the main route to upward social mobility.

A highly important factor in this modernist project has been the large-scale resettlement of Han in the strategically important border regions. The main aim of this book has been to present this project from the perspective of those groups and individuals who themselves participated actively in it, or who followed on the heels of the first state-organised settlers when economic reforms created new attractions in these areas so often perceived as 'peripheral'. When a colonialist and modernist project's cultural and civilising efforts are viewed through the representations of participants in these projects, a fractured picture characterised by contradiction, fissures and plurality emerges. Official Chinese discourse tends to present us with a totalising and monolithic—and positive—image of the civilising project. The popular debate outside China concerning Han migration, to Tibet especially, also tends to present us with a totalising and monolithic—but strongly negative—image of the same project. However, tensions, heterogeneity and contradiction come to the front when the civilising project involving massive migrations of Han to minority areas is seen from the perspective of participating human beings and individuals.

Social discrepancies among different Han immigrants all living within the ethnic minority areas were profound, and only in some

Afterword

contexts did Han interviewees emphasise a common identification and experience as Han in minority areas. On the whole class distinctions between peasants, cadres, workers in state farms and new successful entrepreneurs were much more important than any common identification as Han. Also, regional distinctions between Han from different areas played an important role in daily encounters between immigrants. However, in discussions about modernisation and development—terms frequently evoked by local cadres especially—'Han' as a general categorisation of people with largely similar language, culture and history was often brought in, and all Han immigrants were then praised for contributing to the minority areas with more 'advanced' culture, science, production techniques and trading methods. In spite of the weak expressions of common 'Hanness', immigrants were nevertheless always able in interviews to relate and refer to 'the Han' as a national dominant category of people, and most of them were positive towards further immigration of Han into ethnic minority areas.

For the Chinese government migration towards the sparsely inhabited western regions remains interesting partly because it might help ease the pressure on the eastern and central areas where the need for alternative income is essential for an increasing number of farmers. The large-scale state organised migrations during the Maoist era laid the foundation for new migrations of more Han in later periods of economic liberalisation. However as shown in this book, if indeed the government is interested in promoting further Han migration to ethnic minority areas it does not need to actively support or organise such migration. They will continue anyway as long as there are job opportunities in those areas, and possibilities for supplementing incomes for some of the hundreds of millions of peasants with scarce land resources, and for other people laid off from their jobs. The government has also so far done nothing to prevent these migrations towards the western regions, and now also into some of the neighbouring states. With new state projects such as the one to 'develop the western regions', and with a number of Chinese scholars recommending further organised migrations of qualified personnel in particular into the western minority areas, there is no reason to expect that the number of migrants will decrease as long as there is peace in these areas.

The large-scale migrations of Han during the period of the PRC have definitely left their mark on most minority areas in China, and whether it is regarded as good or bad the process is probably irreversible. Increasing globalisation and trade might work in favour of even more migration to those of the border areas which are developing economically. The poorest areas may, on the other hand, experience out-migration of an increasing number of ethnic minorities also. While many locals belonging to ethnic minorities express satisfaction with the more open society and economy that allow them too to compete on the market, engage in trade, move and take up new kinds of jobs, new tensions tend to arise when local non-Han find that they are squeezed out of markets and outnumbered by Han recruited from outside to work in construction, the tourist industry and other new enterprises.

Interestingly, minorities in the areas researched tended to be much more critical towards the recent economic and individual immigrants than towards the Han who were organised by the state and resettled in, for instance, state farms before the late 1970s. This might reflect the fact that it is legitimate in China to criticise low-status individual peasant migrants in cities for all kinds of evils (criminality, low education, too many children, uncivilised behaviour....). It might also be related to the increased competition from recent incoming migrants on the labour market, which often works against members of ethnic minorities in rural areas. This competition might be strengthened even more when previously powerful units, such as the state farms, lose their impact as state institutions and have to lay off larger numbers of people owing to their integration into the global market economy. Even though an increasing number of Han born and raised within state farms are no longer entitled to work there, most of them will remain within the minority area and they might start to argue for a status as a new 'local *minzu*'.

Beyond doubt Han immigration in minority areas—especially in those areas where immigration has been on a large-scale and where immigrants possess vital positions related to the economy and governance—has serious implications for the implementation of minority rights and autonomy law in China. With the revival of previous forms of local authority (connected to religious institutions, for instance) and renewed emphasis on ethnic identity supported by increased global contacts and awareness of indigenous rights, resentment against Han immigrants might develop. At the same time the strained situation for millions of laid-off workers and peasants in China pushes them to search for other means of income wherever they are available. Deepening social discrepancies resulting from unequal opportunities for immigrant Han and local non-Han might well constitute a major challenge for political legitimacy in several minority areas on China's borders.

BIBLIOGRAPHY

Appadurai, Arjun (1996), *Modernity at Large*, Minneapolis: University of Minnesota Press.

Bachman, David (2004), 'Making Xinjiang Safe for the Han? Contradictions and Ironies of Chinese Governance in China's Northwest' in M. Rossabi (ed.), *Governing China's Multiethnic Frontiers*, Seattle: University of Washington Press.

Barfield, Thomas, *The Perilous Frontier: Nomadic Empires and China, 221 B.C. to A.D. 1757*, Oxford: Blackwell.

Barnett, Doak A. (1993), *China's Far West: Four Decades of Change*, Boulder, CO: Westview Press.

Bass, Catriona (1998), *Education in Tibet: Policy and Practice since 1950*, London: Zed Press.

Bauman, Zygmunt (1998), *Globalization: the Human Consequences*, Cambridge: Polity Press.

Becquelin, Nicolas (2000), 'Xinjiang in the Nineties', *The China Journal* 44 (July): 65–91.

Benton, Gregor and Frank N. Pieke (1998), *The Chinese in Europe*, Basingstoke: Macmillan.

Bernstein, Thomas P. (1977), *Up to the Mountains and Down to the Villages*, New Haven and London: Yale University Press.

Blum, Susan D. (2000), 'Tales From the Fields of Yunnan: Listening to Han Stories', *Modern China* 26 (2 April): 148–65.

—— (2001), *Portraits of 'Primitives': Ordering Human Kinds in the Chinese Nation*. Lanham, MD: Rowman & Littlefield.

Bovingdon, Gardner (2004), 'Heteronomy and Its Discontents: "*Minzu* Regional Autonomy" in Xinjiang' in M. Rossabi (ed.), *Governing China's Multiethnic Frontiers*, Seattle: University of Washington Press.

Broegger, Benedicte (2000), 'Occasions and Connections. The Chinese Clan Associations as Part of Civil Society in Singapore', thesis, Department of Social Anthropology, University of Oslo.

Brown, Melissa J. (1996) (ed.), *Negotiating Ethnicities in China and Taiwan*, Berkeley, CA: Institute of East Asian Studies.

Bruner, Edward M. (1986), 'Experience and Its Expressions' in V. W. Turner and E. M. Bruner (eds), *The Anthropology of Experience*, Urbana: University of Illinois Press.

247

Bulag, Uradyn E. (2004), 'Inner Mongolia: The Dialectics of Colonization and Ethnicity Building' in M. Rossabi (ed.), *Governing China's Multiethnic Frontiers*, Seattle: University of Washington Press.

Cao Chunliang *et al.* (eds) (1998), *Zhiqing gushi* (Stories from Intellectual Youth), Guangzhou: Huacheng chubanshe.

Carter, Paul (1992), *Living in a New Country: History, Travelling and Language*, London: Faber & Faber.

Chambers, Ian (1994), *Migrancy, Culture, Identity*, London and New York: Routledge.

Chen Guoqiang (1990), *Chongwu renleixue diaocha* (Anthropological research in Chongwu), Fuzhou: Fujian jiaoyu chubanshe.

Chen Guoqiang (1992), *Jianshe Zhongguo renleixue* (Establishing Chinese anthropology), Fuzhou: Fujian jiaoyu chubanshe.

Chen Han-seng (1949), *Frontier Land Systems in Southernmost China*, New York: Institute of Pacific Relations.

Chen Liankai (1991), 'Hanzu bu yi gai cheng "Huazu"' ('It is inappropriate to change "Han Nationality" into "Hua Nationality"'), *Sixiang zhanxian* (The Ideological Front) (2): 84–7.

Chen Shu (1986), 'Han er hanzi shuo' ('Explanation of the Terms *Han* and *Hanzi*'), *Shehui kexue zhanxian* (The frontline of social sciences) (1): 90–7.

Chen Xiguang (1991), 'Zhongguo chengshihua de jincheng yu renkou qianyi' ('The Process of Urbanisation and Migration in China'), *Sixiang zhanxian* (The ideological front) (1): 9–15.

Chen Yimin and Tong Chengzhu (1992), *Zhongguo renkou qianyi* (Migration in China), Beijing: Zhongguo tongji chubanshe.

Chen Yuning (1988), 'Jindai Neimenggu diqu de "yimin zhibian" ji qi yingxiang' (The 'Immigrant consolidators of the borders' and their influence in modern times in Inner Mongolia), *Xibei shi di* (History and Geography of the Northwest) (3): 6–11.

Cheng Jiang (1998), *Lao zhiqing* (Veteran intellectual youth), Beijing: Shiyou gongye chubanshe.

Clarke, Graham E. (1994), 'The Movement of Population to the West of China: Tibet and Qinghai' in J. M. Brown and R. Foot (eds), *Migration: The Asian Experience*, Basingstoke: Macmillan.

Cleverley, John F. (1991), *The Schooling of China: Tradition and Modernity in Chinese Education*, Sydney: Allen & Unwin.

Clifford, James (1992), 'Travelling Cultures' in L. Grossberg, C. Nelson and P. Treichler (eds), *Cultural Studies*, London and New York: Routledge.

——— (1994), 'Diasporas', *Cultural Anthropology* 9 (3): 302–38.

Cohen, Myron L. (1994), 'Being Chinese: The Peripheralization of Traditional Identity' in T. Wei-ming (ed.), *The Living Tree: The Changing Meaning of Being Chinese Today*, Stanford University Press.

Cohen, Robin (1997), *Global Diasporas: an Introduction*, Seattle: University of Washington Press.

Cohn, Bernard S. (1996), *Colonialism and its Forms of Knowledge: the British in India*, Princeton University Press.

Commission for Editing Historical Annals in Xiahe County, Gansu Province (ed.) (1997), 'Xiahe Xian zhi' (Annals of Xiahe County), Xiahe: unpublished draft.

Croll, Elisabeth J. and Huang Ping (1997), 'Migration For and Against Agriculture in Eight Chinese Villages', *The China Quarterly* (149): 128–47.

Dan Qu (1994), *Labuleng Si jian shi* (A brief history of Labrang Monastery), Lanzhou: Gansu minzu chubanshe.

———— (1998), *Labulang Shihua* (A historical narrative of Labrang), Beijing: Minzu chubanshe.

Daunton, Martin and Rick Halpern (eds) (1999), *Empire and Others: British Encounters with Indigenous Peoples, 1600–1850*, Philadelphia: University of Pennsylvania Press.

Davin, Delia (1999), *Internal Migration in Contemporary China*, New York: Macmillan Press.

Davis, Sara (2003), 'Premodern Flows in Postmodern China', *Modern China*, vol. 29 (2): 176–203.

Day, Lincoln H. and Ma Xia (eds) (1994), *Migration and Urbanization in China*, Armonk, NY: M. E. Sharpe.

Deng Ke (2001), 'Wo yao wo de xuexiao bu liulang' (I want my school not to 'lead a vagrant life'), *Nanfang Zhoumo* (Southern Daily).

Dikötter, Frank (1992), *The Discourse of Race in Modern China*, London: Hurst & Co., 1992.

———— (1997a), *The Construction of Racial Identities in China and Japan: Historical and Contemporary Perspectives*, London: Hurst & Co.

———— (1997b), 'Racial Discourse in China: Continuities and Permutations' in F. Dikötter (ed.), *The Construction of Racial Identities in China and Japan*, London: Hurst & Co.

Dillon, Michael (1999), *China's Muslim Hui Community: Migration, Settlement and Sects*, London: Curzon Press.

Dodd, William Clifton (1992), 'Zai Xishuangbanna chuanbo jidujiao jianwen' (Experiences from Christian missionary work in Sipsong Panna), in *Banna wenshi ziliao xuanji* (A collection of material concerning the cultural history of Sipsong Panna), edited by the Working Commission for Editing Material Concerning the Nationalities' Cultural History, Kunming: no publisher.

Dongfang State Farm (1988), 'Zengqiang chang qun tuanjie, gong jian bianjiang wenming' (Strengthening the unity between state farm and people and building in common the border civilisation), *Minzu gongzuo* (*Minzu* Work) (July): 18–19.

Duara, Prasenjit (1988), 'Superscribing Symbols: the Myth of Guandi, Chinese God of War', *Journal of Asian Studies* (47): 778–95.

——— (1996), 'De-Constructing the Chinese Nation' in J. Unger (ed.), *Chinese Nationalism*, Armonk, NY and London: M. E. Sharpe.

Dunne, Nancy (1999), 'Tibet lobby upset at World Bank scheme', *Financial Times*, 13 May.

Ebrey, Patricia (1996), 'Surnames and Han Chinese Identity' in M. Brown (ed.), *Negotiating Ethnicities in China and Taiwan*, Berkeley: Institute of East Asian Studies, University of California.

Economy Department of National Minzu Commission *et al.* (ed.) (1992), *Zhongguo minzu tongji* (Statistics on China's *minzu*), Beijing: Zhongguo tongji chubanshe.

Editing Commission of 'A General Survey of Gannan Tibetan Nationality Autonomous Prefecture' (ed.) (1986), *Gannan Zangzu Zizhizhou gaikuang* (A general survey of Gannan Tibetan Nationality Autonomous Prefecture), Lanzhou: Gansu minzu chubanshe.

Elman, Benjamin A. and Alexander Woodside (eds) (1994), *Education and Society in Late Imperial China, 1600–1900*, Berkeley: University of California Press.

Fan Wenwu and Deng Zhiren (1993), 'Minzu tuanjie you xinpian' ('A new chapter for the unity of the nationalities'), *Minzu gongzuo* (*Minzu* work) (May): 26.

Fei Xiaotong (1981), 'Ethnic Identification in China' in Fei Xiaotong (ed.), *Toward a People's Anthropology*, Beijing: New World Press.

Feng Jianjiang (1993), 'Zai Xibei xiao chengzhen de mangliu' ('The flow of people into townships in the northwest'), *Renkou yanjiu* (Population Research) (2): 60–2.

Fong, Rowena and Paul R. Spickard (1994), 'Ethnic Relations in the People's Republic of China: Images and Social Distance between Han Chinese and Minority and Foreign Nationalities', *Journal of Northeast Asian Studies* (spring): 26–48.

Frankenberg, Ruth and Lata Mani (1996), 'Crosscurrents, Crosstalk: Race, "Postcoloniality", and the Politics of Location' in L. Smadar and T. Swedenburg (eds), *Displacement, Diaspora, and Geographies of Identity*, Durham, NC: Duke University Press.

Gaubatz, Piper Rae (1996), *Beyond the Great Wall: Urban Form and Transformation on the Chinese Frontiers*, Stanford University Press.

Giersch, Pat C. (2001), 'A "Motley Throng": Social Change on Southwest China's Early Modern Frontier, 1700–1880', *The Journal of Asian Studies* 60 (1, February): 67–95.

Gladney, Dru C. (1994), 'Representing Nationality in China: Refiguring Majority/ Minority Identities', *The Journal of Asian Studies* (1 February): 92–123.

———— (1996), *Muslim Chinese: Ethnic Nationalism in the People's Republic*, Cambridge, MA: Council on East Asian Studies, Harvard University.

———— (1998), 'Internal Colonialism and China's Uyghur Muslim Minority', *Regional Issues*, no. 1. <http://www.uyghuramerican.org/research-analysis/internalcol.html>.

Grunfeld, A. Tom (1996), *The Making of Modern Tibet*, Armonk, NY: M. E. Sharpe.

Guojia minwei minzu wenti wu zhong congshu bianwei hui (ed.) (1980–92), *Guojia minwei minzu wenti wu zhong congshu* (The Nationality Commission's Five Kinds of Collections on Issues Related to China's Minority Nationalities), vols 1–403, Beijing: Beijing minzu chubanshe.

Hansen, Mette Halskov (1999a), 'The Call of Mao or Money? Han Chinese settlers on China's Southwestern Borders', *The China Quarterly* (158, June): 394–413.

———— (1999b), *Lessons in Being Chinese: State Education and Ethnic Identity in Southwest China*, Seattle: University of Washington Press.

———— (2001), 'Ethnic Minority Girls on Chinese School Benches: Gender Perspectives on Minority Education' in Lu Yongling, R. Hayhoe and G. Petersen (eds), *Education, Culture and Identity in Twentieth Century China*, Ann Arbor: University of Michigan Press.

Hao Haiyan *et al.* (eds) (1998), *Zhongguo zhiqing shi chao* (Poems of Chinese intellectual youth), Beijing: Zhongguo wenxue chubanshe.

Harrell, Stevan (1994), 'Introduction: Civilizing Projects and Reactions to Them', in S. Harrell (ed.), *Cultural Encounters on China's Ethnic Frontiers*, Seattle: University of Washington Press.

———— (ed.), (1995), *Cultural Encounters on China's Ethnic Frontiers*, Seattle: University of Washington Press.

———— (2001), *Ways of Being Ethnic in Southwest China*, Seattle: University of Washington Press.

Hechter, Michael (1975), *Internal Colonialism: the Celtic Fringe in British National Development, 1536–1966*, London: Routledge and Kegan Paul.

Hill, Ann Maxwell (1989), 'Chinese Dominance of the Xishuangbanna Tea Trade', *Modern China* 15 (3): 321–45.

———— (1998), 'Merchants and Migrants: Ethnicity and Trade among Yunnanese Chinese in Southeast Asia', New Haven: Yale University Southeast Asia Studies.

Ho, Ping-ti (1954), 'The Salt Merchants of Yang-chou: a Study of Commercial Capitalism in Eighteenth-Century China', *Harvard Journal of Asiatic Studies* (17): 130–68.

Hoh, Erling (2000), 'Hear our prayer', Far Eastern Economic Review (13 April): 24–5.

Honig, Emily (1992), Creating Chinese Ethnicity: Subei People in Shanghai, 1850–1980, New Haven: Yale University Press.

Hou Zurong (1995), 'Li Foyi xiansheng qi ren qi shi' ('Mr Li Foyi, the man and his work'), in Jinghong wenshi ziliao (Historical Material from Jinghong), edited by the Commission for Editing Historical Material, Jinghong: No publisher.

Hsieh Shih-Chung (1989), 'Ethnic-Political Adaptation and Ethnic Change of the Sipsong Panna Dai: an Ethnohistorical Analysis', Ann Arbor, MI: UMI Dissertation Services.

Huang Tianming (1965), Bianjiang xiao ge (Song of dawn at the borders), Beijing: Zuojia chubanshe.

Hyde, Sandra Teresa (2001), 'Sex Tourism Practices on the Periphery: Eroticizing Ethnicity and Pathologizing Sex on the Lancang' in Nancy N. Chen, Constance D. Clark, Suzanne Z. Gottschang and L. Jeffery (eds), China Urban: Ethnographies of Contemporary Culture, Durham, NC: Duke University Press.

Jankowiak, William R. (1993), Sex, Death, and Hierarchy in a Chinese City: an Anthropological Account, New York: Columbia University Press.

Jhaveri, Nayna (2001), 'Transnational Ecological Reconstruction and Citizenship in China's Western Regions', paper presented at Second International Convention of Asian Scholars, 8–12 August, Berlin.

Jinghong State Farm (ed.) (1992), Lü chao: zai beihuiguixianshang. Yi ge chongpo jinqu de xiandai shenhua (The green tide: on the Tropic of Cancer: a modern fairy tale of a breakthrough in a Restricted Zone), Chongqing: Guoji wenhua chuban gongsi.

Kolstø, Pål (1995), Russians in the Former Soviet Republics, London: Hurst & Co.

Land Reclamation Department (1997), 'Zhigong duiwu' (The team of workers), Jinghong: unpublished draft.

Latour, Bruno (1993), We Have Never Been Modern, Brighton: Harvester/ Wheatsheaf.

Lattimore, Owen (1932), 'Chinese Colonization in Manchuria', Geographical Review, 22, 2: 177–95.

———— (1940), Inner Asian Frontiers of China, Oxford University Press.

———— (1950), Pivot of Asia: Sinkiang and the Inner Asian Frontiers of China and Russia, Boston: Little, Brown.

Lavie, Smadar and Ted Swedenburg (1996a), 'Introduction: Displacement, Diaspora and Geographies of Identity' in S. Lavie and T. Swedenburg (eds), Displacement, Diaspora, and Geographies of Identity, Durham, NC: Duke University Press.

Bibliography 253

(eds) (1996b), *Displacement, Diaspora, and Geographies of Identity*, Durham, NC: Duke University Press.

Lee, James (1978), 'Migration and Expansion in Chinese History' in W. H. McNeill and R. S. Adams (eds), *The Human Migration: Patterns and Policies*, Bloomington: Indiana University Press.

(1982), 'Food Supply and Population Growth in Southwest China, 1250–1850', *The Journal of Asian Studies*, 41, 4: 711–46.

Li Debin, Shi Fang and Gao Lin (1994), *Jindai Zhongguo yimin shiyao* (The essentials of the history of migration in Modern China), Harbin: Harbin chubanshe.

Li Xiaofang (1996), *Neidi ren zai Xizang* (People from the heartland of China living in Tibet), Lhasa: Xizang renmin chubanshe.

Li Xiaoxia (1998), 'Lun Xinjiang Hanzu de difanghua de xingcheng ji qi tezheng' (A discussion of the formation and characteristics of the Han's regionalisation in Xinjiang), *Minzu yanjiu* (*Minzu* research) 3: 39–45.

Liao, T'ai-ch'u (1949), 'Rural Education in Transition. A Study of the Old-fashioned Chinese Schools (Szu Shu) in Shantung and Szechuan', *Yenching Journal of Social Studies*, 4, 2 (February): 19–67.

Lipman, Jonathan N. (1997), *Familiar Strangers: a History of Muslims in Northwest China*, Seattle: University of Washington Press.

Litzinger, Ralph A. (2000), *Other Chinas: the Yao and the Politics of National Belonging*, Durham, NC: Duke University Press.

Liu Weihua *et al.* (eds) (1995), *Aiguozhuyi jiaoyu shouce* (Handbook in patriotic education), Beijing: Chenguang chubanshe.

Long Xijiang (2002), 'Lun Zhongguo tese de minzu lilun' (A Discussion of a Special Chinese Theory of Nationalities) [Internet source] 2001 [cited 04.03.02 2002]. Available from <http://www.unirule.org.cn/Academia/neibu99-12-long.htm>.

Lu Li and Wang Xiuyin (1986), 'Cong wo guo wushi niandai you zuzhi de yimin kenhuang tanxi yimin gonggu wenti' (An exploration of the stability of migrants based on the organised migrations of people sent to open up wasteland in our country in the 1950s), *Renkou yanjiu* (Population research), 4: 28–31.

Ma Jiang (ed.) (1993), *Gannan Zangzu Zizhi Zhou muxu zhi* (Gannan Tibetan Autonomous Prefecture Gazetteer of Animal Husbandry), Lanzhou: Gansu minzu chubanshe.

Ma Litu (1958), 'Zheng shi Hanzu dali bangzhu he zujin women de minzu fanrong' (It is the Han nationality who has helped and promoted our nationality's prosperity), *Minzu gongzuo ziliao yuebao* (Nationalities Work Monthly Magazine) 1: 39–42.

Ma Rong (1987), 'Migrant and Ethnic Integration in Rural Chifeng, Inner Mongolia Autonomous Region, China', PhD thesis, Brown University, Providence, RI.

———— (1991), 'Han and Tibetan Residential Patterns in Lhasa', *The China Quarterly*, 128 (December): 814–35.

———— (1993), 'Economic Patterns, Migration, and Ethnic Relationships in the Tibet Autonomous Region, China' in C. Goldschneider (ed.), *Population, Ethnicity and Nation-Building*, Boulder, CO: Westview Press.

———— (1996) *Xizang de renkou yu shehui* (Population and society in Tibet), Beijing: Tongxin chubanshe.

Ma Xia and Wang Weizhi (1993), *Migration and Urbanization in China*, Beijing: New World Press.

Makley, Charlene Elizabeth (1999), 'Embodying the Sacred: Gender and Monastic Revitalization in China's Tibet', PhD thesis, Dept. of Anthropology, University of Michigan, Ann Arbor.

Malkki, Liisa (1992), 'National Geographic: The Rooting of Peoples and the Territorialization of National Identity among Scholars and Refugees', *Cultural Anthropology*, 7, 1: 24–44.

McKhann, Charles F. (1995), 'The Naxi and the Nationalities Question' in S. Harrell (ed.) *Cultural Encounters on China's Ethnic Frontiers*, Seattle: University of Washington Press.

McMillen, Donald H. (1981), 'Xinjiang and the Production and Construction Corps: A Han Organisation in a Non-Han Region', *The Australian Journal of Chinese Affairs*, 6: 65–96.

Melvin, Neil (1995), *Russians beyond Russia*, London: Royal Institute of International Affairs.

Miao Zishu *et al.* (ed.) (1987), *Labuleng Si gaikuang* (A survey of Labrang Monastery), Lanzhou: Gansu minzu chubanshe.

Mueggler, Erik (2001), *The Age of Wild Ghosts: Memory, Violence, and Place in Southwest China*, Berkeley: University of California Press.

Oakes, Tim (1998), *Tourism and Modernity in China*, London and New York: Routledge.

Office in Charge of the Fourth Census of Jinghong County (ed.) (1990), 'Renkou ziliao fenxi huibian' (A collection of analysis of census material), Jinghong: unpublished.

Olwig, Karen Fog (1997), 'Cultural Sites: Sustaining a Home in a Deterritorialized World' in K. F. Olwig and K. Hastrup (eds), *Siting Culture: the Shifting Anthropological Object*, London and New York: Routledge.

———— (1998), 'Contested Homes: Home-making and the Making of Anthropology' in N. Rapport and A. Dawson (eds), *Migrants of Identity: Perceptions of Home in a World of Movement*, Oxford: Berg.

Ong, Aihwa (1996), 'Cultural Citizenship as Subject-Making: Immigrants Negotiate Racial and Cultural Boundaries in the United States', *Current Anthropology*, 37, 5 (December): 737–63.

Ong, Aihwa and Donald Nonini (eds) (1997), *Ungrounded Empires: the Cultural Politics of Modern Chinese Transnationalism*, New York and London: Routledge.

Pan, Lynn (1994), *Sons of the Yellow Emperor: a History of the Chinese Diaspora*, New York: Kodansha International.

Pasternak, Burton and Janet W. Salaff (1993), *Cowboys and Cultivators: the Chinese of Inner Mongolia*, Boulder, CO: Westview Press.

Peng Xun (1992), *Renkou qianyi yu shehui fazhan* (Migration and Social Development), Jinan: Shandong daxue chubanshe.

Pepper, Suzanne (1996), *Radicalism and Education Reform in 20th-Century China: the Search for an Ideal Development Model*, Cambridge University Press.

Peterson, Glen, Ruth Hayhoe and Yongling Lu (eds.) (2001), *Education, Culture, and Identity in Twentieth-Century China*, Ann Arbor: University of Michigan Press.

Postiglione, Gerard A. (ed.) (1999), *China's National Minority Education: Culture, Schooling and Development*, New York and London: Falmer Press.

Prakash, Gyan (1990), *Bonded Histories: Genealogies of Labor Servitude in Colonial India*, Cambridge University Press.

Qian Wenbao (1996), *Rural-Urban Migration and its Impact on Economic Development in China*, Aldershot: Avebury.

Qiao Wenbo (1993), 'Xiahe Xian lishi tuntian yu liangshi jiaoyi gaikuang' (A brief account of Xiahe's history of garrison troops opening up wasteland and grain trade) in 'Xiahe wenshi ziliao' ('Historical material from Xiahe'), edited by Xiahe Commission for Editing Historical Material, Lanzhou: unpublished.

Qie De'er (1991), 'Xiahe Xian xumu gongzuo huigu zhi qidi' (An inspirational review of the work with animal husbandry in Xiahe County), in *Xiahe Xian dang shi ziliao* (Xiahe County Party history material), edited by CCP Xiahe Commission's Office in Charge of Collecting Party History, Lanzhou University.

Rapport, Nigel and Andrew Dawson (1998a), 'Home and Movement: a Polemic' in N. Rapport and A. Dawson (eds), *Migrants of Identity: Perceptions of Home in a World of Movement*, Oxford: Berg.

—— (1998b), 'The Topic and the Book' in ibid.

—— (eds) (1998c), *Migrants of Identity*, Oxford/New York: Berg.

Rhoads, Edward J. M. (2000), *Manchus and Han: Ethnic Relations and Political Power in late Qing and early Republican China, 1861–1928*, Seattle: University of Washington Press.

Ricoeur, Paul (1984), *Time and Narrative*, vols 1–2, University of Chicago Press.

Rosaldo, Renato (1993), *Culture and Truth: The Remaking of Social Analysis*, Boston, MA: Beacon Press.

Rouse, Roger (1991), 'Mexican Migration and the Social Space of Postmodernism', *Diaspora* 1 (1), p. 8–23.

Rowe, William T. (1984), *Hankow: Commerce and Society in a Chinese City, 1796–1889*, Stanford, CA: Stanford University Press.

—— (1989), *Hankow: Conflict and Community in a Chinese City, 1796–1895*, Stanford, CA: Stanford University Press.

Sautman, Barry (1997), 'Myths of Descent, Racial Nationalism and Ethnic Minorities in the People's Republic of China' in F. Dikötter (ed.), *The Construction of Racial Identities in China and Japan*, London: Hurst.

—— (1999), 'Expanding Access to Higher Education for China's National Minorities: Policies of Preferential Admissions' in G. A. Postiglione (ed.), *China's National Minority Education: Culture, Schooling, and Development*, New York and London: Falmer Press.

—— (2001), 'Peking Man and the Politics of Paleoanthropological Nationalism in China', *The Journal of Asian Studies*, 60, 1: 95–125.

Schein, Louisa (1997), 'Gender and Internal Orientalism in China', *Modern China*, 23, 1: 69–98.

—— (2000), *Minority Rules: the Miao and the Feminine in China's Cultural Politics*, Durham, NC: Duke University Press.

Schwarz, Henry G. (1963), 'Chinese Migration to North-West China and Inner Mongolia, 1949–59', *The China Quarterly*, 16 (November–December): 62–75.

Scott, James C. (1998), *Seeing like a State: How Certain Schemes to Improve the Human Condition Have Failed*, New Haven: Yale University Press.

Shapiro, Judith (2001), *Mao's War against Nature: Politics and the Environment in Revolutionary China*, Cambridge University Press.

Sipsong Panna Land Reclamation Department (ed.) (1991), *Shanguang de zhuren* (The Shining Masters), Jinghong: no publisher.

—— (ed.) (1992a), *Jiaolin qunxing* (Stars of the Rubber Plantation), Jinghong: Sheng xinwen chubanju.

—— (ed.) (1992b), *Lü haichao: Xishuangbanna kenqu xinwen zuopin ji* (The green tide: a collection of news articles from the reclamation area of Sipsong Panna), Kunming: Yunnan Sheng xinwen chubanju.

—— (ed.) (1990), *Banna qing* (Friendship in Banna), Jinghong: no publisher.

Skinner, William G. (1976), 'Mobility Strategies in Late Imperial China: a Regional Analysis' in C. A. Smith (ed.), *Regional Analysis*, New York: Academic Press.

—— (1977), 'Introduction: Urban Social Structure in Ch'ing China' in W. G. Skinner (ed.), *The City in Late Imperial China*, Stanford, CA: Stanford University Press.

Soerensen, Birgitte Refslund (1997), 'The Experience of Displacement: Reconstructing Places and Identities in Sri Lanka' in K. F. Olwig and K. Hastrup (eds), *Siting Culture*, London and New York: Routledge.

Solinger, Dorothy J. (1999), *Contesting Citizenship in Urban China: Peasant Migrants, the State, and the Logic of the Market*, Berkeley: University of California Press.

Somers, Margaret R. (1994), 'The Narrative Constitution of Identity: A Relational and Network Approach', *Theory and Society*, 23, 5 (October): 605–51.

Suo Dai (1992), *Labuleng Si fojiao wenhua* (The Buddhist culture of Labrang Monastery), Lanzhou: Gansu minzu chubanshe.

Tapp, Nicholas (2002), 'In Defence of the Archaic: a Reconsideration of the 1950s Ethnic Classification Project in China', *Asian Ethnicity*, 3, 1: 63–85.

Thoegersen, Stig (2001), 'Learning in Lijiazhuang: Education, Skills and Careers in 20th Century Rural China' in Lu Yongling, R. Hayhoe and G. Petersen (eds), *Education, Culture and Identity in Twentieth Century China*, Ann Arbor: University of Michigan Press.

Thomas, Nicholas (1994), *Colonialism's Culture: Anthropology, Travel and Government* Cambridge: Polity Press.

Tian Fang and Zhang Dongliang (1989), *Zhongguo renkou qianyi xin tan* (A new study of migration in China), Beijing: zhishi chubanshe.

Tibet Support Group UK (1995), *New Majority: Chinese Population Transfer into Tibet*, London: Tibet Support Group UK.

Tu Wei-ming (1991), 'Cultural China: The Periphery as the Center' in Tu Wei-ming (ed.), *The Living Tree: the Changing Meaning of Being Chinese Today*, Stanford, CA: Stanford University Press.

Upton, Janet L. (1999), 'The Development of Modern School-Based Tibetan Language Education in the PRC' in G. A. Postiglione (ed.), *China's National Minority Education: Culture, Schooling and Development*, New York and London: Falmer Press.

Wang Jianmin (1997), *Zhongguo minzuxue shi* (The history of ethnology in China), vol. 1, Kunming: Yunnan jiaoyu chubanshe.

Wang Jianmin, Zhang Haiyang and Hu Hongbao (1998), *Zhongguo minzuxue shi* (The history of ethnology in China), vol. 2.

Wang, L. Ling-chi (1991), 'Roots and the Changing Identity of the Chinese' in T. Wei-ming (ed.), *The Living Tree: the Changing Meaning of Being Chinese Today*, Stanford University Press.

——— and Wang Gungwu (1998), *The Chinese Diaspora: Selected Essays*. Singapore: Times Academic Press.

Wang Mingming (1997), *Cunluo shiye zhong de wenhua yu quanli: Min Tai san cun wu lun* (Village visions of culture and power: three villages and five theses of Fujian and Taiwan), Beijing: Shenghuo-dushu-xinzhi, san lian shudian.

—— (1996), *Shequ de licheng: Xicun Hanren jiazu de ge'an yanjiu* (The course of a community: a case study of Han clans in Xi village).

Weiner, Myron (1978), *Sons of the Soil: Migration and Ethnic Conflict in India*, Princeton University Press.

Wellens, Koen (1998), 'What's in a Name? The Premi in Southwest China and the Consequences of Defining Ethnic Identity', *Nations and Nationalism* 4, 1: 17–34.

Wiens, Harold J. (1967), *Han Chinese Expansion in South China*, Hamden, CT: Archon Books/Shoestring Press.

Williams, Dee Mack (1996), 'The Barbed Walls of China: A Contemporary Grassland Drama', *The Journal of Asian Studies*, 55, 3 (August): 665–92.

Xiao Ji (1996), 'Gaoyuan meng xun—jin Zang daxuesheng suo' (Dream searching on the High Plateau—a literary sketch of university students going to Tibet) in L. Xiaofang (ed.), *Neidi ren zai Xiazang* (People from the heartland of China living in Tibet), Lhasa: Xizang renmin chubanshe.

Xie Benshu (1994), *Minzu diqu aiguozhuyi jiaoyu jianming duben* (A brief reader in patriotic education in minority regions), Kunming: Yunnan renmin chubanshe.

Xu Jieshun (1992), *Han minzu fazhan shi* (The history of the Han nationality's development), Chengdu: Sichuan minzu chubanshe.

—— (1994), 'Han minzu yanjiu yu Zhongguo wenhua' ('Research on the Han nationality and China's civilisation'), *Minzu yanjiu* (*Minzu research*), 8: 35–42.

—— 1998, *Hanzu minjian fengsu* (Folk customs of the Han), Beijing: Zhongyang minzu daxue chubanshe.

Ya Hanzhang (1991), 'Jiefangchu Xiahe jian zheng de jingyan he jiaoxun' ('Experiences and lessons from the establishment of government in Xiahe during the early period of Liberation') in Z. Qingyou (ed.), *Xiahe Xian dang shi ziliao* (Material concerning the party history of Xiahe county), Xiahe: Zhonggong Xiahe Xian wei dan shi ziliao zhengji banshichu.

Yang Xuezheng and Gerong Lamu (1995), *Fo guang li de shihua rensheng: Zangzu* (A people nurtured by the Buddhist halo: the Tibetans), Kunming: Yunnan jiaoyu chubanshe.

Yunnan Province Commission of Nationalities Affairs (ed.) (1955), *Yunnan Sheng shaoshu minzu diqu jinji* (Taboos in Yunnan Province's minority areas), Kunming: no publisher.

Zhang Li (2001), *Strangers in the City: Reconfigurations of Space, Power, and Social Networks within China's Floating Population*, Stanford, CA: Stanford University Press.

Zhang Qiyun (1978 [1934]), *Xiahe Xian zhi* (Annals of Xiahe county), Taibei: Chengwen chubanshe.

Zheng Xiaoyun and Yu Tao (1995), *Muyu shengshui de nüxing: Daizu* (Women bathed in holy water: the Dais), Kunming: Yunnan jiaoyu chubanshe.

Zhuang Kongshao (2000), *Yin chi: Zhongguo de difang shehvi yu wenhua bianqian* (Silver wings: local society and cultural change in China), Beijing: San Lian Shudian.

No author (1993), 'Xiahe Xian gongshang xingzheng guanli zhi: jianguo qian—1990' (Annal of the administration of Xiahe County Department for Industry and Commerce: from before the founding of the country to 1990), Xiahe: unpublished report.

—— (2001), 'Di er dai yimin de jiaoyu wenti' (Educational problems among the 'second generation of immigrants'), *Nanfang Zhoumo* (Southern Daily), 7 June.

CHARACTER LIST

ba bai jia maimairen	800 families of traders	八百家买卖人
bao'an siling	security command	保安司令
ban fan	‹half-Tibetans›	半番
bendi minzu	local minzu	本地民族
budui nongchang	military state farms	部队农场
chadui	school graduates who went to live and work in the countryside	插队
chaosheng youjidui	‹guerrilla of people having too many children›	超生游击队
chengbao	contract	承包
chi ku	eat bitterness	吃苦
danwei	work unit	单位
dagong	work in unskilled labour, doing odd jobs	打工
Daizu	the Dai nationality	傣族
danao	brains	大脑
di er dai	the second generation	第二代
difang ganbu	local cadres	地方干部
difangzhuyi	local nationalism	地方主义
diu lian	loose face	丢脸
fan	barbarian, foreign	番
fan fengjian douzheng	the battle against feudalism	反封建斗争
fen	unit of area, 1/10 mu	分
fen chang	branch of state farm	分场
fen jia	divide the family	分家
gongzuo	working; having a definite work position	工作
Hanizu	Hani nationality	哈尼族
hanhua	sinicise	汉化
Hanzu	the Han nationality	汉族
hu	non-Han peoples in the Northwest, barbarians	胡

hunanren de naozi hen huoyue	the brains of the people in Hunan are rather dynamic	湖南人的脑子很活跃
hunxue er fazhan de	developed through the mixing of blood	混血而发展的
hunxue er xingcheng de	formed through the mixing of blood	混血而形成的
jishengwei	Family Planning Committee	计生委
jiazhang	head of the family	家长
jianban	wooden painted ritual relic	简板
kuzao	dull	枯燥
laobaixing	common people	老百姓
laojia	‹old home›, place of family's origin	老家
linchang	state-owned forestry farm	林场
lian	face	脸
liudongrenkou	floating population	流动人口
man	barbarian	蛮
meishenme teshude	there is nothing special about them	没什么特殊的
mendang hudu	a marriage well-matched in social and economic status	门当户对
meili de Xishuangbanna	beautiful Sipsong Panna	美丽的西双版纳
mei you hao wanr de	nothing to do for fun	没有好完儿的
minsuxue	folklore	民俗学
minzu xingge	the nature of an ethnic group	民族性格
minzu diqu	minority area	民族地区
minzu ganbu	minority cadre	民族干部
minzu shibie	classification of the nationalities	民族识别
minzu tuanjie	unity of the nationalities	民族团结
minzu xiongdi	brother nationalities	民族兄弟

minzu zizhiqu	minority autonomous region	民族自制区
minzuxue	ethnology	民族学
minzu gongzuo	minority work	民族工作
mosuoren	Mosuo people	摩梭人
mu	unit of area, 0.0667 hectare	亩
naozi bu tai hao	they do not have the brains for it	脑子不太好
naozi suzhi tai di	the quality of their brains is not very high	脑子素质太底
ni ye shi waimian lai de	you are also from the outside	你也是外面来的
nongkenju	Land Reclamation Department	农垦局
nongmuchang	agricultural and livestock husbandry state farm	农牧场
putongxuexiao	ordinary school	普通学校
putonghua	standard Chinese	普通话
qingmingjie	tomb-sweeping day	清明节
renmin gongshe	people's commune	人民公社
ronghe	amalgamate	融合
shantou hanzu	mountain Han	山头汉族
shaoshu minzu	ethnic minority/minority nationality	少数民族
shaoshu minzu diqu	minority area	少数民族地区
shaoshu minzuxue	the study of ethnic minorities	少数民族学
shangshan xiaxiang	up to the mountains and down to the villages	上山下乡
sheng	raw	生
sheng fan	‹raw Tibetans›	生番
shehuixue	sociology	社会学
shi	city	市
shu	cooked	熟
shu fan	‹cooked Tibetans›	熟番
sixiang	minds	思想

suzhi gao	high level of education/civilisation; of high quality	素质高
ting wo de hua	do as I say	听我的话
tusi	minority hereditary headman	土司
wenhua	culture	文化
wenming	civilisation	文明
xia	Chinese	夏
xiagang	off-duty	下刚
xian	county	县
xianzai zhu de difang	current place of residence	现在住的地方
xiao ziyou	a bit of freedom	小自由
xibu da kaifa	The Development of the Western Regions	西部大开发
xing	family name	姓
Xishuangbanna	Sipsong Panna	西双版纳
xuetu	apprenticeship	学徒
yi	barbarian	夷
yi liang wei gang	take grains as the key	以粮为纲
yi nong wei zhu	take agriculture as the most important	以农为主
yinyang xiansheng	yin-yang specialist	阴阳先生
youhui zhengce	preferential policies	优惠政策
yuanshi shehui	primitive society	原始社会
zhaoxu	seek son-in-law to live with the wife's family	招婿
zhibian	supporters of the borderlands	支边
zhibian qingnian	intellectual youth in support of the borderlands	支边青年
zhichi bianyuan	supporters of the borderlands	支持边缘
zhiqing	intellectual youth	知青
zhou	prefecture	州
zhongdian xuexiao	keypoint school	重点学校

INDEX

Aini people, *see* Akha people

Akha people: 33–4, 39, 55, 56, 72, 76, 85–6, 114, 185, 219–20, 238; in state farms, 211–12, 216–18

Apa Ablo, 47–8

Appadurai, Arjun, 26–7

Bachman, David, 20

Bauman, Zygmunt, 81

birth control, 64, 112, 114, 115–19

Blang people, 33, 34, 39, 237–8

Blum, Susan, 15–16, 191–2

Buddhism: in Sipsong Panna, 94–6, 221; in Xiahe, 28, 29, 30, 41, 88–91, 111, 153, 199, 223, 233; of Han, 91, 92–6, 111

Bulag, Uradyn D., 19

Bulang people, *see* Blang people

Burma, 4, 69, 145, 235

cadres, minority, 48–51

Chen Han-seng, 33, 50 n.10

Chiang Kai-shek, 174

Chongqing, 59, 60

Clifford, James, 181–2

Cohen, Myron L., 136

colonialism: European, 5, 6, 8, 242; in Chinese history, 6–7, 8–9, 14–15, 18–2; internal, 5–7, 242–3

Communist Party, Chinese, 10, 12, 48, 51, 94, 112, 120, 194, 200–2, 204, 214, 243

Dai people, *see* Tai people

Dalai Lama, 206

Daoism, 90–1, 92, 93, 96–7, 126

Deng Xiaoping, 153, 174

Dodd, William Clifton, 32

education: of Han, 57, 61, 97–9, 101–11, 120, 153, 157, 226; of minorities, 40, 85, 90, 100–1, 102, 103, 104–6, 109–11, 113

Engels, Friedrich, 194

Erlang, 90

ethnology, Chinese, 11–12

fieldwork: discussion of, 10–16

floating population, 34, 45, 63–4, 166–7, 168, 228

Fong, Rowena, 192

forestry centre, 53; *see also* state farms

Gannan Prefecture: history of, 27–31, 51, 154, 198

Gaubatz, Piper Rae, 29

Giersch, Pat, 9, 29

Gladney, Dru, 5

Great Leap Forward, 30, 33, 42, 47, 51, 59, 178, 200, 213

Guandi, 90

Guomindang, 32, 48–9, 50–1, 174

Hainan Island, 53

Han: as a *minzu*, 98–9, 183, 184–5, 186–7; definition of, 15–17, 193; (re)classification of, 114–15, 117, 136

Han Dynasty, 18

Hani people, *see* Akha people

Harrell, Stevan, 39

Henan, 59, 68

home, old, *see* laojia

Honig, Emily, 137, 139

265